Surviving Mummy

T0365570

Veena Masud

Order this book online at www.trafford.com/05-1015
or email orders@trafford.com

Most Trafford titles are also available at major online book retailers.

Note for Librarians: A cataloguing record for this book is available from Library
and Archives Canada at www.collectionscanada.ca/amicus/index-e.html

Printed in the United States of America

ISBN: 978-1-4120-6114-8 (sc)
ISBN: 978-1-4269-9746-4 (hc)
ISBN: 978-1-4269-9747-1 (e)

Library of Congress Control Number: 2011917585

Trafford rev. 10/04/2011

www.trafford.com

North America & international
toll-free: 1 888 232 4444 (USA & Canada)
phone: 250 383 6864 ♦ fax: 812 355 4082

Preface

This book is a personal reflection on the first eighteen years of my life and of a time way beyond. The events before my birth came from the numerious stories told to me by Nan a frail old woman with whom I spent many hours during my early years.

In my thirst to know, I asked question after question and listened intently, visualizing her words so that they have remained as fresh as if I too had lived through those times.

The compulsion to write was initially inspired by a deep need to reflect and put issues to rest as I entered the middle stage of my life.

So apart from being emotionally therapeutic, writing this book was a wonderful experience in renewed self-discovery. I indulged in memories that were sometimes happy, sometimes thoughtful and reflective, and at times so very sad.

Writing took some of the homesickness away. It coated the bruises with a soft comforting balm as I recalled with freshness, the sweet clay smell of rain soaked soil, the warm balmy breeze against my skin, the soothing malaise of the tropical island and the gentle rhythm of the soulful island beat.

In writing this book I did not aim to judge, malign or indulge in the melancoly. I truly believe that it is a story that is eventful and interesting enough to hold a reader's attention, and so I wanted to share it.

I take this opportunity to thank the many people who have touched my life in very special ways. In particular, a little girl I hardly knew. She gave me her picture because she believed I loved her so very much and that I needed to know she loved me back. The cantankerous old gardener who believed that women should be hidden behind the veil and yet he gave me the seeds of flowers, which he said, would spring up year after year and would remind me that he wanted to give me flowers but was too poor to do so. Every summer for the past fifteen years his flowers greet me and bring a touching lump to my throat.

My very special thanks to Ellen Beck, I am convinced that it was through Divine guidance that I was drawn to her to edit this book. Apart from her expert help and guidance, Ellen's sensitivity and gentleness reached out to me and gave me the courage to go ahead and publish my thoughtful thoughts.

Veena Masud

This book is humbly dedicated to........

All children, may you have the courage and the will to find the beautiful side of life and living, and to survive in the some-times cruel and thoughtless adult world.

My dear friend Fatima Lakhani who nagged, pushed, cajoled and eventually threw down the gauntlet, not too gently and challenged me to write. Fatima remained an absolute thorn in my side till this book was completed. Fatima epitomizes the true meaning of the word 'Friend'.

My son Kamal, who taught me more than he would ever know and for whom life is worth living.

Chapter 1

Gainder was my maternal grandmother's grandmother. Gainder's parents lived in a village on the coast near a seaport somewhere in India, most likely Bombay, Madras or Calcutta, as those were the ports where most of the ships carrying the indented laborers from India to the West Indies loaded their human cargo. Gander's mother, no one remembers her name, was frantic with worry. She could not find her husband. This gentle, thoughtful, kind man was a good husband, but he had not been home in several days.

When none of the family could find where he had gone, Gainder's mother decided they were not looking in the right places and went in search of him herself. Heavily pregnant with their first child, she lumbered around the village, asking people if they had seen him as she shouted his name out loudly. But no one had seen him or knew where he was.

Then someone suggested he might have gone to the docks. There had been much talk about people going to new, faraway places where they could get good pay for working the land. Perhaps he had decided to go there on an impulse. Gainder's mother could not believe that her good man would do that without telling her. He would never leave like that, would he? He had never mentioned ships taking people to other places to work. "Still," people said, "yu never know wat goin' on in a man head, dey head does be full of all kinda tings dat they doe tell dey 'ooman."

Now not so certain that her man would not leave without telling her, she sadly and reluctantly went towards the docks, her head reeling and spinning with the thought that he may have actually been tempted by the idea of a new prosperous beginning in some far off land.

As she neared the docks, she saw the huge sailboats looming threateningly and yet dangerously alluringly. Could he have really got caught up in the excitement of travelling to a new land and been tempted to go on to the ship? She decided to go on board the huge iron vessel to see for herself, still wondering why he would want to be on a ship full of people going to some far-off land.

Perhaps there was another reason why he had decided to board the ship. He may even unsuspectingly have been lured there. Gainder's mother was confused. Again and again she reassured herself that he would not, could not, possibly have gone without telling her. After all, they were very much in love, very happily married, and very excited about the upcoming birth of their baby.

Pushing her way through the throngs of people, she clambered aboard the ship, as quickly as her heavy body would allow to have a quick look. Desperate and wild-eyed, she searched everywhere, frantically calling his name until she became hoarse.

In what seemed like just only a few minutes later, the ship bellowed out its loud horn, the creaking gangway was pulled up, and the ship began to pull away from the pier. Gainder's mother had no idea where the ship was heading, only that she must find her husband. She screamed and wailed, but all in vain, as he was nowhere to be found.

Now she had no way of getting off the ship. What a frightening and utterly dreadfully hopeless situation for her to be in! She thought she would go mad. She ran crazily around pushing through the pack, hoping that someone would hear her pleas. She shouted hysterically to the sailors and the captain to let her off the ship, but no one listened. Her dry hoarse voice was lost in the shrieks, shouts, and rumble of the engine as the ship heaved and groaned out of the harbour. She tried to throw herself overboard, but was pulled back and taken down inside the belly of the ship to a tiny cubicle with ten other people.

Too tired to fight anymore, she sank to the floor and fell into a deep, dark depression as the ship sailed further and further away from her family, her man and the only home she had ever known.

Life on the ship was a living torturous hell. Cramped and stink with the stench of unwashed bodies, the human cargo suffered their journey with crawling bugs sucking mercilessly on their dry rough skin as they slept and ate the gooey mess that was served up in surroundings that reeked of stale urine, and putrid feces. There was no surprise that squabbles broke out amongst the passengers, and tempers remain on edge.

In this melee of confusion, Gainder's mother depressed and tired, huddled quietly in her corner, venturing out only for the occassional meal, if one could call it that, when hunger churned and gnawed like a wild ravenous beast inside her belly.

The journey seemed endless. One hopeless day merging into another. Because of her intense emotional trauma and physical discomfort, the baby was born prematurely not long afterwards. It was a tiny, sickly-looking little girl, who for all intents and purposes, should have not survived but somehow tenaciously did.

Her mother named her Gainder after the bright golden yellow flower of her homeland now left far behind. As she gazed down upon her tiny, helpless baby, Gainder's mother made a solemn promise to live and make a home for her child in that faraway place. With hot tears streaming down her face she consoled herself by saying that perhaps this was what God had planned for her and maybe it was for the best. Surely the ship must be heading to a better place, why else would so many people willingly go there she reasoned.

After the long and otherwise uneventful journey, mother and baby arrived in Trinidad, a tiny tropical island in the West Indies. Out of her desperate need to survive and make a life for her child—the only link she now had with her lost husband—she made friends with her fellow passengers, some of whom had been vaguely familiar faces from her village.

To support herself and her child, Gainder's mother found a job on the sugarcane plantations. When she was not thinking of Gainder, she thought about her husband and wondered what could have happened to him. Did he ever return home? Was he frantically worried and looking for her, as she had looked for him? She would never know. He would always remain her wonderful, loving, gentle husband. But life had to go on. "As de 'Book' say, "yu have to make de best of it; it is a test the Almighty does give yu when He want yu to be strong, life go be better de next time round, if dey is such a ting", the preacher man consoled.

Life was not easy toiling in the cane fields. Planting and cutting the cane from early morning to late evening was hard work. Her hands and feet became blistered and sore from the razor sharp cane leaves and the dry rough stalks. She got used to it, however, and adjusted to a laborer's way of life; she had no other choice. She shared one of the communal huts that had been built for the laborers and their families by the English gentry. This was the only life she knew now. It was difficult, but she had her baby, a part of her husband whom she still loved so much.

The Indian immigrants were ambitious, determined, and tenacious as they worked hard in the fields with a focused vengeance. They had made the sacrifice of leaving the comfort of the familiar to go all that way, half way across the globe to make a better life for themselves and their families. The initial hardships were a means to an end, the start of a prosperous, happy new life. One day they or their children would have the life they had always dreamed of. They would work hard and earn money until the time would come when they could buy and own land.

Owning land meant that it would enable them to earn more money, and they too would become rich landowners. The money would pay for their children's education. They knew that education was the key to elevating their social and economic status. This was the determined obsessive dream they all shared.

Gainder's mother never forgave herself for boarding that ship in search of her man. Every day she chastised herself for being impatient and not having more trust and faith in him. If she had just waited at home like a dutiful wife, sooner or later he would have returned and she would not have found herself in this difficult and at times unbearable situation.

But strong and determined, she bravely faced the challenges of bringing up her daughter all by herself. Although it was difficult being both mother and father to her child, she never thought of making a new life for herself with anyone else because she was still faithfully committed to the man she had left behind. She missed the love and companionship of her husband, especially when she saw other couples holding hands and sharing intimate moments. When her body began to ache with longing, she would work even harder until she was too tired to feel the need for a man in her bed.

Despite her weak and sickly early years, Gainder grew into a very beautiful young lady—tall, slender, and with the light-colored skin that was favoured by the large Indian community that had settled on the island. She had a reserved air about her that some people took to be one of superiority and even arrogance. But it was not that at all, she just had strong ideals and principals and an inherent sophistication, thanks to her mother's fine example.

In was a blessing that Gainder had at first been sickly-looking and thin. It saved her from having to join the workforce in the sugarcane fields. She wanted a better life away from the cane her mother slaved over. Because nature had blessed her with the desired and enviable looks and with her air of aristocratic elegance, she had her pick of all the eligible young men in the surrounding villages.

She eventually chose the most ambitious one and married him with her mother's blessing. That he also happened to be good looking was an added advantage. They made a handsome couple, one that was destined by the heavens to make all their dreams come true and live happily ever after.

As Gainder and her husband began their married life, the government in England began introducing new laws that abolished slavery and gave indented laborers new rights. This brought about many changes in Trinidad. The indented laborers were now able to buy or rent small pieces of the farmland on which they had toiled and so Gainder and her husband seized this opportunity and acquired several acres of land and ten children to go with it over the next twelve years or so.

Not only did they complement each other as soul mates, they also shared an instinctive knowledge of business. With this mutually ambitious drive and understanding, they prospered. Soon they were able to establish themselves as successful sugarcane farmers and hiring their own workforce.

With the abolition of slavery, the Africans who had been brought to the islands as slaves were free to work anywhere. There was little need then to bring in more indented laborers from India and China and so fewer and fewer new indented laborers arrived on the island. Since the indented Indian laborers who were already there wanted to own their own land, it became difficult for Gainder and her husband to get the kind of people they wanted to work the sugarcane fields. They were reluctant to hire the Africans who were once slaves, they had seen and heard things about these seemingly strange people who had come from Africa.

The black-skinned people were different from the Indians with whom they were familiar. Living a carefree life, these people were rumoured to share their women and have loose morals, which resulted in far too many chubby little illegitimate picanninies running around without clothes. These people also looked shiny and sweaty all the time, and people said that they even had a funny smell. Gainder and her husband were convinced the blacks were lazy, good-for-nothings who only liked to sing, dance, and drink too much. They feared that they or their children would be murdered in their beds, for as little as the price of a bottle of rum.

When it became increasingly difficult to hire laborers to work the cane fields, Gainder and her family decided to stop cane farming and acquire still more land. Land was money, they both reasoned. They were far-sighted enough to know that the land they had acquired would be worth much more by the time their children grew up. They continued to buy and sell land, always at a profit. Being acutely business-minded, they also opened a general store that supplied dry goods, spices, and cloth from India to the large Indian community. While Gainder looked after the shop, her husband kept a close eye on the land and property side of their business. Life was good.

Having achieved financial and material success, Gainer and her husband now turned their thoughts to educating their children. All six of their sons went to the local missionary school. Their four daughters did not go to school. They helped in the shop and learned to embroider, cook, and tend the goats, chickens, and ducks that they kept in the yard.

Ironically, all four girls eventually developed keen heads for business and a flare for making money, and either ran their own businesses or became business heads for their husbands later on in their lives. The boys, on the other hand, ended up looking after the property they inherited with lazy indifference. In time, the financial security that their parents had worked so hard to achieve for the boys would eventually dwindle away.

By this time the religious seminaries in England, Scotland and Ireland had sent their missionaries out to the island with the mission to save the pagan souls of the islanders. These missionaries set up the only organized schools on the island and they insisted that the only way to gain admission and get an education was to be 'baptized' and accept the "Lord Jesus Christ as the only Savior."

Most of the Indians on the island, whether Hindu or Muslim, chose to appear Christian in order to get into the schools. Initially they were 'pretend Christians' at school and would continue to practice their own religions at home. But as time went on, they became part-time Hindus, part-time Christians, part-time Muslims, or part-time whatever religion or fad their friends happened to be following that month. Peoples' names aptly reflected this religious confusion. Names like Mohammed Singh, John Hussain, or Terry Patel were not unusual.

Instinctively prone to a joy of life and having a good time, these people caught on and celebrated the festivals and cultures of all the different religions with equal exuberance. They celebrated with such fervor and zest that one might have thought they had been born into the religious or cultural festivals they happened to be honoring that particular season.

With the population expanding and the economy of the country also surging forward, the government in England decreed that major developments should begin to improve the facilities on the island. Roads were laid from north to south and east to west. As luck would have it, the main road running north to south cut through Gainder and her husband's property, for which they were richly compensated.

Halfway along that north south road in the small town of Caripachima, Gainder's husband built a rambling wooden house with wide verandas all around it. Delicate wooden carvings that had been painted white decorated the arches on the eaves, giving the house an ornate lacy look. Framing the back of the house were tall cedar trees and the bright blossoms of the Flame of the Forest. At the front of the house, large beds of phlox, hedges of multicolored hibiscus, croton, bougainvillea, and other wildly exotic tropical flowers added a profusion of color.

In time, their children grew up and married suitable young men and women in keeping with the family's acquired financial status. Caripachima however still remained the center of the family's activities for Christmas, Diwali, Eid, Easter, carnival, birthdays, weddings, and so on. The children had children and the family grew into one of the largest on the island.

One could always meet someone somewhere who was related or who had some claim to kinship. It was known as a pumpkin vine family, its tendrils stretching far and wide, curling around, climbing up, and encircling everyone with whom it came in contact. People were proud to be a part of the family.

I must have been very young when I paid my first visit to Caripachima. I remember feeling very disappointed that the old house I had heard so much about was not as big or as interesting as I had imagined it would be. The descriptions must have been romantically glorified my young mind reasoned. In actuality, the house was old, worn, and decidedly dilapidated. I suppose it had aged with its owner. By then the only people living in the house were Gainder, Roy, who was the last of her sons, and a maidservant who looked almost as old and fragile as Gainder herself. In fact, I remember thinking that they needed a maid for the maid.

The furniture in the house was dark and old and had cushions that were dank and damp to the touch. The pattern of the fabric was almost completely worn off from so many years of wear. The window drapes were heavy with dirt and dust. The floor looked as though it had not been polished in years, and the few tattered rugs were so threadbare it was hard to believe they had been plush rugs at one time. Everything seemed old, dusty, and aged, just like its ancient inhabitants.

When we walked in, Gainder was lying on the sagging old couch with the maid hovering confused and uncertainly behind her. Mummy pushed me forward, shouting loudly to remind the old woman who I was. I hated the thought of having to kiss her dried-up, leathery cheek. To make matters worse, I could see quite a few long, wiry hairs on her chin. Mummy kept pushing me toward her. Gainder reached out her long bony hand and with a surprising amount of strength pulled me to her. Too embarrassed to do otherwise, I leaned forward to kiss her as her rheumy eyes looked deeply into mine. Feeling suddenly ashamed, I quickly kissed her. She touched my hair and told Mummy what a pretty child I was.

I remember Mummy later sadly lamenting about how things had changed for the old woman. Her children had quarreled, demanded, and taken their share of the money and then squandered it all after their father had died. It was sad that at this old age Gainder had nothing at all to her name, and was totally dependent on the few visits her children could make when they felt they had the time or when guilt overcame them.

Roy, who had managed to lose his wife earlier, she had run off with someone else, lived with Gainder but he was very often drunk and always had a ready excuse for not earning a living.

It was generally thought that Gainder was about a hundred and nine years old at that time. She lived for another four years and then died peacefully in her sleep. I remember hearing family members say the doctors could find nothing that could have caused her death. It was believed she just switched off her will to live. And while Gander and her husband at the peak of their lives, had epitomized the indented Indian labourer's dream, Gander must have died a sad, lonely, and totally disillusioned woman.

Chapter 2

Nan was Mummy's grandmother, the third of Gainder's four daughters. I grew up with Nan in the house. As a young child, I was very attached to her. She was old and lonely and I was alone. We spent long hours together. She would spend that time telling me stories about my roots, the members of the family, and how things were in Trinidad when she was a young girl.

I was fascinated to know how the family had ended up in Trinidad, so far away from India. Nan enjoyed telling me these old stories, so I begged to hear them over and over again until I knew them word for word. I felt as if I knew everyone she spoke about. I felt their pain and their joy. I relived their experiences as Nan described them, always so colorfully and with many chuckles. At times she would gaze into some long lost memory and shake her head sorrowfully. Yet Nan had a wonderful sense of humor, which had helped her cope with the many challenges she had had in her life.

Nan said that she was very attached to her mother when she was a little girl and spent many hours helping her in the shop. She told me about the strange and wonderfully exotic merchandise that was brought in from India to sell in the shop. Items like huge bags of fragrant rice and pulses, pungent spices that were used for cooking, strange herbs used as elixirs to cure all sicknesses and with promises that "if taken regularly even death could be avoided". There were typical Indian cooking and household utensils, and that very strange nut seed that made your lips turn bright red when you chewed on it. Nan could not remember what it was called, or perhaps she never knew. Many years later I found out she was talking about the slightly narcotic betel nut or 'paan' as it is called today in India. "It was good for deejeshion an ah did not have to colour mey lips to look pretty. De 'nut seed' did dat for mey," Nan recalled.

Nan took great pride in being her mother's favorite child. "Ah was de brightest of dem all," she would boast in her soft, trembling old voice. "De boys in de family were all useless. Ah was de one who had de head for business, and ah should da been de one to go to school. Ah was cheated out of an eddoocation," she lamented all her life. She thought the biggest injustice of her life was not having been given the opportunity to learn to read and write. "Mey ma and mey barp didna know better. Dey still had dem old-fashioned ideas from India. Baa we ar' living in Trinidad, de Englishman country, an dey didna think, an ah end up wid no eddoocation. Bah! Chut!" she irritatingly exclaimed. For that reason, Nan wished she had been born a boy. But despite that major error on nature's part, Nan had a very happy childhood. She loved to play and had numerous friends in the neighborhood.

Many Chinese people had also immigrated to Trinidad as indented immigrants from mainland China. This influx happened around the same time these people were flocking to cities like San Francisco and Vancouver on the West Coast of North America. The Chinese people did well for themselves in Trinidad. Even more business-minded and closely-knit than the Indian community, they established very successful laundry cleaning services and the inevitable merchandise stores for their communities.

Nan had vivid memories of their stores, which she said were filled with a strange combination of things. From the peculiar stench of weird looking, dried-up 'dead animal things' that they used in their cooking, she had no other word to describe what she saw, to very beautiful, ornately decorated ceramic jars, vases, bowls and platters to cheap china bowls and dishes that can still be found in Chinese stores and restaurants anywhere in the world today.

There were also many other interesting things that Nan had never seen before, like the many varieties of Far East bric-a-brac, hand-painted bamboo umbrellas, wind chimes, delicate lace, paper lanterns, fans, and colorful kites with fierce faces of ancient heroes, mythical animals, and gods. Paintings and embroidered wall hangings of beautiful, misty unearthly-looking scenes from far-off China hung on the walls. All these things added to the mystique of the Chinese shop. Walking in there, she said, was like taking a trip far away to the distant east. Everything seemed strangely dark and foreign, very, very smelly, but yet so tantalizing exciting and so addictive that one had to go back again and again.

The Chinese people clung to their old traditions and culture much more than the other indented communities. They maintained their Cantonese language and lived quietly and unassumingly in small, dark, crowded rooms behind their shops.

They were not a warm and friendly people and never really interacted socially with the rest of the community. They seemed to look upon the rest of the population with a deep sense of suspicious alienation. When it did become necessary to interact with others, the male members of the families were the ones to do the mingling, and even this was done reluctantly and only when necessary and only for business purposes.

The women remained well in the background. There was nothing pretty or feminine about them. They all seemed to have the same bland worried faces framed by greasy jet-black hair that was cut just like a boy's. One would sometimes get fleeting glimpses of them as they dashed in and out of their shops or when they came out to beckon their wayward offspring. They always appeared to be scolding their frisky, energetic children in high-pitched, shrill, singsong voices, pulling their ears or slapping them lightly on their heads.

The children also seemed to look the same, with their round heads, flat, rosy faces, small slanted eyes, and short, straight, wiry, jet-black hair. Nan said that one never heard much laughter from the grown-up Chinese people, but when they were little, the Chinese children were playful and rowdy like other children. They sometimes came out to join in games with other children, but one could not actually say they were friends with them.

This little playful interaction continued while they were children, but once they reached puberty, they adopted the stern, rigid, quiet ways of their grown-ups. Nan assumed that they must have been forbidden to mix with people of other races for fear they might fall in love and want to marry out of their culture. To lose their culture would have been a totally forbidden and unforgivable act of treason. They still thought of China as the fatherland to which they owed their first loyalty and allegiance.

Nan said that the one trait of the Chinese people that was very commendable was that they never let anyone of their own kind down. They were always there for each other, welcoming the newly arrived immigrant families into their homes and supporting them until they were able to set up their own businesses in other parts of the country. They never did seek work on the sugarcane plantations, as they did not want to work for anyone who was not Chinese. They never interfered with anyone else, never expected anything from any of the other ethnic groups, and they never helped anyone other than their own people. They were a tight lot and remained that way until the mid nineteen fifties.

Next to Nan's home lived a large extended Chinese family who had their own shop. Although Nan's father and the head man of the Chinese family greeted each other politely every morning, they were never what you would call friends. The children of both families, however, would sometimes play together. Nan said hide and seek was their favorite game. Both families owned large yards around their houses with storage sheds and outhouses. There were also huge piles of wood and logs, all wonderful places to hide behind or under. The children ran, laughed, and shouted together, but were always careful to never enter each other's homes. That would have been a breach of the unspoken rules and ethics.

The Chinese family had many dogs. They were friendly animals who also joined in the games with the children, chasing and barking with frisky delight as if they, too, understood the excitement of the chase. Nan loved the dogs. While there were animals reared for meat in her yard there were no actual 'pet' animals in her home. So Nan felt as if she shared these pets with her neighbors. But she noticed something strange; every so often one of the dogs would disappear. When she would ask about it, she would be told that it had run away or that it had died. The explanation was good enough and Nan never thought anything more of it.

One day while playing hide and seek, Nan ran into the backyard of the Chinese family's home to find a good place to hide. Without thinking, she dashed into the back shed and hid behind a large barrel. It was then that she saw the carcass of one of the dogs she had not seen that day. It was hung up on a hook just like a goat at the meat shop. A butcher's knife, a chopping block, and a large basin lay on a table nearby. Realizing what that meant, she stumbled out of the shed in shock and in horror and hurried back to her home. Nan never played with the Chinese neighbour's children again and mistrusted all Chinese people after that.

Nan grew from a tiny child into a tiny young woman. She was as brown as a berry with smooth skin, long, thick hair that fell to her knees, and sparking eyes. She was also a flirt, much to her mother's chagrin. When her older sister got engaged to the son of a wealthy family friend, Nan's biggest fear, though only fifteen, was that she might be left on the shelf. She just had to get engaged as well. Noting that her new brother-in-law to be had a handsome younger brother, she unabashedly set out to seduce him. Nan's charms were irresistible; the young man did not stand a chance. Before long she, too, was engaged.

Two sisters engaged to two brothers was a recipe for disaster, or so Nan was told. The older family members warned Nan that one marriage would end in sorrow, but she did not listen or care. She wanted that man. She would make sure her life would not have a sorrowful ending.

Both weddings took place on the same day, which was another taboo. Nan's sister, a shy, demure bride, sat with her head slightly bent, too self-conscious to lift her face. Nan, on the other hand believed she was in an enviable position, brazenly looked around and laughed, proudly aware of the fact that she and her new husband made a handsome couple. She believed hers would be the happiest of marriages, especially since it was obvious that her husband was totally besotted and amused by her free-spirited nature.

After marriage, Nan and her sister lived with their in-laws in the family home. Since her husband was the younger brother, he did not have the responsibility of running the family business. That onerous task fell on the shoulders of his older brother, who was married to her sister.

Nan's husband liked adventure and enjoyed nothing better

than to go out hunting in the untamed equatorial jungles of the island. There were deer, rabbits, turtles, tattoos and agotees to chase out and hunt. Wild meat was quite a delicacy at that time, and a hunting trip was an exciting pastime for the well-to-do, idle men-folk who had no real business to look after. Returning home with a couple of slain animals was also a good reason for an elaborate and festive celebration.

Nan did not want to stay at home and miss the excitement she heard so much about when her husband went on these hunting trips, so on many occasions she insisted on going along. Her husband didn't dare refuse her.

They often camped out under the stars or in broken down huts with all kinds of creepy insects, bugs, slimy lizards, and snakes that hung from the eaves. Nan was never afraid; in fact, she enjoyed the thrill of danger. She had her man there to protect her.

Once they sat on what they thought was a tree trunk only to find that it moved under them. She laughingly recalled that it was a huge snake. Another time they met a hunter who decided to join up with them. They settled down to spend the night together in a dilapidated hut they had found. After their evening meal, the three of them wrapped themselves up and lay down side-by-side on the damp floor.

Just as they settled down they realized that they had left their flambeau burning about ten feet away. The two men decided to toss a coin to see who would have to get up from their cozy bed to put it out. The stranger lost the toss and therefore had to put out the light. To their shock and amazement, the stranger did not get out of his sleeping roll to turn the torch off; instead, he stretched his hand out the full ten feet to where the lamp was and quashed it with his thick, bare hands. Nan said she and her husband were too scared to do anything but lie there quietly.

They must have fallen asleep at some point because the next thing they knew it was morning and their companion was nowhere to be seen.

Nan's husband also taught her to smoke. He would ask her to light his rolled-up tobacco leaves and they would sit close together on the wooden stairs of the wide veranda and share puffs until late in the evening. They were also known to have shared the odd ganja joint on special occasions. "It does fix up yu head, make it light, light. Yu tiredness does just melt away, it does also stop yu stomach for hurting and does clear yu lungs out, it does good for many many odder tings " Nan would confide much later when we registered shock that she had smoked a substance that was considered illegal. Nan never did explain what the other 'things' she meant.

Five years and three daughters later, Nan woke up one morning to find that her husband, who was only 27 years old at the time, had died in his sleep. No one knew what could have caused his death. Nan was sure it had to have been the work of black magic and Obeah. There were jumbees everywhere and people were jealous of their love and happiness. How on earth could a man who was so young and strong fall down dead like that? It was unheard of! In retrospect, though, we now know that the family did have genetic heart problems because now, six generations later, some of us have an inherited congenital heart disease. But Nan would never have understood that then, she was sure it had been the work of "Obeah and black tongue."

Nan was heartbroken, her light, her beacon, had gone out of her life. Still, she did not fear for the financial security for her and her daughters. After all, her husband's brother was also her sister's husband. The family had vowed to see that the girls were given their rightful share of the property. Her brother-in-law had also promised to see that they would be married to suitable young men of substance. Nan consoled herself that all would be well for her three daughters, Ismat, Nass, and Little Sparrow. She brushed the nagging thoughts of the warnings she had had five years before……."Two sisters should never marry two brothers; one marriage would surely be sorrowful."

Nan did the cooking for the large extended family that lived together. "She hand does have a sweetness," they said. One day as Nan was preparing lunch; an old traveling man came to the door and called out. "Hello! Hello! Ah was walking by when ah smell de wonderful aroma of de food yu cooking. Ah cannot help but ask if ah could come in and have some." Nan, who was very proud of her cooking, fell for his flattery and offered the old man some of the curried goat and roti.

After eating he saw her three daughters playing and looked very seriously at them. He turned to Nan and in a very quiet voice told her that her eldest daughter, Ismat, would have a peaceful and contented life—not too rich, but not too poor either—with a husband who would adore her. Nass, he said, would have a hard tough life and would live to an old, old age. He looked long at Little Sparrow, the youngest, and then predicted she would be wealthy beyond her wildest dreams if she lived beyond the age of forty. But he warned that a boy child would not be lucky for her. The old man then quickly left.

Nan did not really believe him, but she never forgot his words either. She kept them in her heart, wondering if what he had said would ever come true or if it was just the fanciful raving of a drunken crackpot high on ganja. Nan's three girls were very lively; they had inherited her "joie de vie." She saw to it that all three girls went to school and learned how to read and write. And although she missed her husband, she was by and large quite content.

As time went by, things began to change. The house did not feel as comfortable as it once did. Nan began to feel she had become a heavy burden to the family. Her sister's family had grown and there were now seven of them, all very bold and loud with the arrogant confidence of having their parents alive and there for them. Her sister and brother-in-law now found faults with Nan's daughters all the time, becoming irritated with them for no reason at all, always accusing them of not helping out enough in the house, wasting things, getting in everyone's way, taking more than their fair share, and so on.

Nan felt she had no choice but to marry off both Ismat and Nass very quickly to the first "suitable" young men as soon as they were old enough. These suitors were not from the same class of family, but Nan accepted them gratefully, relieved that the two older daughters would marry, have their own home, and fulfill the destiny that was ordained for them. There was no other way. Her helplessness hurt and depressed her. She was utterly disappointed in her sister. She could never have imagined that a sister would treat her own flesh and blood that way.

A few years later, when things in the house had gotten even worse, she decided she would take Little Sparrow, who was still quite young, and go to stay with her youngest sister in a village called Diamond. She knew they would be welcome there. As they left, nothing was said about their share of the family wealth or their inheritance. Nan refused to ask, deciding to leave it up to the will of God.

This other sister, the youngest of Gainder's daughters, was married to a generous man who was busy worrying about making more money, keeping his wife constantly pregnant, and having a good time with his friends. He was very happy to have Nan come and stay with them. He hoped this would keep his wife from complaining and nagging him all the time about being too busy with his work and friends.

He had a rum shop and a restaurant of some ill repute. One

sure way to make money in Trinidad was to open up a rum shop and serve raw oysters. Quickly knocking back the shots of the rough, strong rum and swallowing the raw oysters was a sure sign of macho manhood. The men boasted that it gave them the virility of a wild bull and they were not above describing how well endowed they were and how they made their women "'purr like she cats."

The family lived in a large rambling wooden house built on thick wooden stilts. A wide staircase led from the front garden up to the veranda that surrounded three sides of the house. Nan's sister was an easygoing, lazy person who was only too glad to have Nan do the cooking, take charge of the kitchen, and supervise the endless cleaning. The cousins were a noisy carefree lot, only too happy to include another little person in their large and boisterous herd.

Nan and Little Sparrow were very happy living with them in their spacious home. There was always something exciting happening and no one ever complained. If things got a little crowded or strained, one could just escape to another part of the house. If the house was untidy, so what? It was a home and everyone was happy there amidst the confusion, noise and mess.

Chapter 3

Victor was the third child of a family comprising of two sons and two daughters. While the story of his family is somewhat sketchy, Victor believed his branch of the family originated from Sindh in what is today Pakistan. All we know is that Victor's grandfather was the second son. When his brother inherited the larger share of the family property, Victor's grandfather refused to work with him. Taking his share of what little money there was, he ran away to seek his fortune in a faraway land. He got on the first ship that was leaving the port. That ship was sailing to Trinidad.

After arriving in Trinidad, Victor's grandfather immediately went to work on the sugarcane fields with the intention of making enough money to become a landowner like the brother he had left behind in India. Although he had refused to work on his brother's land, he didn't hesitate to work on a stranger's land. He justified this by convincing himself that he would one day have enough money to buy his own land. He was known to be a hot-tempered young man with stubborn ideas who kept pretty much to himself.

It appears he eventually earned enough money to buy a large piece of land in Diamond Village. He then retired from working in the fields and proceeded to hire his own laborers to work the sugarcane fields, paddy fields, and vegetable patches. He built a small house on one corner of the land and set out to make a name for himself. As he bought up more and more land, he became a kind of leader in the village—a sort of Trinidad country squire—and the largest landowner. The villagers would turn to him for advice, to help solve their petty squabbles, and to borrow money. The townspeople respected him, for although he was known to be abrupt and strict, he was also fair and just in his dealings with people.

At some point he must have gotten married because he eventually had a son. This son—Victor's father—had no clear recollection of a mother. She may have died soon after his birth. There is very little information about Victor's grandfather after this, but we do know that his son married and had two children, a boy and a girl, before his wife died in childbirth. We also know that for no apparent reason he went blind while still a young man. Mummy thinks it may have been glaucoma because some of his descendants today have this disease and glaucoma is hereditary. But it could also have been cataract. What ever the cause was, he was completely blind and he needed someone to help care for him and the children as well as supervise the workers on the land.

So he remarried, the woman he married was no beauty. She was short and dark, very different from her husband who was by all accounts a tall and strikingly good-looking man. But she was a kind and good woman who tenderly cared for her two stepchildren. In time she had two children of her own—Victor and a daughter. Victor inherited his father's good looks and his mother's dark complexion. He perfectly fit the description 'tall dark and handsome.' Victor's father died when he was fifteen or sixteen years old. Victor and his older half brother inherited the land. The Indian community still held faithfully to the Indian custom of giving the land and property only to the sons, while the daughters inherited the money and jewelry that they were given on their wedding day.

For some reason I used to call this older half brother Green Pa, perhaps because he had a greenish tinge to his aura that only a child could recognize. He also drank a lot. In later years Green Pa's drinking got the better of him.

Green Pa could not make a success of farming and he eventually sold his half of the land. With his small fortune, he idled away his time drinking and having a good time with friends who were happy to keep him company as long as he had money to spend and buy them drinks.

Following his mother's advice, Victor decided he would take on the responsibility of making sure his sisters got married to suitable young men as there were no guarantees that Green Pa would see to their future. All Green Pa could do and think about about were his friends and drinking till the early hours and then to go home to his current paramour. The bottle was definiately his best friend; it was never far from his side.

I clearly recall the last time I saw Green Pa. I must have been about three or four years old at the time. He had come to see Victor. He was an extremely handsome man, who must have been very tall in his youth because he still looked tall even though he was slightly stooped. He had tiny, hair-like blood vessels on his nose, a ready smile and wit, and a distinctive air of assumed elegance with his affected mannerisms, despite the three days of hair growth on his face. In retrospect, he looked like a tall version of a not-so-sad Charlie Chaplain's "Tramp."

Green Pa had arrived unannounced early that morning obviously to borrow money, which we all knew he would never pay back. By now he had depleted all the money he had received from the sale of his land, most probability losing it all on gambling, drinking, and womanizing.

Green Pa pleaded for a small loan to tide him over till his

new venture made money, then he would pay the loan back with interest, he promised. Tired of these 'new ventures', Victor refused to give him any money and there was a terrible row.

Victor's loud voice thundered his reproaches for Green Pa's slothful drunkenness and bad business deals. I heard him say that Green Pa was welcome to come to the house for food and shelter but that he did not intend to ever give him money at any time! Green Pa stormed off in a dejected rage and that was the last we saw of him.

I don't remember hearing where he ended up, but he died a year or two later. When Victor heard of Green Pa's death, he felt bad about the row.

Victor left school when he was about 16, barely finishing Standard Eight. He was astute enough to be able to supervise his holdings and began to make money, which he carefully saved. Victor was the wealthiest young man in Diamond; he loved sporting activities and was known for his generosity, so it was inevitable that he would soon have a group of hangers on. These friends played a lot of cricket together, frequented the bars, and generally made quite a stir in the small village, singing their loud, noisy songs as they meandered their way home every night.

Victor had a passion for roasted salted peanuts and always had a handful of them in his pocket. He could often be seen tossing them high up in the air and trying to catch them in his mouth. Yet despite these obvious frivolous pastimes, Victor stayed focused and never let his love of life interfere with his desire to make a success of his land and farms.

He instinctively knew where to draw the line. As he matured, he took on the role of country squire that his grandfather had assumed, and did so with compassion and great style. The villagers regarded him very highly and trusted him in every way. They spoke of him in such glowing terms and with such respect that one was taken aback to discover that he was still only in his early twenties.

When his mother died, Victor was shattered. The responsibility of his sisters was now squarely on his shoulders, with no older person to give him advice. Green Pa even when he was alive, was never around to help. As it turned out, both sisters married quite young and moved to the north of the island with their respective husbands. By all accounts, they lived contented lives and had many babies.

Nan had seen the young Victor with his friends and would often invite him into the house to have some food or to give him motherly advice. "Be careful of hangers on; don't waste money on yur friends so much; don't drink! It will be de end of yu if yu do; look after yur sisters; be more serious," and so on. Victor loved and appreciated her concern; it reminded him of his beloved mother. He made a point of visiting her every day to listen to her advice, even though he did not intend to ever give up his way of life. He reassured her that he knew exactly what he was doing, she recalled, and he would laughingly tease her if she got too heavy on the advice. Nan adored him. He became the son she never had.

Victor soon began to take notice of Little Sparrow, who had matured into a pretty, soft, pink-cheeked, smiling young woman. He began to come around more and more until he was spending most of his spare time with Nan and her daughter. It was some time, however, before he summoned up the courage to asked Nan if he could marry Little Sparrow. Nan said it had been the only time she had seen him nervous. "How could he tink ah go say no to dat marriage? He don know full well dat ah care for him, dat ah love him as mey own son." Victor explained that he was frightened she would say no because she obviously did not approve of his lifestyle. He was sure she would send him packing.

The wedding took place with great celebration. It was the event of the year in Diamond. It was said that Victor had his pocketful of peanuts even on his wedding day and had tossed them up in the air to catch them in his mouth even more frequently that day.

Always one for show, Victor arranged for a beautifully decorated horse-drawn buggy to take his new wife home. Peoples' eyes popped of their sockets when he came down the stairs carrying his bride in his arms. Nan followed closely behind, saying this was not the thing to do and begging him to be careful lest he fall on his face with his bride in his arms, "Yu go break yu neck and kill yu wife even befor yu really married," she scolded gently. But Victor was in his element. He loaded Little Sparrow into the carriage and then before Nan realized what was happening, swung her up also and deposited her next to Little Sparrow. He then got in the front seat, grabbed the reigns of the buggy, and took them both to their new home in galloping style. Nan was in a state of shock but recovered quite quickly and enjoyed Victor's high spirits on his wedding day.

When she was old, Nan would relate this story again and again, shaking her head from side to side in fond memory of Victor's wanton enjoyment of his wedding day. Perhaps she recalled the gay abandon she had displayed on her own wedding day. Nan would laugh and a far away look would come into her eyes as she related this story.

Victor began to rent out his land in the village. He made investments in town and began to buy up land and build houses, which he then either rented out or sold for a large profit. He did not really have a job as such, but paid regular visits to his agents, negotiated land deals, and dealt with his building contractors when necessary. He no longer hung out with his friends. They dropped in from time to time, but not as often as they used to. Victor had settled down to married life.

Little Sparrow lived a very contented life. Nan looked after the house while she and Victor played at being married. Victor's passion for Little Sparrow never waned. He was always picking her up and dashing up to their bedroom for lovemaking no matter what time of the day it was because, as he would announce, when he wanted her he just had to have her.

In time they built their home, which became the largest house in the village. It had four large bedrooms upstairs with a study, drawing room, dining room, and a large veranda. On the shiny wooden floors were huge, darkly polished armchairs with over stuffed cushions, glossy wooden rocking chairs with smoky glass tables dotted around. Several potted palm trees and ferns completed the décor with the lacy white curtains that hung from the many windows and doorways.

The large open area downstairs had ample space where friends and family could get together and sit in hammocks, soft cushioned armchairs, or the ever-present rocking chairs. The house was built on a slight incline so that all the rooms would get the early morning sun and fresh morning breezes. The kitchen was build apart from the main house to keep the cooking smells from the living rooms. There were two outside latrines and two bathrooms, all with running water. The latrines were a source of pride since they were the most modern bathroom facilities in the village at that time.

Victor was a very serious cricket player who loved the game passionately. In truth, however he was quite a lousy cricketer; he always got bowled out for zero or almost zero but his redeeming quality as a cricketer was that he did bowl reasonably Ok. When he realized that other teams did not want him on their team because they found him more of a handicap than an asset, he created his own cricket team, ambitiously calling it The MCC after the famous English Team.

Victor bought all the best cricket equipment and gear available on the island and then purchased a piece of land on which to make his own cricket pitch. He arranged for his own team to play teams from other villagers. These teams were always willing to play against Victor's team because they were guaranteed to win the match and feted to the lavish parties he gave after each match.

Victor even went so far as to have an annual cricket award ceremony in the village for the best team in the village—his team, the only team in the village. At this award ceremony, Victor presented the highest scoring batsman, the best fielder, and the person who took the most wickets with cash prizes. Then he ceremoniously presented himself, as Captain, with the largest trophy celebrating the best team in the village.

This was all done in great humour and the whole village indulged him. He could afford it, they said. Let him have his fun. He displayed the large photographs of each of these award ceremonies all over his house.

Victor had yet another passion, - music, but he was a lousy musician. He did not have the patience to learn to play any of the instruments he bought, so he would hire a few musicians to accompany him whenever he sang. Victor would sing lustily at the musical evenings he would hold at his home almost every Saturday evening, getting so carried away that he would carry on singing until 6 o'clock the next morning.

Nan would have to arrange hasty breakfasts for the guests and the musicians who had been patient enough to last the night. More than likely Victor had paid them to sit and listen to him, so they could not really leave. I clearly remember some of these musical sessions. When I was little, I would peep curiously through the wooden slats of the study window at the group of noisy, happy, carefree throng, high on music and most probably rum.

Victor also loved books; he would buy lots of them to fill up his study. While growing up, I realized that despite his wild carefree streak, he did possess quite a questioning mind. The books he collected were mostly about religion. He owned holy books about all the big religions and many other books on religious thought and philosophy.

Years later I was quite surprised to find quite a few first editions amongst his prized books. Special books that he had heard about and wanted to read he would order directly from England. During quiet times, he could be found standing up beside a bookshelf, with one arm leaning on the shelf reading, and it was not unusual for him to break away from some trying or boring meeting that was held at home and rush upstairs for a half-hour break to read. I think in his later years he regretted not continuing his schooling and getting a better education. His thirst for knowledge was never quenched.

Clara, my Mummy, was born in that very carefree, happy atmosphere. Exactly a year and twenty days later, Fifi was born, and four years later, Dora followed. During each of Little Sparrow's pregnancies, Nan would quietly recall the prophetic words of the strange old fakir so many years before. After the birth of each baby girl, Nan would breathe a sigh of relief, silently thanking God that it had not been a baby boy.

Little Sparrow however was sad each time another girl was born. She so wanted to give Victor a son. She rejected the foolish superstition about a baby boy being unlucky for her. Victor, on the other hand, was adamant about not wanting a son. All he wanted was Little Sparrow, his cricket, his music, and his books—in that order.

Chapter 4

Nass was the second of Nan's three daughters. When she was a little girl, the old *faqir* had foretold that her life would be hard, and so it was. She was married off very young to Naaj, the first young man who asked for her hand. He was the son of a simple but honest farm worker who owned a small pocket of land surrounded by tall, thin trees down south in the dark, damp little village of Moruga.

Nass lived with her in-laws, who were very proud of the fact that their only son had married the granddaughter of the grand old matriarch, Gainder. Things went very well at first. Nass was happy and her husband was devoted and loving. Her mother-in-law, however, was very much the ruler of the roost. She could not bear anyone else receiving attention, so it was not long before she began to resent the attention her son Naaj was paying to his new wife. The mother-in-law soon began finding faults with Nass. At first they were little, niggling faults, but then they became more serious. Her mother-in-law seized every opportunity to fill Naaj's ears with complaints about Nass. She accused Nass of being lazy and a spendthrift. She also said Nass could not manage the house, that she had no idea how to cook, and that she expected to be waited on hand and foot. She even insisted Nass had airs and graces. In reality, Nass never had airs and graces. The prediction that her life would be hard was forever in her thoughts, so she was always prepared for the hardship and challenges that she knew her life would have.

Fed up with hearing his mother's non-stop complaints, Naaj appealed to Nass to keep the peace by helping more in the house and in the fields, and doing whatever his mother wanted of her. So Nass, willing to please her man, began to help even more in the house. Seeing that Nass was now bending to her wishes, her mother-in-law made her work like a slave. Nass now had to do all the housework, sweep, dust, tidy up, wash the clothes, and cook for the men folk returning from the fields.

Meanwhile, her mother-in-law would spend most of the day lounging in the hammock on the front porch, barking out orders to Nass, nagging her non-stop, and criticizing almost everything she did. When the mother-in-law was not lazing in the hammock, she was visiting her friends in the neighbourhood, comparing notes on useless daughters-in-law. The old hens were convinced their lazy good-for-nothing daughters-in-law had far too many airs and graces for their own good and were being spoiled by their soft gentle husbands and caring, loving mothers-in-law. They agreed that keeping them busy all day would keep them in their place.

New to the business of cooking and cleaning, Nass made many mistakes even though she tried hard to remember everything. She either burned or undercooked the food or forgot to pick up the washing from the line and close the windows when the rain came rushing down. She pounded the cocoa beans improperly, sweetened the tea too much or not enough, made tea when coffee was the order of the day, and so on.

Forgetting to fill the lamps with oil before dark was by far the worse crime Nass could have committed. The first time it happened, Naaj was so fed up with his mother's constant complaints, he did the only thing he could do. He took off his belt and beat Nass. He swung the belt left and right, left again and right again, hitting harder and harder as he got into the rhythm of his temper. Blinded by his own fury, he was now convinced that his mother was right. Nass was lazy and unwilling to help. Perhaps she did these things deliberately just to annoy his poor helpless old mother, who had given her life of hard work just for him. He had no choice but to straighten Nass out and teach her a lesson once and for all. He would not, could not take the constant complaints. He would show her who was boss. She would have to change her careless, thoughtless ways. If sweet talk did not make her understand, then perhaps the belt would, as his mother had suggested, "Yu have to show dem who is boss, yu can't be soft with dem, dey go sit on yu head and den yu go never wear de pant in yu own house ".

After the first beating, it became easier for Naaj to beat his wife and this soon became the pattern of Nass's life. She would get the belt across her back for any and every little thing. And then she had to help in the fields as well. In the scorching sun and blinding rain she worked the fields with Naaj and his father and then came home to finish the housework.

Through all of this, Nass discovered she loved planting. She tenderly and lovingly sowed beans, peas, vegetables, and fruit trees. Her flower garden soon became an obsession. It was a profusion of wild tropical colours, the prettiest in the village. Every chance she got, she would be out in the garden weeding and planting. Everything she planted grew and flourished. She began to quietly sell off some of her vegetables and fruits, hiding the money she earned under the bed in an old, rusty Jacob's English Biscuit tin.

In time, Nass got used to the beatings. By day she would be beaten; by night she would be arm in arm with Naaj. They would sit in the hammock in the porch and look up at the stars, sing love songs, laugh, and joke. She bore two boys, Evans and Ramsey. They settled into this routine. Nass could not imagine any other life. She loved her husband and was strangely contented.

Many years later when both her father-in-law and mother-in-law had died, the land was left to Naaj. It was then that Nass came into her own. By now she was an expert cook, could tend the fields, sew, manage the finances, and generally be in charge. Having been used to seeing his mother take control, Naaj was quite at ease with Nass looking after all the affairs. He had a fair amount of free time in the afternoons and it was during this time he would go to the rum shop to meet with friends and catch up on news.

The rum shop was the centre of village life. Filled to capacity, a peg or two or three was the order of the day after a long, hot day in the fields. The men laughed loudly at their raucous and bawdy jokes, made fun of other men's wives, and boasted about their manhood and the amount of money they had or hoped to have. It was all in good fun. Sometimes Naaj would forget to come home. There would always be that last one for the road or the last joke that had to be heard. Nass would either go herself to call him or send the boys to call him. When he did come home, he was usually in a drunken state, he ranted, raved, and swung his belt for good measure to keep Nass in place just as his dear mother had advised. He would then have his dinner or breakfast and take Nass off to bed.

The boys were used to this behavior; it was how most of the other families in the village lived. Their lives appeared to be the same as their friends and there was comfort in that. Evans and Ramsey both attended the village school. After finishing seventh standard, Evans, the more easy going laid back one, went to the nearest town of San Fernando to become a bookkeeper's apprentice to escape the hard life of a farmer. He lived as a paying houseguest in the home of another senior accounts clerk and his family of three pretty young daughters.

Inevitably he got one of the clerk's daughters Jessie, preg-nant and he ended up having to marry her. Jessie was a comely, plump thing with no desire except to have a man in her bed and be married. They continued living with Jessie's parents and eventually had four daughters. Evans was not ambitious and was content to remain a bookkeeping clerk. It was an easy, uncomplicated life. He was the dutiful son-in-law, listened to his wife, and did everything that was required of him.

Many years later, when his wife reminded him that he was entitled to a share in the family land, Evans went to Moruga and demanded his share. Nass was astute enough to send him packing. "How dare yu come here lookin' for land! Did yu help wok the land? Did yu stand by me? No, yu run off to da town. Yu gone an' marry a town gul, who doe care for yu mudder. Yu wer shame of we country people and now yu want mey land? Get lost! Ah don't want to see yu face again!"

Jessie, his wife, did not encourage him to mix with his side of the family after that. She called them "country bookies" and so Evans remained estranged from the family, seeing them only when they took the time to visit him. He never even showed up for family weddings or funerals. Later we got to know some of his daughters at school and we met them on the few occasions when they visited their grandmother, usually to ask for money.

Nass eventually gave Evans' daughters some of the gold jew-elry she had collected over the years, "Dey fadder is a fool but dey still mey granddaughters after all and I never had a gul child, so ah have to do the right ting!".

Ramsey was more sensitive to Nass and took a stand when her beatings became worse. This did not endear him to his father. Not wanting father and son to end up fighting, Nass decided that since Ramsey was a good student, he should go to college in town. They could not afford the fees, so he was packed off to Little Sparrow and Victor. Victor was a loving and generous family man and insisted that Ramsey was welcome to live with them and get a good education, something that Victor himself had yearned for after he had wasted his youth on cricket and chumming around with friends.

Ramsey graduated from college and went on to the Teacher's Training College. He loved woodwork and spent many an hour in the garden shed cutting, sawing, joining, and polishing pieces of furniture. I remember as a child we always got beautiful wooden bits and pieces as presents—coffee tables, tea trolleys, child-size rocking chairs, bookends, and the like. He used different shades of wood so his designs were always distinctive and much appreciated. Ramsey had also inherited his mother's love of planting. He became a member of the horticultural society and an expert in orchid and croton growing, winning many prizes for his orchids at the annual flower shows.

Living with Victor and Little Sparrow, Ramsey grew even closer to Clarla, Fifi, and Dora. This closeness remained all throughout their lives. He was the brother they did not have. Being a practical, man-about-town kind of person, Ramsey was always on hand when they needed him. He fixed their cupboard doors, mended leaks, helped them get an honest car mechanic, obtained builders for them, designed their gardens, and escorted them to the cinemas to see the latest Hollywood movies.

While at teacher's training college, Ramsey met Lucille and fell in love. Nass was not at all happy that Lucille was another town girl. Jessie was a painful example of what town girls did to poor country boys. She even went so far as to tell Ramsey that Lucille's father had a touch of the 'old tar brush,' A term that meant he had some black African blood running through his veins. This was more than she could take. Naaj, of course, agreed with her.

Lucille initially was not very happy with Ramsay either, as he was only the son of a villager, and who had worked the fields, as this was very much a peasant and well beneath her town girl status. Love got the better of them though, and eventually they decided to get married. The wedding was a quiet affair at Victor's house in Diamond. Nass and Naaj refused to attend.

Nass was desperate to travel. All her life she wanted to visit India, the land of her forefathers, and other places like London with its beautiful palaces and the Queen. The old English Jacob's biscuit tin box under the bed had been filled and emptied into a bank account many times. There was well over $10,000, a large sum for a poor humble village farmer.

In one of his sentimental moments, Naaj decided to surprise Nass and use the money in the bank to buy two plane tickets to London, England so she could see the Queen. The next day he went to the bank and withdrew the money. On the way home he decided to stop at the rum shop for a quick drink. He never came home that night.

Frantic with worry, Nass called up Ramsey who rushed to Moruga with the family from Diamond. The men and the villagers formed a search party. Much later that evening, Naaj's charred body was found near a pond not too far from their land. No one could understand how he could have been burned when there was a pond nearby. The mystery was never solved.

Later, when Ramsey and Nass went to the bank, they found out that Naaj had withdrawn all the money and was later seen at the rum shop patting his pocket and boasting that he was going to take his wife on an airplane. It was quite a shock to the family and must have been extremely difficult for Nass. She believed that her husband had been so tragically murdered and all her hard backbreaking savings had gone with him at the same time.

I have very vivid memories of happy Sundays in the old rain-stained mildewed wooden house in Moruga before that sad time. When I was little, Fifi would come to Diamond in her big, fancy Statemans car and take us all for a long drive through lush winding tropical forest roads down south to Moruga to see Nass.

As we neared the house, Fifi would slow down the car, sound the car horn loudly, and drive slowly past the house to turn the car round. In that short space of time, we would hear Nass shouting to the boy servant. "Go catch a fowl, go get a duck and kill it quick, quick. De family come to visit." There was always so much excitement in her voice as she shouted out the instructions.

With Fifi's big car parked outside, the whole village could see that her rich family had come from the town to visit. Nass made a big fuss. The fowl or duck was quickly killed and as she was busy cooking it, she'd order the boy servant, "Go cut a pine. See if the sapodilla ripe and pull down the coconuts. Hurry up, yu lazy slouch." The poor little fellow would try to do all these things at once. If he happened to walk past Nass, she would pull his ear because he was "such a slow coach."

We children would leave the hustle and bustle and cooking smells in the kitchen to escape outside. It was an adventure to walk through the swampy fields and see rice growing or pull up a pineapple from its thorny bush, pick pigeon peas, and dig up yams and sweet potatoes. I loved the damp, earthy smell of the muddy fields and the brightly coloured tropical birds. It gave me such a sense of freedom! It felt like I was in the Garden of Eden I had heard and read about.

After we had eaten the fowl or duck with the sweet, sticky lagoon rice, pigeon peas, and sweet potatoes, there was fresh pineapple, custard apple, and sapodilla to follow. Nass would bake pone, a mixture of pumpkin, yams, coconut, sugar, and condensed milk. How we loved to eat the hot, glutinous, sticky pone! We kids washed all this down with coconut water while the adults added just a nip of rum to their coconut water.

After consuming the heavy lunch, the grown-ups would all go into one of the bedrooms, lie together on the bed, and bring Nass up to date on the latest news and gossip in the family. Tired from our romp through the fields, we children would all sit together in the old hammock singing all the latest songs we had heard on the crackley radio. The grown-ups were far too busy talking and munching nuts and fruit to remind us to keep quiet.

As evening approached, Nass would grind freshly dried cocoa beans and boil the dark brown mess with water before sweetening it with condensed milk. The house and yard would be filled with the thick, velvety smell of hot chocolate. We would be given huge enamel mugs of the best tasting hot chocolate you could ever imagine, with chunks of fresh bread and tinned New Zealand salted butter.

As Nass got older, she could not manage the land anymore and had to sell the property. She bought a house in the small town of Princes Town to be close to her older sister Ismat. With only herself to worry about, Nass decided she would now realize her long-time dream of traveling. She traveled all over the world by herself. She saw the Queen of England, made friends everywhere, and had a wonderful time. She was a brave, strong, resilient woman who had learned to be happy and content with her lot in life.

Nass is still alive. At nearly 100 years of age, she does not travel anymore but insists on living on her own in the house in Princes Town. It is now quite old and run down, but she is still a fiesty stubborn old woman and will not budge from there.

Ramsey has kept two maids to look after her, as she suffers from arthritis and needs help to walk. Quite cantankerous and difficult now, she shouts and waves her walking stick at them all the time. Ramsey visits her every day to feed her; otherwise, she refuses to eat.

Lucille never visits her. But Clara and Fifi often visit too. On occasions, to give the maids a break, they would bring her home to Diamond to stay with Clara for a few weeks. Her memory is still quite sharp, although she mixes up her dates. She often relates stories from her past and always says that when she does her gardening the next day; she will send us some vegetables and flowers. I visit her every time I go home. She always remembers me and asks about my son and husband. She is convinced I am the prettiest girl in the family and tells everybody so, much to my embarrassment.

On my last trip to Trinidad, I brought a cutting of the very Croton bush she planted in her yard many, many years ago. It grows outside my bedroom window. Every time I look at it, I remember those times in Moruga and Nass' strong survival instinct. A good lesson to all of us.

Chapter 5

Little Sparrow and Victor were very happy with their life. Victor continued to prosper by buying up property in different towns in the southern part of the island. He built or repaired the houses and rented them out. This was his main source of income. Of course, little Sparrow believed deep inside that having a son would complete their family. It was the one great sadness in her life. She shared these feelings with Nan, who told her time and time again that having a son was not everything. She did not tell Little Sparrow that if she had a son her life could be in danger.

Nan had told Victor about the old man's prophecy years before and he too insisted he did not want a son. He tried to convince Little Sparrow that his girls were all he wanted and needed. Little Sparrow was never truly convinced that he meant this and continued to quietly grieve, thinking that she had failed her husband by not giving him a son.

Little Sparrow was very much the lady of the manor—the squire's wife, if there was such a thing in Trinidad. The people in the village loved and respected her. The women turned to her for advice and help just like the men turned to Victor. She set up a "sou sou," where the women in the village would contribute a small amount of money every month and the total collected was given to each of them in turn so that they could "do things."

She was always there for the women when their babies were

born or their children got married. She shared their joys and their grief. They listened to her advice on how to cope with their drunken or wayward husbands and difficult mothers-in-law, what curtains would match, or what furniture they should buy. They even asked her to speak to their husbands on their behalf. For Christmas, Eid, and Divali she collected clothes and toys for the needy. She enjoyed helping the women in the village and was happy that she and Victor could make a difference in their lives.

Victor's spontaneous joy of life endeared him to all. His love of sport, especially cricket, drew many of the young men in the village to seek his company. But he had yet another dimension to his personality—his love of reading and collecting books. He had become a compulsive reader whenever he was at home, trying to catch up on his education. He could be found at seminars, debates, and intellectual gatherings.

In his quest for knowledge, he even set up and organised some of these sessions, inviting the people he wanted to talk to or hear speak. Over the years he also learned the art of public speaking and in time was considered a very eloquent speaker himself.

I suppose Victor's fascination with religion was natural. Coming from India, he had lost the religion of his forefathers and had become part of a multi-religious community. The only way to get an education was to attend the local missionary schools and pretend to be a true believer of that particular school of thought. Victor collected as many books as he could on different religions. He became an avid reader and read every book he could lay his hands on. He would compare different points of view and ways of thinking and discuss their similarities and differences. He argued his points so well that one was always convinced that he really knew what he was talking about and that his views and interpretations were the correct ones.

Victor loved the fact that he was now gaining a reputation as an orator. He enjoyed speaking and reveled in performing his speeches before an audience. He emphasized each point dramatically and emphatically, his voice rising and falling to punctuate his words, then effectively building up to his concluding arguments. Having made his point, he would then humbly stand back, head slightly bowed with a shy smile, and wait for the accolades and applause. He was never disappointed. The more they clapped and cheered, the better he got. He actually looked taller and more massive as he stood on the stage behind the podium with his big voice resounding throughout the hall.

Little Sparrow found all this quite humorous. She would laughingly shake her head when she heard about these sessions, never actually having seen Victor "perform." Fifi however accompanied Victor on many of these tours and enjoyed the experience as much as he did if not more. Clara and Dora found the whole thing far too showy and very embarrassing. They often teased Fifi by saying, "You are just like your father. You enjoy all this centre stage show business nonsense." Their taunts never bothered Fifi; she loved the whole affair and would continue to be a part of it. It did not matter one bit what her sisters thought of the whole thing. No doubt because of this support, Fifi became Victor's favorite child, taking the place of the son he never had.

Victor helped set up schools by contributing money to their building funds and helping to maintain some of the costs. He made rounds to all these schools to ensure that everything was going smoothly. Other like-minded people joined him in these efforts and they soon formed an organization whose function was to check out the standards of the schools they supported.

These, of course, were private schools that did not come under Government controls. Later on, as the members of this organization grew, they began to meet formally every month at one of the member's houses. Eventually the association became the "Society for the Unification of all Religious Thought," a subject that was very close to Victor's heart. They continued to look after the schools, but also had other meetings where they shared their views and beliefs. They hoped that in time the whole island would understand that everybody could live in perfect harmony despite their religious inclinations.

Victor was approached several times by political parties to stand in the local elections. He always refused, preferring to work on the sidelines and not identify himself with any one particular party. That way he could be friends with all and not have to be concerned with what party formed the government. They all appeared to be fundamentally the same anyway. He also believed that becoming involved in politics would interfere with the hobbies and pastimes that were nearest and dearest to his heart. He did, however, have very private affiliations, which he shared with no one except Little Sparrow and Nan.

For Nan, looking after Victor and his family was a privilege. She considered herself blessed. Her only fear was that something terrible would happen to Little Sparrow before her fortieth birthday, as the old man had predicted. She was no longer worried about Little Sparrow having a boy child. Dora, the last of the three girls, was now eighteen years old and it did not look as though Little Sparrow would ever get pregnant again.

Little Sparrow's fortieth birthday was approaching and Nan had planned a big celebration. Little Sparrow had survived her fortieth year. Now it was plain sailing. She would live to be a hundred and she would be rich beyond her wildest dreams! Life would be perfect. Nan was overjoyed. Relatives near and far were invited to the party. Nass and Ismat along with their husbands and children would all come to Diamond to spend the whole week leading up to the big day.

The day arrived. Nan had the butcher come home early that morning to slaughter the goat. It had to be a special one, young enough so the meat was tender, and big enough to feed the whole clan with some extra for them to take home as well.

Nan did all the cooking herself, preparing everyone's favorite dish. Curried goat meat, crabs cooked with coconut milk spinach and okra; pigeon peas and rice; pounded-up half-ripe bananas; sliced sweet potato; red kidney beans cooked gumbo-style with tomatoes and West Indian herbs; stewed chicken Trinidad style; and all the extra trimmings Nan insisted had to accompany the meal. The grand finale, the piece de resistance, was her special butter pound cake, large enough to accommodate forty candles. The birthday party preparation was a labor of love. She was not celebrating the birthday as much as she was celebrating the new lease on Little Sparrow's life.

The party was a success. The food was exceptionally good and everyone was jolly. The best Scottish whiskey was brought in for the occasion—no cheap rum today. The villagers all came to pay their respects, showering Little Sparrow with blessings and good wishes for a long and happy life. Everyone got quite inebriated and Victor and his group of musicians led the merrymaking until the wee hours of the morning.

A few months went by. Life had returned to normal. Then Little Sparrow woke up one morning feeling decidedly unwell. She felt nauseated and then fainted. She was quickly rushed to the doctor, who without hesitation told the family that Little Sparrow was pregnant. Pregnant at forty! Little Sparrow was shocked. How could she be pregnant at forty? It must be the time of a woman's life when her menses stopped, she insisted. But no it wasn't. She really was pregnant at forty.

As Little Sparrow adjusted to the idea that she was to have

another baby, her excitement grew. Even Victor began to feel a little thrill. Perhaps it would be a baby boy. Maybe God had decided they were to have a son after all. Only Nan was uneasy. She could not forget the old man's prophetic words. She became quiet and withdrawn. No one could understand this change in her. She was too afraid to tell anyone how frightened she felt as she tried to carry on as usual.

A few months later, in her sixth month of pregnancy, Little Sparrow began to get swollen feet and hands. She felt tired all the time, so she went to the Doctor for her check-up, only to be told that it would be better if she went to the hospital for a few days to do some tests. After all the tests had been done, she was told that she had very high blood pressure and that it could affect the baby. She was advised complete bed rest. A week later, Little Sparrow went home but continued to feel unwell. She began to swell up even more. She was then advised to stay in hospital until the birth of the baby.

Three weeks later Little Sparrow went into premature labor. A tiny little baby boy, so blue that it looked black, was born dead. Little Sparrow never knew. She died of a massive heart attack during the delivery. Victor was devastated. He was like a broken man. He stopped eating, forgot to have a bath and change his clothes, cried like a baby a lot of the time, and refused to sleep in his bedroom.

Nan had lost her favorite daughter, the child who had given her so much joy in her life. It was hard for her but she had to be strong for Victor. Pulling herself together, she shouted and bullied him to carry on again. "It is God's will," she told him. She reminded him of his strong faith and his three daughters who were suffering just as he was.

Clara, Fifi, and Dora could not believe or accept the death of their loving mother, who had been such a safe and stable rock in their lives. Fifi was hysterical and grieved loudly and dramatically. Clara and Dora suffered their loss quietly, wearing black clothes for two years in her memory. They turned to Nan for comfort. She was the only one who appeared strong and in control. Nan had no choice. She had been warned so many years before that this might come to pass. The old man was right. God had given her a difficult test and she would face it bravely.

Chapter 6

Rookie was a pocket-sized beauty, all four feet eleven inches of her. Her mother had come from some sort of East Indian stock that was diluted with a touch of Spanish and a bit of indigenous Carib blood. No one was quite certain what kind of origins her father had but it certainly had made him a good-looking man. He had smooth, fair skin with light brown, wavy hair. Rookie's doll like perfection came from both her mother and father's side of the family.

There was never any doubt that Rookie's beauty had gone to her head. From the time she was little, she teased, showed off, and flirted with every male who came her way. She was notoriously wild, to put it mildly and no one could control her. She behaved as though the world belonged to her and her alone. She believed her good looks were her passport through life and she wanted to have as much fun as she possibly could. She grabbed whatever came her way and claimed it as being rightfully hers. She knew what it was to be poor and to long for the pretty things that other not-so-pretty girls had. She would show them, she vowed. They may have the money, but she had the looks to get all the things she wanted in life—expensive gold jewels, fancy clothes, and a beautiful home with large gardens full of trees and beautiful flowers. Her beauty would be her ticket out of her overcrowded home with the noise and stench of four younger siblings, a harassed, screaming mother, and lazy, good-for-nothing father.

Khris, the grandson of an indented laborer who had immigrated to Trinidad from the sub-continent many years before, fell hopelessly in love with Rookie and begged her to marry him. Rookie, who had had many lovers by the time she was 18, saw no reason to rush into marriage, especially with the offspring of some poor indented laborer. Totally besotted, Khris did not seem to mind her constant ridicule. He just followed her around like a little lost puppy. Occasionally, when Rookie was in a good mood, she would be amused by his devotion and encourage him to stick around. But most of the time she would be quite irritated by the unwanted attention he gave her. He cramped her style and embarrassed her, especially since he was not particularly good-looking. Khris was content to bide his time, certain that she would come around one day.

Khris was not very tall—a mere five foot seven inches—had dark skin, a rather large nose, and a round, bald patch on top of an almost flat head. He was not wealthy, which obviously added to his unfortunate qualities and made him appear even less attractive to Rookie. He had nothing going for him except his kind, gentle, soft manner.

But life is full of many surprises. Things took a dramatic turn for Khris when Rookie discovered she was pregnant. She had no idea who the father of the child was. All her former boyfriends and lovers who were once so devoted were now too busy or otherwise occupied to come around anymore. She found herself alone with no one to stand by her. She lost her joie de vie. Her face became drawn and pale, she lost a lot of weight, and her shoulders slumped under the burden of her predicament. The early morning retching and puking had taken its toll. People began to gossip. They had predicted that she would end up like this, "Wild whore! Good- for-nothing trollop, bringing disgrace to her poor family." If that was what beauty did for a young girl, thank God their daughters were not beautiful!

Rookie's parents were ashamed of the bad name she was giving the family. Being an unwed mother was the most disgraceful thing for a young woman. Rookie's father had to show the village that he disapproved and that he was not to blame. He came out of his malaise to beat her badly. He took the belt to her in a mad frenzy and then threw her out of the house onto the road, all swollen and bruised. He told her it was better for her to die than to bring this shame to the family name. Rookie had no choice but to leave the house and find somewhere else to live, preferably in another part of the island. She thought of going to see some back street midwife to pull the wretched thing out of her body, but she did not know who to ask for that kind of information and it would cost money she didn't have. She did not know what to do. Lost and helpless, she would turned to the only one she thought might help her—Khris. She would ask him to loan her some money and she would get a job. Someone must surely need a maid. She would start a new life, God willing. So she made her way to where he lived and sat under the mango tree near his house waiting for him to come home.

Khris came home later that evening. He was surprised to see Rookie sitting there waiting for him. "What yu do'in here? Wah happen to yu? Yu lookin' real bad, gul. Who hit yu up so? Tell mey. Ah go mash dey skull in. Tell mey!"

Rookie burst into tears and threw herself into his arms, sobbing out her plight to the first sympathetic person she had found. Khris, of course, had heard the rumors. Seeing her like this, so alone and helpless, his heart filled with protective compassion. He impulsively decided that this was his chance to be her hero and come to her rescue. He offered to marry her and accept the baby as his own. Having no other way out, Rookie readily agreed. At least she would not be alone and on the street. And she would have someone who loved her and who was willing to stand by her when everyone else had deserted her. And so

Rookie and Khris got married. What an unlikely looking couple they made—a beauty with her loving, devoted, grateful beast!

Not long afterwards, a baby girl was born. They called the baby Rita. The family lived modestly in a small house at the junction of the two main roads that crossed in the centre of Diamond Village. Rookie settled down with Khris and tried very hard to become the respectable, loving, dutiful wife. She cared for her husband and looked after their tiny home with care and attention.

Rookie was grateful to Khris and tried to show it every way she could. She even got used to his clumsy touch and awkward lovemaking and in her own way, grew to love him. Their life was adequate. Khris worked hard for his family. They had food on the table, decent clothes to wear, and enough money to get by. After a few years they had another baby girl who they named Ena. The birth of a boy named Winston soon followed. Khris was content; he had made an honest woman out of the most beautiful women in the village. And, as unbelievable as it was, she had grown to love him in her way and he had three beautiful children. Life was good.

Some time later Khris suddenly fell down dead. Just like that. It caused quite a shock in the village. How could this man in the prime of his life and with everything to live for just drop down dead! "You know it must have been de pressure of being married to that woman." People began to talk about Rookie. Her past life had caught up with her. "She must have been too demanding or insatiable in bed," they speculated. "He heart done gone and give up on he. She to blame, dats for sure."

Rookie ignored the talk. She hardened herself to the bad talk and carried on, as only she knew how. No one really knew how Rookie made ends meet after that. She caused a few tongues to wag as people wondered how she could live with three children to support with no obvious income coming in. Khris had not left her very much money; in fact, the little money he did leave her was used to bury him. Rookie somehow managed to run her home and send all three children to school. The village gossips whispered that she had gentlemen friends who paid discreet calls to her late at night.

The two girls, Rita and Ena, finished standard seven at the local village school and then went on to learn cooking and sewing, skills that their mother hoped would bring them good, decent husbands. Rookie was determined that her girls would have opportunities she did not have. Snaring the right kind of husband would be the best way out of their impoverished lives. She watched over them like an overprotective hawk, lest they fall by the wayside as she had done.

Rita grew up to be a very tall and stunningly beautiful girl. It was not long before she married a boy from a respectable family in the village. The boy's parents were not too happy with his choice, since they knew of Rookie's reputation and that Rita was conceived out of wedlock. But there was nothing they could do to stop him from marrying her, and because they did not want to lose their son, they reluctantly agreed to the marriage.

Rookie was delighted with the marriage. It was a very quiet affair with only the parents of the couples attending. After the wedding, Rita and her husband decided to leave Diamond Village to make a fresh start in another part of the island, far away from the prying eyes of people who had nothing better to do but to gossip and mind other people's business. Rita had had enough of that in her young life. Being Rookie's daughter had not been easy. Everyone expected that she would be a chip off the old block and just as wild and wanton as Rookie had been in her young days.

Rookie's other daughter, Ena, was not at all pretty. She had inherited her father's unflattering looks. She was not only unattractive with her big nose and flat head, but she was also thin and tall with a sour, irritable disposition. Ena had no lady-like talents to her credit either. She had no friends but developed a very close bond with her mother. She was also very devoted to Winston, her younger brother. She cared for him lovingly, like a mother would do. In her eyes, he could do no wrong. She demanded his devotion and made sure he knew how much she cared for him.

As a result, Winston was a rather pampered little boy when it came to his mother's and sister's affections. He was not a particularly good-looking child, having taken more after his father, but he did have Rookie's sparkling eyes and charm as well as a charismatic, likeable personality.

To his credit, he did go regularly to school and enjoyed studying. Being a bright student, he won a scholarship to attend college where he majored in English Literature. His love of drama and acting and that led him to perform in many plays. Shakespeare was his forte; he loved the sounds of the old English words and phrases and the way the poetic prose fell easily off his lip. He could actually feel the sound of the letters as he rolled the syllables around in his mouth. It was like gargling with words, he thought. He had a beautiful, resounding voice that seemed perfectly suited to Shakespeare.

As a little girl I remember hearing him recite lines from Hamlet, Julius Caesar, and Twelfth Night. He acted out the roles of all the characters, changing his voice and tone for each one. But his absolute favourite character was that of the jealous but romantic husband Othello. Playing the part of a husband tormented by his wife's unfaithfulness suited his temperament to a tee. The role was written just for him, he thought. He loved showing off.

Winston's other literary passion was Greek Mythology. He relayed the adventures of the Gods and Goddesses with such clarity and vision that one might have thought he had been a part of that era or perhaps had incarnated as one of the heroes. Listening to his stories was like stepping back in time. I remember visualizing Pegasus galloping across the sky and hiding behind the clouds. I could hear Neptune's voice in the roar of the waves, see Medusa's face hidden in between the leaves of the pommcetay tree in the backyard, and Cassiopeia flung up to the heavens to remain there forever as a beautiful collection of stars.

Winston lived a Bohemian lifestyle. To him, life was for fun. He believed it should be lived one day at a time, fully, and with gay abandon. The fact that he had no money was never a problem. He would always find delicious food to eat, a shoulder to lean on, and a warm bed to sleep in. It did not matter if it was under the trees or the starry sky.

The well-to-do young men of his college belonged to the Freemason and Lodge fraternities. Charming and popular Winston was also invited to join. He and his young friends participated in activities that rich young men did at that time. Several times during the week they would drink and smoke to excess. On Saturday nights they would dance then every Sunday they would go to the beach. And they would try with the obsessive determination of their youth to get laid whenever and wherever possible.

At that time it was very difficult to get their respectable girlfriends to go all the way with them. Since no one wanted to have to pay for sex, their safest bet was to make friends with bored housewives who had raging libidos. By all accounts, Winston had quite a few of those frustrated housewives on his list. He was the Casanova of the village, and although many husbands must have heard rumors, they could not prove he was the one responsible for their wives' nervous excitement and glow of sexual contentment.

Winston had a close call once when a poor unsuspecting husband came home early from the office one day. Winston had to beat a hasty getaway by jumping out the window. After doing this, he brazenly knocked on the front door and invited the husband to go out for a drink to the nearest rum shop. Of course, the husband readily agreed. Winston was great company; he always had good, raunchy stories to tell about other people's horny wives.

Clara had heard of Winston and his antics. She could not avoid it as everyone in the village talked about him and his activities. "Look at dat Winston boy, ole Rookie's son. Dat man sure take after he mudder. He does keep the women sweet." Because he was a man, he escaped the ridicule his mother had endured; instead, he was regarded with quiet, almost jealous amusement.

Winston had also noticed Clara. Self-conscious with attractive looks and pompous airs, she thought it beneath her to acknowledge any advances made by the simple young men of the village. She had much bigger fish to catch. She already had many admirers from the town where she was attending high school. But she was vain and very much aware of the looks and remarks the young men in the village were making. She pretended not to notice, but secretly enjoyed the stir she caused.

Winston saw through her act. He got his friends to tease her while he quietly hung back and looked on. Clara would turn red in the face, stick her little button nose up in the air, and sashay on. One day he decided to make a move. He went up to her and tried to chat her up. Clara looked at him scornfully and with as much contempt as she could muster, told him in no uncertain terms that she would have nothing to do with him and he should just get out of her way. With a toss of her head, she flounced away, muttering to herself, "Who on earth does he think he is?"

Winston was more than a bit taken aback. How could she possibly resist him? Everyone said he was irresistible. He had all those married women in the village crazy about him. "Who did she think she was?" The more he thought about it, the more obsessed he was about getting her to notice him. He started waiting for her on street corners, near bus stops, and anywhere he thought he might get a chance to see her. Whenever he tried to talk to her, she snubbed him. He tried everything he could think of to get her attention, but Clara continued to ignore him. To an outsider, it was obvious that she was very aware of him and was quite bothered—even flattered—by his attentions, even though she continued to appear to look right through him.

One day when he had almost reached the end of his tether, he marched up to her and grabbing her arm said, "I have every intention of marrying you." She roughly shook off his hands and replied in her haughtiest tone, "Not if you were the last man on this earth." They had, in their own way, declared war.

Chapter 7

Clara was now quite perturbed and more than a little frightened by Winston's relentless pursuit of her. There was no way she would ever be attracted to him. He was not particularly handsome—although he did have a certain charm—and he was short—only five feet seven inches tall. Besides his looks, there was his wild reputation. There was talk that he had barely left his mistress' bed when her husband came home early from work one day. No way would she demean herself by even talking to such a shameless womanizer. He must have a lot of nerve to think that she would ever fall for him and marry him.

There was never any doubt that Clara was the catch of Diamond Village. All the old mothers with sons of marriageable age hoped that one of their sons would be the one to catch Clara's eye. As Victor's eldest daughter, she would have 'means' one day. She was attending the best high school on the island and she was smart.

Clara had another claim to fame, it was her portrayal of Portia in the court scene of the Merchant of Venice in the school play. She spoke her lines with such emotion, confidence, and conviction that one might think she had written the words herself. Everyone agreed that her performance was the best the school had ever witnessed. Her voice and diction were greatly admired. She was exactly the way Portia was supposed to be. Clara was quite proud of that performance and reminded everyone about it as often as possible. Fifi and Dora would patiently watch her enact the scene over and over again so she could reassure them, and herself, that she was really as good as everyone had said she was.

Clara was more than just attractive. She had the good fortune to have a perfect, heart-shaped face and a smooth coffee-colored complexion that included an enviable blue-black mole on her left cheek, which was surely a sign of good luck, or so the old wives claimed. Her pretty smile displayed perfect pearly white teeth. Clara was most proud of her twenty-three inch waist. She reveled in the fact that she had the tiniest waist of all her friends. Her round breasts and full shapely hips accentuated her tiny waist.

Clara had thick, wavy, long hair that she wanted desperately to cut. Victor would not hear of it, so Clara kept trimming her hair little by little until it was shoulder-length. Victor did not notice at first because she always had it pinned up at the sides. One day, however, as she was brushing it out, it suddenly dawned on him that her hair looked considerably shorter than it used to be. He asked Little Sparrow, who had to have been aware of Clara's actions, if she knew what had happened to Clara's hair. Little Sparrow played innocent. "I have no idea," she said. "Clara's hair looks the same to me. Perhaps it is your imagination," she suggested.

A few days later, Victor asked Clara out right what had happened to her hair. Clara innocently reminded him about the fever that she had had a few months before. Her hair, she explained, had fallen out in big clumps due to her weakness after that illness. She had trimmed it a wee bit to help strengthen it and make it grow again. Surprisingly, Victor did recall a fever, but he thought it had been well over a year ago. Still unsure, he decided to take her word for it. He then left it at that, reminding her that she should have proper food and get hot coconut oil massages to help her hair grow back quickly.

Of course, Clara's hair never did grow back to its former length; by some strange miracle, it stayed shoulder-length. Victor probably realized he was beaten and decided to concede defeat with dignity. The deed was already done and, therefore, not worth a bitter and tearful confrontation.

Clara, however, had one physical blemish that she believed marred her perfection—the thumb on her left hand. She called it her "looly" finger. Clara had been born with ten fingers like everyone else. They were a little stubby, but otherwise normal. She was about eight years old when the accident occurred on coconut-picking day. Coconut-picking day came every few months. The skinny little yard boy would climb like a monkey to the top of the coconut palms that were at the back of the house and pull down the huge bunches of young coconuts. Great care was taken to pick the nuts when they were just the right size and age so that the milk would be at its sweetest and the jelly inside still soft and tender. This particular kind of coconut water was the best remedy for flushing out the kidneys and clearing up any urinary tract infections, or so the old wives said. Little Sparrow made sure that first thing every morning the whole family had some pure coconut water to drink.

On coconut picking days, Little Sparrow would sit under a shady tree in the yard and supervise the pulling down of the nuts. All the parts of the coconut, including its leaves, were important. Little Sparrow would ensure that just enough of the fronds were cut down to make "cokeya" brooms for sweeping the yard and that the boy did not get carried away and cut down all the nuts. Some of the nuts had to remain on the trees to mature and dry for the next harvest. When the nuts were dry enough, they would be picked. By then, the jelly would have hardened and become oily. The hard, oily jelly would be grated and squeezed so that the oil could be extracted. This oil made an excellent conditioner that guaranteed long, thick, shiny hair. The course fiber found inside the shell of the dry nut was formed into balls, which were excellent for scouring pots and pans, rubbing out stubborn stains, and stuffing mattresses and cushions.

Everyone was busy on coconut picking-day. Many chores had to be done and all hands were busy. The girls were expected to help by fetching and carrying. On that particular day, there was a huge mound of young nuts waiting to be sorted into piles to be distributed to relatives, friends, and neighbors. Clara called out to the yard boy to cut open a nut for her to drink. It was always a thrill to cut open the freshly picked nut and then drink straight from the coconut. The water was sweetest and freshest at that stage. The yard boy was busy sorting out the nuts and could not immediately cut open the nut for Clara. He called out to her, telling her he would be there in a little while.

Clara was always very impatient. When she wanted some-thing, she wanted it then and there. Deciding she would not wait, she picked up the big, sharp cutlass, which she knew she was not supposed to touch. Holding the nut with her left hand, she brought the cutlass down heavily to cut it open. But instead of cutting the nut, she chopped half an inch off her thumb. She screamed more from shock than pain, and dropped the cutlass. The half-inch piece of her thumb was lost in the pile of nuts and fronds. Her hot blood gushed and squirted everywhere. Little Sparrow screamed and ran towards Clara. Nan came running out of the kitchen. She scolded Little Sparrow for allowing such a thing to happen, and warned her that Victor would be furious that this terrible thing had happened because of their lack of attention to the children.

Overly dramatic as ever, Fifi started to scream and stomp her feet as if her finger had been cut off. Little Dora cried quietly, more frightened by the shouting and screaming than by the disfigurement of Clara's hand. Clara was now crying, more because of what Victor would say when he came home and found out she had not listened when they had told her to wait.

Iodine was quickly poured over the thumb to kill the germs. Then the thumb was wrapped in a clean cloth. They looked for the wayward piece of flesh in case the doctor could sew the pieces together, but they did not find it. It was lost somewhere in the pile of coconut husks and dust. The finger healed quickly and neatly, but it was a long time before Clara could look at it without crying.

As she grew older, Clara looked after her 'looly' finger with the same delicate meticulous care that she looked after the rest of her fingers and hands. She regularly filed and polished the little bit of nail that still sprouted out of the rounded stub. This looly finger never detracted from her beauty; in fact, no one really noticed it much, even though Clara was always very conscious of it and kept her fingers curled up when meeting new people, hoping they would not notice it.

When Winston could not get Clara to talk to him, he decided to make friends with Fifi, hoping that he could somehow get to Clara through her sister. He hoped that Fifi would be his ally. It seemed like a good plan. He caught up to Fifi when she was coming home from school and told her how much he had fallen in love with Clara. He admitted that he had been wild, but that Clara was the one he had always been searching for. She was the love of his life. If she did not give him a chance, he would surely die of a broken heart like some lovesick Romeo. Fifi was totally taken in by Winston's charm and the story of this Casanova's unrequited love touched her heart.

Flattered that she had been asked to be the important go-between in this love story, she agreed to help him. She was convinced that Winston deserved a chance. He must really care for Clara if he was prepared to go to such great lengths to woo her, she thought. She was convinced that Winston was a sweet, caring person who just needed a fair chance. She could not understand why people said he was so wild. She decided she would love to have him as her brother-in-law. She went to talk to Clara on Winston's behalf to plead his case and to tell her how much he loved and admired her. Fifi could not understand why Clara acted so snooty and haughty. She tried to persuade Clara to at least talk to Winston, but Clara would not give in. While Fifi was sad that Clara would not listen to Winston, she was loyal to her sister and her wishes. She finally agreed that if Clara was adamant that she wanted no part of Winston, then she would support her sister. And so from that day on, she also snubbed Winston.

Quite despondent now and in total despair, Winston approached Dora, who was much younger that Fifi and Clara and was the most romantic and gentle one of the three sisters. Dora felt sorry for Winston and pleaded with Clara to "just talk to him. He is really quite nice. Don't listen to what people say." Clara would not budge or soften.

Dora, like Fifi, had also developed a soft spot for Winston. She found the whole thing wonderfully romantic, straight out of a novel.... a desperately in love, reformed, romantic hero ready to die for the love of his lady fair. She quietly suggested to Winston that he talk to Victor. "If you love her so much, why don't you ask Pa if you could marry her? Pa likes nice, straightforward people. It is better to be up front." Winston liked the idea very much. Why had he not thought of this before? He took young Dora's advice, went to Victor, and told him that although he had no money and no real family name, he loved Clara very much. He said he had sown his wild oats and was now ready to settle down and be a good and dutiful husband to Clara.

Victor, who had been observing the goings on for some time,

found the young man charming. So what if he had had a "good time and had sown his wild oats?" That was not such a bad thing. Most young men did that sort of thing. He had not really hurt anyone. He would make a good husband, he said to himself. As for not having money, that, too, was no problem. Victor had enough and would see that his daughter got everything she needed. If Winston kept his job as a schoolteacher and continued to study, they would have a good life together with good prospects. "In all fairness," he told Winston, "I cannot decide for my daughter, but I will talk to her."

Victor did talk to Clara and asked her to at least get to know Winston. If after six months she did not want to have anything to do with him, Victor agreed that he would not push her into a marriage she was dead set against. Winston received permission to visit the house and meet Clara at home. Clara was very upset with her father, so she went to Little Sparrow and complained. Little Sparrow, who also had a secret soft spot for the soft-spoken, charming Winston, convinced Clara that no harm would be done and that she would herself send him packing after six months if Clara wanted her to. She thought Clara should give him a chance. She would have nothing to lose.

Disappointed with her parent's decision, Clara went to her room and sobbed. It was not that she hated Winston; she had been quite excited when he had pursued her. It was her pride. She had said so many things to him, chased him away, insulted him, and now she had to be polite to him? How could she face him and the people in the village after she had said so many horrible things? She was sure everyone would laugh at her. They would surely remember the taunts she so carelessly threw at him. Her friends would also tease her. She had made so many jokes at his expense and now he had her parents' permission to come courting. What terrible, terrible irony! She would never live that shame down. Clara shared her anguish with Fifi. Always the one to rescue the downtrodden and suffering, Fifi promised to do everything she could to sort out the situation, she had an inspired ploy.

Fifi went to Victor and told him she had heard that Winston had TB, the dreaded disease that carried a great taboo. People stayed far away from those who had the disease. No one wittingly married into a family that had someone with TB. Victor was smart and caught on to Fifi's plan. He boxed her ears for saying that Winston had TB when he did not. Poor So Clara had to reluctantly agree to give Winston a chance. This pleased Dora very much and sent Winston to high heaven.

When Winston first began to visit the house, Clara would not come out to meet him. She stayed in her room while Winston sat and talked with the family. He would tease Nan and commend her on her cooking, take little presents of English chocolates and flowers for Little Sparrow, talk politics and religion with Victor, tell Dora about the movies he had seen, and promised to take her to see the latest movie if she could talk Clara into going as well.

By now only Clara and Fifi were immune to his charms. But how long could Clara stay away from someone who always seemed to be hanging around? In time, curiosity brought her out of her room when he was visiting and within three months, both she and Fifi eagerly participated in the lively chitchat when he came around. Although she stubbornly refused to admit it to herself, Clara now found herself quite looking forward to his visits.

A month or so after she had begun to be comfortable talking to Winston without feeling self-conscious, for some reason Clara was home alone when Winston came to visit. When he realized they were alone, he sat close to her and began to gently stroke her arms and tell her how deeply he felt for her. Clara found it hard to breathe. He seemed to be suffocating her. Her heart began to beat very fast. Seeing her lick her dry lips, Winston seized the opportunity and quickly grabbed her and kissed her passionately for the first time.

He kissed her lips, her eyes, her ears, and her neck. His hands were busy too, as they found their way inside her blouse. Clara did not know what had hit her. She could not pull away. She said she tried to fight him off, but he was too strong and his hold too tight.

Perhaps it was during that moment of wild passion that Clara began to realize that she had in fact fallen in love with him. The family must have noticed the change in her because not long after that, sensing her change in attitude towards Winston, they asked her if she would marry him. She said yes and yes and yes. And so the real courtship began.

Victor had a father-to-son chat with Winston. He knew that Winston was unable to support a wife and look after his mother and sister Ena on just his salary, so Victor offered to build them a small house next door to his own home. That way he could see that his daughter was well settled and happy and should she need anything, she only had to run next door.

Rookie was delighted with the turn of events. Now she was finally accepted. Her son—the whore's son – was not only going to marry the most eligible girl in the village but he would get a house in the bargain too. Ena, who was as sour as ever, showed little emotion. The only thing that mildly pleased her was that now there would be someone else to do the housework. She chuckled at the irony of it. Little Miss Proud, Miss Full of Herself with her nose in the air, who thought she was too good to talk to anyone beneath her, was about to marry her short, ugly, little brother and they would all live together like one happy family in a brand new house. "Ha!" she snickered. "We will see how Miss Tiny Waist Portia likes washing clothes in a wooden tub. I bet she doesn't know a pot from a pan."

The wedding took place six months later, after the house was built. Winston and Clara went for a two-week honeymoon to the beach resort of Mayaro. And what a honeymoon it was! Winston was the perfect lover. Clara fell in love with her husband over and over again. The nights of heady love and the days on the sand whispering sweet nothings to each other were more romantic than anything written in the romantic novels Clara loved to read. There was sure to be a happy-ever-after ending to this story.

Chapter 8

Fifi, who was a year and one month younger than Clara, took great pride in the fact that she looked like Victor, with her almond-shaped eyes, long, straight nose, and finely shaped rosebud lips. Despite her delicate beauty, Fifi was very much the tomboy in the family. She accompanied Victor on many of his visits to seminars, debates, and lectures. One was never sure whether she was truly interested in these things or whether she had developed and inculcated these interests just to be near him.

Fifi desperately wanted to please Victor and be the son he never had. She loved the fact that everyone said she was just like her father, and made every effort to emulate all his habits and even his foibles. For a while, she even tossed peanuts until Little Sparrow got wind of it and made her stop. Fifi also tried her hand at playing cricket, but when she quickly got bowled out and ended up fighting with the boys in the team, Little Sparrow had to put a stop to that too.

Fifi loved to sing with Victor's group of singers in the musical sessions held at home. In fact, she would sing the loudest and carry her notes the longest until she was nudged to shut up. All this singing and carrying on came to an abrupt halt as Fifi grew up because Victor did not want her sitting with the male band members, some of whom were young boys and keen young men with watchful eyes. But it was obvious to all that Fifi did all these things just to impress her Pa and assure him that he had no reason to miss having a son.

Fifi was also what Trinidadians called "own way" in the West Indian vernacular. This meant that she never listened to anyone or took anyone's advice. She was also labeled "stubborn and hardened!". She paid attention to no one and listened to no one other than herself. Time and time again, Fifi would do things that would get her into trouble like climbing trees, tearing her new dress, and getting scraped and scratched. She was famous for visiting friends and family without asking and staying outdoors longer than she was allowed.

But there was also a kindness and gentleness about Fifi. She would give her pocket money to the needy and look after the washerwoman's little snotty-nosed baby so that the washerwoman could go to work for an extra three hours every evening. Fifi would get into trouble big time when she, in trying to help someone would completely forget to go back home on time.

Fifi's sense of family loyalty was unquestionable. She could not accept anyone in her family being in the wrong and would blindly defend them to the very end. Fifi would argue her point of view with the same fierce determination as her father. It was this very stubbornness which caused her to receive many beatings. Even though she was his favorite, Victor would not take her nonsense and firmly believed she had to be kept in line. He was afraid that if he gave her a little leeway, she would be totally out of control and would one day shame him and the family name. Little Sparrow had much more faith in Fifi. Although she also found her to be exasperating at times, she knew that Fifi meant well and couldn't help being soft and kind to people less fortunate than she.

Fifi refused to listen to reason—or perhaps didn't remember there were things she should not do—so she got the cane, usually around her ankles. The beatings had no effect on Fifi; she would just do the same thing again. Every time Fifi did something that deserved a beating, she took her licks and did not make any excuses or apologize for her so-called misdemeanors.

Fifi, like her father Victor, was very dramatic. So long before she even got her licks, she would begin to scream loudly and run around the house to get away from Victor and his cane. Fifi's hysterical screaming aggravated Victor, so she invariably got a few extra lashes just for screaming so loudly. In fact, Victor would not stop the beating until Fifi stopped screaming. Unfortunately, Fifi would always forget this. Strangely, once the caning was over, Fifi appeared just fine. No one who saw her afterward could ever believe she had just been screaming her head off as though a crazy battalion were chasing her.

Dora, the most placid, peace loving, and sensitive of the three sisters, would get very upset during these beatings. She would cry softly and beg Victor not to hit Fifi, promising that "Fifi would never do it again" on Fifi's behalf. Clara, on the other hand, was never involved, "how could I ever condole any of Fifi's silly shenanigans or making excuses for her stupid ways," she would disdainfully remark. So during Fifi's punishment she stayed removed from the noise and confusion, would calmly and coolly tell Fifi that she deserved the beating and that if she did not want to get a beating again, she would just have to behave herself and not make such a spectacle of herself. "What would people say seeing you make such a spectacle of yourself," she chided.

Clara was her mother's favorite. In her mind, that made her right and perfect. Clara always got her own way. All she had to do was run to Little Sparrow and ask charmingly with a cute little pout, admittedly now and then she did have to beg a little, but that was no problem. She knew just how to handle Little Sparrow and always got what she wanted in the end.

At times Fifi would deliberately do things to ruffle Clara. When Clara got upset, she would throw a mammoth tantrum. She would stomp off, throw things around, hit herself against the wall, and then run to Little Sparrow. Little Sparrow would then appeal to Fifi's better nature and ask her to please control herself to keep the peace and try not to upset Clara. Fifi did not think this was fair and said so time and time again. In the end, Fifi was usually the one who gave in, not just for the sake of keeping the peace, but also because she was ready to give in and say sorry. Everyone knew that if you sweet-talked Fifi and gave her attention, she would give invariably give in to your requests.

Clara, Fifi, and later Dora, went to Naparima Girls High School—the best high school for girls in Trinidad at that time—in the town of San Fernando about five miles away from Diamond. This meant they had to travel to school by bus. While Fifi made many friends at school, soft-spoken aloof Clara had fewer friends. They were both good students.

While Clara mastered Shakespeare, Fifi excelled in needlework class, learning to crochet with such skill that her pieces were often displayed. She was a star pupil. Fifi continues to crochet even now. Whenever she is traveling or on tour, out comes her crochet bag and she makes little doilies, which would later be joined together to make bed covers, tablecloths, tray cloths, or tea cozies. We were all given a set of Fifi's handiwork when we got married and we treasure these delicate would be heirlooms.

After Clara got married and went to live in the new house her father had given her, Victor heartily congratulated himself on his success as a husband-finder for his first daughter. He was convinced he had received divine inspiration and was very pleased with the fine match he had made. He now began to look for a similar match for Fifi.

He was sure this would prove to be a difficult task, as Fifi did not appear to be at all interested. He was sure that without his intervention, her tomboyish ways would deter young man from being attracted to her

Victor kept his eyes open for likely candidates, but he could find no one who fitted the profile of the kind of husband he had in mind for her. He wondered if he would ever find a suitable match. There was no doubt that Fifi was kind, considerate, loving, and self-sacrificing almost to the point of being stupid. This in particular bothered Victor and Little Sparrow. They had to find Fifi a husband who would understand and appreciate all these qualities and yet keep a firm eye on her in case she forgot herself and got into trouble over some silly, thoughtless thing.

Later that year Victor went to one of his debate seminars where he noticed a smartly dressed young man sitting quietly to one side, waiting for his turn to speak. Victor wondered how one so young could have been selected to speak at such a prestigious gathering. Then he remembered the passion that had driven him when he was that age. Before too long it was the young man's turn to speak. He spoke like a true orator and held those in attendance spellbound with his voice and his wit. It was obvious he was a very confident, intelligent, and well-read young man.

Victor sat quietly through the entire speech, too excited to even breathe. He had found a husband for Fifi. He could hardly contain himself. He would speak to him immediately after the seminar. It never occurred to Victor that his actions were somewhat strange or that this young man may have already been spoken for or that he may not even want to get married.

Excited at the thought of what he was planning, Victor found the young man's speech frustratingly long. At long last the speech ended. Victor quickly went up to the young man before anyone else could reach him. He fortunately remembered to first congratulate him on his fine speech and then, not wanting to waste any time, Victor very straightforwardly asked him what he was doing and what were his plans for his future. Noman, although taken aback, explained that he had been given a scholarship to study at the teacher's training college and had graduated at the top of his class. He went on to tell Victor that he was at the moment teaching at the college but that this was only temporary, as he was hoping to save enough money to study Law.

There and then, Victor made Noman a proposition. "Come meet my daughter. If you find her pleasing, you can marry her and I would pay for your studies". Noman was in a state of shock. Did this sort of thing actually happen? Was this man for real? Noman decided to tell Victor a bit about himself. Perhaps Victor might decide to withdraw his offer if he knew his background.

Noman was the eldest of four children. A brother named Peter was born after him. A sister called Barbs followed, and then came brother Joie. Joie had been born without any legs and their mother had died when Joie was born. Their father, Parpi, worked the small plot of land far out in the country where they lived in a little hut covered with karat palm leaves. Noman told Victor that his family was so poor they barely had only one balanced meal a day. He was the only member of the family who earned any money and, therefore, could not consider marriage. He was responsible for looking after all his siblings. Peter had to be educated, Barbs had to get married, and little Joie had to be taught a trade so he could one day earn a living. Parpi suffered from asthma and was not in good health. His own marriage would have to come later.

Victor laughed at Noman's fears. He was now even more convinced that Noman needed a break and that he was the perfect young man for his daughter. What courage! What strength of character! What a brother to have! What a son to have! What next best thing to a son if not a son-in-law, he asked himself? The fact that Noman looked like Clark Gable did not even cross Victor's mind. He told Noman he would foot all the bills if he married his daughter, but of course he understood that Noman should at least see Fifi before making up his mind. Even Victor knew that two people had to be attracted to each other before a marriage could be contemplated.

It was difficult to refuse such an offer, especially if one was ambitious and poor, but Noman still hesitated. He could not understand why anyone would want to do such a thing. Noman decided that this man must be a crazy loony with a strange ulterior motive. Rich people did no go around buying poor men as husbands for their daughters!

Victor invited Noman to dinner the following Sunday. Noman politely agreed to go to the dinner. This might be the answer to his prayers, but in the meantime, he decided to do some research of his own. Who was this man? Why would a daughter agree to such a marriage? Why did such a man want to or need to buy a husband for his daughter?

Noman remembered that while he and Victor had been talking at the seminar many people had stopped by to greet Victor, to ask after his health and his family, and to make plans to meet up sometime. Perhaps there was more to this eccentric man than he thought. There was no doubt that Victor was well known and highly respected. Maybe he should consider this crazy proposition. It would certainly be the answer to his ambitious prayers. He would think about it. He still had a few days to find out the real reason Victor may have for making this very strange proposal to someone he did not know. At the back of his mind,

Noman was sure the daughter must be the problem. Perhaps she was so ugly or so fat that no one wanted her.

Victor did not think his idea was in any way strange or peculiar. To him, it was a straightforward agreement. Both young people should meet and if they found each other pleasing, it would be a good match. So what if he supported and helped Noman with his career? He could afford it. God knows this young man needed a chance. He was brilliant, he was smart, and Victor was happy to be his benefactor.

Fifi was not told who Noman was or why he was coming to the house. All that was said was that he was a young man who had spoken brilliantly at the seminar and that Victor had invited him home to chat and join the family for dinner. Fifi was unconcerned. She had to help some people in the village that day, so she was out when Noman arrived. Noman met the other members of the family and chatted easily with Little Sparrow and Nan. Being a little more astute than the others, Dora wondered why Victor had invited this young, handsome man to the house when he had never done that kind of thing before. She remembered that Winston had not been invited into the family; he had invited himself into the family. Dora recalled that Victor more often than not, discouraged young men from calling. She was convinced there had to be more to this dinner than just Victor's appreciation of the young man's skills as a speaker. Dora anxiously waited for Fifi to come home so she could run out into the yard and warn her. She was sure that the man was intended for Fifi.

As usual, it was well past sunset when Fifi came home, rumpled and sweaty. Dora could not contain her excitement as she ran out to the road and whispered that Pa had invited some young man called Noman to dinner, most probably for her, Fifi. Foie quickly dashed upstairs and peered from behind the door to see what this Norman fellow looked like. Surely he did not look like Clarke Gable, as Dora had said. But to her surprise, he really did look like Clark Gable. Maybe it was the neat moustache that he wore and the slick way he combed back his hair. Fifi fell in love right then and there.

For Noman it was not love at first sight. He found Fifi passably pretty and a little awkward. Her slightly unkempt hair was hanging limply down her back and she looked decidedly self-conscious as she smiled shyly at him. But Noman had done his research and had heard good reports about Victor; he had also come to know that they were very distantly related. Now that he had met Fifi, he began to think that marrying her and getting his education as part of the bargain was perhaps not such a bad idea after all. He realized there was a method to Victor's madness. Without hesitating, he told Victor immediately after dinner that he would marry Fifi.

Noman began to visit the house regularly. Fifi waited excitedly for these visits and began to take greater care with her appearance. She curled her unruly straggly hair, polished her half bitten nails and tried to cover up the numerous cuts and scratches that she some how managed to get on her bare arms and legs. She spent more time at home, hoping that Noman would surprise her with yet another unexpected visit.

Noman enjoyed the time he spent at Diamond. He admired Victor and enjoyed talking to him and learning from him. He was pampered and spoiled by Little Sparrow and Nan. And now that he was getting to know Fifi better, he began to like what he saw. She may not share his intellectual dreams, but she was nice enough looking, kind, and most of all, had made it obvious that she was totally besotted with him. He liked the fact that she wanted to please him. It was something he had never experienced in his life. For so long he had been the serious, responsible head of his own family with no mother or big sister to do special things just for him. This was totally new to him and he was getting to like it very much indeed!

Fifi could not wait to get married! Very quickly she became absorbed with the wedding plans. Organizing her trousseau was such fun. She chatted about it non-stop, much to everyone's annoyance. She wanted everything she saw, and Victor and Little Sparrow indulged her. Fifi was sure everyone would envy her for snagging this handsome man.

On the day of the wedding, however, all Fifi's excitement quickly drained away. She was nervous and terrified about what the night would bring. Finally, Clara had to convince her to come out of her room for the brief ceremony and the lavish festivities. All too soon it was time for Fifi to leave for her honeymoon, but Fifi refused to get into the car. No amount of persuasion could make her do so. Clara had done the big sister thing and told her what to expect on the honeymoon. It frightened Fifi that a man could get that close to her and do those apparently repulsive things. Clara had told her that the first time it had hurt so much it felt like she was being torn apart down there. Oh Lord, it was horrifying unthinkable!

Noman looked on with amused tenderness. He tried to hold her and gently take her into the car, but she pulled away. Some time later, she finally agreed to go on her honeymoon but on condition that Victor go with them. So, Victor and Clara accompanied them to their honeymoon retreat.

When they arrived at the honeymoon lodge, which was the same place Clara and Winston had been for their honeymoon, Victor explained that he and Clara would return home since there was no room for them in the cottage. He assured Fifi that they would return the next day, which was only a matter of hours away, to take them back home. With that, they quickly got into the car and drove off. Fifi sat on the outside steps of the cottage with Noman, howling and crying her eyes out. It was quite some time before Noman was able to persuade her to go inside. He promised he would not do anything she did not want him to do. Somewhat appeased, Fifi finally decided to go in. She knew she could not stay on the steps all night.

The next day Victor received a telephone message from Noman saying that Fifi had agreed to spend a few more days before returning home, and that she said they must not worry, as everything was fine. Their honeymoon lasted three weeks, one week longer than planned. When they returned home, it was obvious that Fifi was not the same silly, young girl who had left home for the first time three weeks before.

Chapter 9

Dora, the third and last of Victor's and Little Sparrow's daughters, was born five years after Clara and four years after Fifi. Although there were only those few years difference in their ages, Dora always felt even younger and very different from her older sisters. While they were gregarious and outgoing, Dora was quiet, self-conscious and shy.

Most people considered Clara very attractive, admiring her sense of style and elegant carriage. She always seemed to know exactly what to say and do. She freely gave advice on the latest fashions, hairstyles, diet fads and any other style-related subject. If one had any questions, one would automatically turn to Clara because she was sure to know all about it and have all the solutions. She took her role as everyone's and in particular her sister's beauty and fashion advisor very seriously. And the fact that she always looked so well groomed obviously led her sisters, particularly Dora, to believe that she really knew what was in vogue. Even Fifi, who did not take much notice of the fashion scene because she was too busy going about her rounds in the village, occasionally stopped by to ask for Clara's helpful advice.

Both Fifi and Dora soon realized that if anyone did not agree with or wear what Clara thought was fashionable in Clara's eyes, that person had "absolutely no taste and knew nothing about what was going on." Clara would inform the person about their

fashion faux pas with such conviction that one would automatically feel gauche, awkward, and decidedly unattractive. Not
wanting to be accused of having bad 'taste,' the two younger
sisters always consulted Clara before altering their clothes or
changing hairstyles.

Clara was the first one in the family to dare pluck her eyebrows
like Greta Garbo. She also applied bright red lipstick and nail polish like Joan Crawford. Her real passion, however, was shoes.
She particularly loved the high-healed, strappy sling backs. She
knew she would have to walk carefully as she balanced on the
thin heels, and would sway her hips ever so slightly to help keep
her balance. Clara also loved to wear "V" shaped necklines just
that bit deeper than they should have been so she could display
a hint of her tempting ample cleavage.

Knowing very well that she attracted the attention of the
men in the village, Clara secretly relished the attention she got.
In reality, Clara was a tease. Her sexy way of dressing contra-
dicted her prudish manner of speaking. Dora was in awe of
Clara. She desperately wanted to do as Clara did but was not
brave enough to do it.

Victor was not at all happy with the make-up and sexy clothes
Clara wore and tried to voice his disapproval on many occasions.
He taunted her, saying she looked like a cheap streetwalker.
Sometimes he even used the word 'whore' to taunt her. While
Victor knew in his heart she did not really appear that way, he
hoped that if he said she looked like a whore, she would be
shamed into dressing more modestly or rather to his liking. But
Clara turned a deaf ear to him and continued to dress exactly
the way she pleased, leaving Little Sparrow to sort it out with
Victor. She knew Little Sparrow would eventually convince him
she did not mean any harm and that it was just her style.

Victor also did not approve of the influence Carla had on her sisters, Fifi and Dora. They copied her style of dress and make-up, which did not suit them at all. They failed to realize that what might have look well on Clara did not necessarily look good on them. In truth, they did not possess the panache to carry off Clara's style. As Clara often remarked, "they did not have the right figure." Clara's idea of the 'right figure' was the hourglass shape of 36-23-36 that she possessed.

In most aspects of her life, Dora was much more under Carla's influence than was Fifi. Dora shared a room with Clara and they would talk late into the night. Or, rather, Clara would talk. She would relate stories about the ways of the world that she had gleaned from the flashy fashion magazines she bought with her monthly pocket money and which she read from glossy cover to glossy cover with avid interest. Dora listened intently; impressed that Clara knew so much and was so in touch. Clara also shared her secrets and fantasies with Dora, who didn't have many original thoughts of her own and lived vicariously through these fantasies. There was no other excitement in Dora's quiet life.

Dora had the darkest complexion of the three sisters—having inherited it from Victor's mother—and had become very self-conscious about it. This was exacerbated by constant reminders from the family not to stay out too long in the sun. Clara would also inform her that certain colours or styles would not suit her because of the dark shade of her skin.

Practically everyone remarked on Clara's outstanding attractiveness and compared Fifi's perfect features with many of the great beauties of the time. But all that was ever said about Dora was "Pity Dora is so much darker than her sisters." In fact, Dora was no less pretty than the other two. She had lovely, wide, light-brown eyes fringed with thick, long eyelashes, a nice, straight nose, lips that were soft and full, and a beautifully shaped, innocent face. The problem was that she felt very unattractive and totally overshadowed by Clara and Fifi. This caused her to be withdrawn and introverted, always hanging back in the shadows and never allowing her true personality to shine through.

Under Clara's expert guidance, Dora applied many creams and herbs to improve her complexion. She even cut her hair in the same style as Clara's. Dora worked harder to look attractive than either of her other two sisters. Little Sparrow and Nan repeatedly told her that she need not do all those things to become beautiful, that beauty emanated from within. But that only convinced her that she lacked beauty and needed all the help she could get from whatever magic cream she could buy. Dora even went so far as to drink the juice of the "bitter gourd plant" because someone told her it would make her fairer. Then there was the time she wore a facemask of baking soda mixed with lemon juice every day for two weeks. She even drank copious amounts of milk—which she hated – in an attempt to have that elusive light skin. Nothing really worked, however, and in time Dora reluctantly began to accept her skin colour. She realized she would never be 'fair' and there was nothing she could do to change her natural skin tone.

Dora was a gentle and loving soul. She hated rows and loud arguments or the showy, dramatic antics in which Victor and Fifi reveled. She would get very embarrassed whenever Fifi would sing at the musical evenings they had at home, especially when she bellowed out her high notes. Dora could not handle noisy family gatherings and would quietly slip away to sit in a corner, happy to just observe rather than take part. But the family rows and arguments affected her the worse; she would get stomach pains and curl up with her hands on her ears and rock back and forth to make it stop or go away.

As she got older, Dora timidly tried to make peace during disagreements. She got on very well with Winston and Noman. They were the older brothers she did not have and they treated her like a little sister. She was especially close to Winston. When-ever there was a disagreement between Carla and Winston, she would be the go-between and carry messages between them. She would beg Clara not to get upset with Winston. And he, in turn, would always bring her little treats when he visited and take her to the movies whenever he and Clara went. Dora was very instinctively intuitive but kept this special gift to herself when she was young, afraid that she would be laughed at. This insight would assist her later on in life in many situations that affected her own family.

Dora was seventeen years old when Little Sparrow died. To-tally heart broken, she kept her sorrow to herself, sharing it only with Clara. At the funeral, Clara and Dora held on to each other, sharing their loss, while Fifi screamed and wailed, rolled on the ground, and had to be held back from throwing herself into the grave. Dora was so upset by Fifi's open display of noisy grief that for the entire period of mourning she hid inside her room. On several occasions she told Fifi to stop making scenes, but Fifi refused to listen. Fifi logically maintained that this was the proper way to grieve and saw no harm in people knowing how badly she hurt. "There is no shame in grieving," Fifi insisted. "Only shame in keeping it suppressed. You could get sick like that," she declared. Not able to argue with that, Dora remained silent.

With Little Sparrow now gone, Victor wanted to see Dora settled like her sisters. Normally he would have waited for Dora to be at least twenty years old, but he was so disorientated after the death of Little Sparrow that he panicked and kept thinking he must get Dora married off while Nan was still alive. Nan had taken Little Sparrow's death badly and had aged overnight. So Victor was once again on the lookout for an eligible bachelor for the last of his daughters.

Victor went into town every day to see his banker, lawyer

or the real estate agents. During these trips he would visit his friends and relatives who lived close by. On one of these visits, he met Larry, the son of a distant relative. Larry, unlike both Winston and Noman, was very much a town boy. Lanky and light-skinned with reddish brown hair, he was nicknamed Reds. Larry had all the smooth graces of a "party-going town boy." He was a great dancer and knew all the latest dance steps. It was said that no one could Cha Cha Cha or Rumba like him. He went dancing every Saturday night at the top nightspots and had many a girlfriend hanging onto his arm. Every year for the Trinidad annual street extravaganza carnival, he danced in the street for days, spending what little money he had on elaborate costumes. He was even crowned carnival king one year.

Larry was the seventh in his family of nine brothers and sisters. Both his parents had died when he was still a young boy. His brothers and sisters were very close and they helped and supported each other. Pearly, his eldest sister cared and tended him like a mother. At twenty-two years of age, with little money for a college education, Larry was articled to a firm of accountants and hoped to one day qualify as an accountant and open his own firm.

This time around, Victor asked Dora's permission to invite Larry home to meet her, even though he was not sure this good-looking, sophisticated young man would fancy a dark-skinned, quiet girl like Dora. But to Victor's surprising, Dora was just the kind of girl Larry wanted. He was fed up with the loud, smart-mouthed party girls he had been hanging around with. He had seen their wild, sexual morals and their greed for money and position. What he wanted was someone who would be a good, kind, and gentle mother to the kids he wanted to have. Larry wanted many children; he had come from a large family and knew the close camaraderie and emotional security that having siblings provided. He agreed straightaway to marry Dora. Victor did not even have to dangle an extravagant dowry to temp this young man. To Larry, money did not figure prominently in this decision; he wanted only the comfort and security of a loving home and a gentle wife.

Dora was very happy with the match and was thrilled to be marrying him. Larry was light-skinned, tall, and good-looking. She could not believe he had taken a fancy to her. It was a quiet wedding, as Little Sparrow had only recently passed away and the year of official mourning had not yet expired. Larry planned to take Dora to Barbados for their honeymoon, which meant they would have to go by airplane.

It would be the first time anyone in her family had been on a plane. It was so exciting Dora could not believe her good fortune. The ugly ducking had grown up and had found a handsome prince who wanted to take her to an exotic place for their romantic honeymoon.

The whole family planned to go to the airport to see the couple off. They were excited but also a little nervous. Dora was going on a plane. Would it be safe? Nan was not at all happy. She said it was not natural to fly. "Dem crazy young people ar taking dey lives in dey hands," she complained. But no one listened to her, as they were too caught up in the excitement. Victor thought it was a thrilling adventure. It was something he dearly wanted to try himself but was too afraid to do so. He never did sum up the courage to fly.

The family got dressed up in their best clothes to go to the airport north of the island. It took two hours to get there, but they all went and waived Dora and Larry off with such enthusiasm that anyone observing them would imagine the couple was leaving forever. Fifi and Nan both cried. As usual, Fifi sobbed the loudest and most dramatically. Nan quietly dabbed away tears from her wrinkled brow. She had already lost a daughter. If, God forbid, something happened to Dora, it would kill her in an instant, she thought.

Dora and Larry had a wonderful honeymoon and returned with marvelous stores to tell of kind people and beautiful beaches and food, so much better than that of Trinidad. They had taken a cruise on an old pirate ship. "It was just sooooo wonderful," Dora enthused to everyone. She was finally beginning to come out of her shell. She was happy and grateful to this man who was happy to be married to her.

Dora and Larry made their first home in one of Victor's small flats downtown near the High Street. Dora learned how to keep house while Larry went to his office. He had another year to qualify as an accountant and then hoped to get a better job. In the meantime, he took on evening jobs doing the books for a few small businesses. Every Saturday there was horse racing at the Union Park Race Club, a very exclusive private racetrack, where Larry did the accounts on weekends. With all this moonlighting, he earned a fair amount of money and hoped to soon begin building a home for the large family he wanted.

Meanwhile, Fifi and Noman had also settled in one of Victor's flats across town from Dora. Fifi was less organized at keeping house than Dora was, but she was extremely devoted to Noman. She stayed up all night with him as he studied, making cup after cup of coffee or hot chocolate and listening to him as he read her his notes. Noman loved this attention and devotion.

The two sisters living in town missed their family, so during the day when Noman went to the law offices where he was articling and Larry was at his office, Fifi would run away to see Dora and keep her company. Perhaps that was why her housework was never done. No one ever understood why Fifi felt she had to run away to visit her family. She later admitted she did not tell Noman about her visits to her family because she did not want him to think she had any other interests besides him.

Chapter 10

Clara had settled down to a wildly passionate and blissful married life with Winston. They lived in the house her father had built for them next door to the family home in Diamond. It was a simple but functional house with three bedrooms, a drawing room that merged into a small dining room, and a tiny but compact kitchen at the back. The house was built on seven-foot high stilts. The front steps led down from the front gallery to a flower garden and from the back veranda of the house, the back stairs led to the small kitchen garden.

Underneath the house was an open space with a large striped canvas hammock strung from two of the supporting pillars. Large wire baskets of leafy ferns adorned the front and sides of the house. The not-so-tidy front garden overflowed with scented flowering shrubs of hibiscus and croton, beds of anthurium lilies, phlox, and showers of gold. Wild purple orchids clinging to the old, rotting tree trunks added an exotic jungle touch.

The back garden was a splash of different shades of green dotted with colourful vegetables. There were tidy rows of pigeon peas, leafy corn stalks, ladyfingers, broad and shiny dasheen leaves, peppers of all varieties, red and orange Jamaican pimento, purple aubergines, and blood red tomatoes. Rambling vines of pumpkin, marrow, cucumber, and miniature bitter gourd curled and climbed their way onto the wire fence at the back of the house, making the garden cozy and cool. The fresh smells of damp earth, wet manure, and the variety of vegetables were intoxicating.

Surrounding the house and garden was the usual array of fruit trees that one might find in a tropical island country estate—coconut palms, sapodilla, mango, chennet, orange, and kaimet. Because several of these trees were either in bloom or bearing fruit, there was always an abundance of fresh fruit available to eat or share with family, friends, and neighbours.

Bees and butterflies flittered among the bright flowers, competing with the iridescent hummingbirds for the juicy nectar, while yellow birds, kiskadees, parakeets, and blue and yellow birds picked at the ripened corn, peas, and fruit on the trees. At the crack of dawn each morning, the family would be awakened by a cacophony of sounds as the birds flitted from tree to tree stretching their wings and practicing their shrieks and whistles while feeding on the abundance of food.

In this idyllic setting, the small country house looked very pretty with its sloping, red, corrugated galvanized roof. On rainy days the dancing rhythm of the rain pitter-pattering on the roof would urge Winston to whisk Clara off to bed, cozy up next to her, and make wild passionate love.

Their first few months were blissfully happy months. Clara was a much-cherished bride and Winston was the epitome of a loving husband, going to his teaching job every morning and rushing home with some small token for Clara in the early evening.

He seized every opportunity to demonstrate his love, affection, and devotion, finding excuses to touch, hug, nuzzle, and hold her. He showed his love in so many different ways, he would help himself to food on her plate, insisting that it tasted so much better than what was on his own plate, he would tenderly stroke caress her, always gentle always lovingly.

Winston had happily and willingly given up his wild Casanova ways, much to the surprise and chagrin of some of the lonely wives in the village. Some of the more cynical, jealous ones even whispered that Winston's lovey-dovey, passionate feelings for Clara were bound to fade and die. "Give it time," they said.

Before too many months had gone by, this open display of love and devotion began to irk Rookie. She had tried to be patient and look the other way when all the stupid hugging, kissing and touching nonsense was going on but she could not get it out of her head so it would have to stop. She would make sure it did because if it did not she would go stark raving mad.

Winston was losing himself and his selfrespect to this clever, manipulative young woman, and on top of all that he was forgetting the mother who had brought him into the world and made so many sacrifices for him. She reasoned.

Irritable and bad-tempered Ena wasn't handling it any better. She was missing Winston's attention and she began to complain nonstop to Rookie. Rookie began to nag Winston whenever and wherever she got the opportunity.

At first Rookie was clever enough to keep her nagging subtle and teasing, telling Winston that it was for his own self respect that he control his emotions. She reminded him that it was not a good idea to give too much attention to a young wife, as they would begin to expect too much. When Winston did not take these gentle complaints very seriously, Rookie decided she had to be more assertive. She became more obvious in her criticism, making stinging comments and being openly nasty to Clara.

Winston was very close to his mother and Ena. He called his mother Queenie, a name she had insisted he call her ever since he was a little boy. She enjoyed nothing more than having her son close to her, giving her all of his attention as she stroked his hair.

Even though Winston's marriage to Clara meant a giant leap upward on the social ladder of the village for him and social acceptability for Rookie and Ena, this did not stop Rookie from being jealous. To keep Clara in her place, she insisted that Clara do all the cooking and housework, while mother and daughter did nothing except find fault with everything she did. Clara, who had never learned how to cook, would often run next door to find out how to make this dish or cook that. Little Sparrow was adamant that Clara should learn to do things for herself as she was now a wife. Clara would get frustrated, and collapse into tears when things did not turn out right.

It was at this point that Ena would choose to tauntingly re-mind Clara that although she had come from a well-to-do family, she now had to work for the so-called under-privileged, lower class people that her family had married her into. Ena would keep rubbing it in until Clara was goaded into answering back.

That was the worst thing she could have done. By the time Winston came home from work, the two co-conspirators had concocted a story about her bad mouth and her rowdy ways. They would tell Winston that Clara had spoken harshly to them and then gone to spend the whole day at her mother's house, returning home just before he arrived.

Winston could say nothing to his mother and sister, and would plead with Clara to understand and try to make the house a happy, loving home. No amount of explaining from Clara would ever convince him that she was telling the truth and they were lying.

To make matters worse, whenever Winston and Clara would

go to their room for a siesta in the afternoon or for an early night, Rookie would pretend she had severe chest pains. She would moan and groan so loudly that Winston would come rushing out so she could rest her head against him until the pain eased and she felt better. This often took several hours.

All during these dramas, Ena would pace back and forth fussing and bawling loudly as if Rookie were really dying. They never let up their possessive behavior and always made their presence felt whenever the couple was together.

When Winston sat with Carla, either Ena or Rookie would sit on the other side. If he bought Clara a little nonsense gift, he had to bring the same for Ena or Rookie. If he had his arm around Clara, he also had to have an arm around Rookie.

What irritated Clara the most, though, was that Winston had to give his mother his entire salary. When payday came, he would promptly drop the envelope into his mother's hands. "Queenie is saving you the trouble of balancing the household budget," he would explain to Clara. "Let her do it. She has the experience".

Clara had no say at all in this matter. She was given only twenty-five cents as pocket money, and if she dared to ask for any more, she would be told to go ask her father. So Clara had to either go without new clothing and necessary toiletries or ask her parents.

And even then, complaints would go to Winston that she was far too wasteful and a spendthrift. Too proud to go to her family, Clara often went without. She could not bear the thought that she had to take handouts from her family when she had a husband.

Ena took every opportunity she could to continue to make

fun of how Clara had now fallen on hard times. Did she miss her expensive silks, perfumes, and make-up? "How needy the extravagant one had now become," she would taunt. Ena mocked Clara and copied the affected way she walked and talked. Rookie found the whole thing quite hilarious and encouraged her daughter's taunting. They laughed loud and long at their cruel jokes.

Clara put up with this situation for several months. She could not understand how Winston could not see anything wrong with what his mother and sister was doing. He thought it was just silly, harmless fun. Clara should not be so sensitive, he would say. She should understand where they had come from and appreciate that they were just trying to have some fun. So what if it was a little joke at her expense? He loved her, he reminded her. That, and their wild passionate nights of love, was all that mattered. He was a four-times-a-night guy, he would proudly remind her. Clara admitted that their lovemaking was something very special; she would get lost in the sensual mood he created. They would make passionate love again and again and she would be temporarily appeased.

But a time came when even the sex could not make her ignore or forget the cruel taunts. Clara had reached the point where she could no longer take it. She told Winston that her father had given this house to her for her wedding and she would not take any nonsense from his mother or sister while they lived there. They should behave or get out. Overhearing this, Rookie and Ena started crying loudly for all the neighbours to hear, noisily packed their meager belongings, and moved to a tiny apartment they quickly found in the not so nice part San Fernando.

Winston was now torn between his wife and his mother, both of whom he adored. He would visit his mother after work, have his meal with her, and then come home to Clara in Diamond. All this made him tired and upset. He became quiet and withdrawn when he was with Clara. He could not make up his mind what he should do. He knew Clara was not to blame, but he could see and feel how his mother felt.

Understanding his dilemma, Rookie played her cards well. She reminded him of all the sacrifices she had made for him after his father had died. She told him he was all she had and that she was old with no one to look after her. When Ena got married, what would she do? Where would she go? She could not possibly live with her daughters. That was not the traditional or the accepted thing to do, and people would talk. She would be disgraced. People would laugh at him and say he did not love his mother. As he was the only son, it was his duty to make Clara understand.

Winston tried to explain to Clara that he had no choice but to live with his mother. He explained the hard life she had had and that he just could not leave her hurt, sad, and lonely for him. "Please, my darling, try for me, for the love we have. Give it one more chance. My mother loves you. She is just worried for me. When you have our son, you will know how it feels. Please, please. I will make sure they know your rights and understand. They mean well; they just get a bit carried away." He begged and promised, holding her tenderly in his arms, caressing her thighs as he spoke. "All will be well, you have my word."

Winston was good at begging; he had it down to a fine art. With his charm, he knew he had convinced Clara they should move into town and share the flat with Rookie and Ena. Winston did and said all the right things and made all the right promises. It was difficult for Clara to resist when he explained it that way and then made passionate love to her to seal the deal. By now Winston realized that all he had to do to get Clara to agree to something was make love to her. She was like putty in his arms.

Clara and Winston moved out of the house and into the cramped flat in town. Things were fine initially, but after a few months, Rookie and Ena began their complaining again. Clara decided to ignore it for the time being. Perhaps the situation would improve when Ena got married.

Rookie was making a desperate effort to get her married off but with Ena's disposition, it was no wonder suitors were hard to come by. One day a sad, quiet, mousy young man was brought in as a prospective suitor. The poor chap was having trouble finding a wife. He was a harmless soul with not much to say except that he drove trucks for a living.

Ena fell in love. She had her truck driver, a man with prospects of one day having a fleet of transport trucks, and so she hastily agreed to marry him. Ena could not believe she was finally going to be married.

The situation in the house improved somewhat as they made preparations for the wedding. Clara excitedly helped in every way she could, thrilled that Ena would be leaving soon. The happy day came and Ena went to live in her new home. Clara was delighted. The troublemaker was finally out of the house!

Shortly after Ena's marriage a new problem arose. Ena immediately got pregnant. It had been two years since Clara's and Winston's wedding and there was still no sign of a baby. Something must be terribly wrong with Clara. Could she be barren? Clara went home tearfully, only to hear that Little Sparrow was not well and that the doctors had said she might be pregnant.

The last thing Clara needed to hear was that her sister-in-law and over-aged mother were both pregnant. Clara fell into a deep depression. Victor decided he had better take Clara to the doctor for a check-up. If there was a problem, hopefully it could be solved. The doctors found that Clara had a very slight tilt to her uterus and that a simple operation would fix it, so she went into hospital for the surgery.

Almost immediately after that, Clara got pregnant. She was very happy but Winston was even happier. A son! How he longed for a son! This would be a blessing from the Gods. He now openly pampered Clara, indulging her in all her fancies. One day she craved exotic Chinese canned lychees. Another day, she longed for imported baked beans, a luxury in Trinidad at that time. Winston obliged. Nothing was too difficult or too expensive for Clara. Even Rookie took some interest in Clara's pregnancy. She could not wait for the birth of Winston's son.

Little Sparrow's pregnancy had taken a bad turn. She was getting bigger and bigger and swelling up with edema caused by her high blood pressure. Little Sparrow was hospitalized. Clara took this badly. She was very close to her mother, especially at this time when they were both sharing the same experience of being pregnant. Little Sparrow's condition worsened and shortly afterwards, she died.

Clara went home to Diamond to be with Victor, Nan, Fifi, and Dora for the forty days of mourning. She was taking the loss of her mother so badly that Nan suggested she remain in Diamond until the time of her baby's birth. Winston did not have a problem with the arrangement. It would be nice to have some respite from the constant bickering between his mother and Clara.

With Clara now in Diamond until the baby's birth and Winston visiting every day, Nan began to enthusiastically prepare for the birth of her first great grandchild. A baby in the family would certainly ease some of the pain of losing Little Sparrow. The impending birth would also be a balm to soothe Victor's aching heart.

One morning a few weeks later, Clara woke up to the first labor pains. She needed her mother and began to cry as she made her way downstairs to call Nan. With her eyes blinded by tears, she missed her footing and tumbled all the way down to the bottom of the stairs. The pains began to come in earnest, strong and hard. Clara was quickly rushed to the hospital where after a long and hard labor she gave birth to a tiny baby girl. The baby was too weak to breathe and died moments later. The baby was never given a name and thereafter was always referred to as Baby.

Clara took the death of her baby badly, insisting that if Little Sparrow had been alive, her baby would have survived. She drew some consolation from the fact that Baby was buried beside Little Sparrow in the same crypt. Later on, a beautiful marble headstone with both their names and their simple sad epithets was erected.

A few weeks later Winston took Clara back to the cramped little flat in town. He had been gentle and kind all throughout the ordeal. He promised that more babies would come and all would be well in the end. Just like a fairy tale, they would all live happily ever after.

Chapter 11

Considering the passionate feelings Winston had for Clara, it was inevitable that she would become pregnant again almost as soon as she moved back in with him. She was relieved she had conceived so soon, she had blamed herself for Baby's death. Winston was beside himself with excitement. He had once again proven his manhood. Now it was up to Clara to make sure she did not lose the baby this time. He was certain he would become a father to a healthy, robust son who would eventually prove to be a chip off the good old block.

Ena was also very pleased with life. Everything seemed to be going her way. She had given birth to a strong, healthy baby girl and was expecting again. Her husband had bought two trucks and was in the process of buying a third. He hired his trucks out to transport goods and other materials from the north to the south of the island. It was a good business, but it was not easy trucking across the hilly island where roads were often washed out or filled with potholes caused by heavy rains and mudslides. A trucker's life could be tough, but being away from home also had its good points. He could hang out with the boys, enjoy one too many beers, and be away from Ena's endless nagging.

Ena did not mind her husband being away. She would spend this time with Rookie, showing off her baby—who cooed and sang loudly—and boasting about the good times she was having with all the money she now had at her disposal.

True, the life of a trucker's wife was lonely at times, but it was a small price to pay for the comforts she now enjoyed. She made sure to display all the wonderful, expensive gifts that her husband had given her upon the birth of their baby. She had recently received a pair of large, dangly earrings with an artificial emerald that looked like a "real, real" stone. She moved her head from side to side to make sure Clara took notice.

Clara knew all the talk and show was for her benefit. She also knew that Ena's life was not the bed of roses she made it out to be. Clara had overheard Ena argue with her husband. She was always pushing him to take more of the long hauls and earn more money. She wanted gold bangles and a thick heavy twenty two karat gold chain like Clara had.

Ena also kept up her demands on Winston, which he didn't seem to mind. She always seemed to need something urgently when her husband was away, and used this as an excuse to borrow money from Winston. She never intended to pay this money back. Clara knew this, but could not say anything. Rookie, or rather, Ena, totally controlled Winston and he found it difficult to say no to either of them.

Although Clara's pregnancy was progressing well and she was looking forward to having her baby, things were not easy. She had no emotional support from Winston where his mother and sister were concerned. She needed to see the doctor more often and have better food, new maternity clothes, and other things that were necessary at this time. Winston would casually tell her that she should ask Rookie for what she needed.

When she did, Rookie would always refuse her. Rookie would complain to Winston that she had given Clara all she had asked for and could not understand why she was still complaining and demanding things all the time.

Rookie suggested that perhaps Clara wanted him to move out of the house, away from his mother. "You should never have married such a girl," she now told him. "She has too many airs and expects too much. What is so wrong with asking her rich father for the extravagant things she wants, even though she does not really need them?"

What Rookie was saying made a lot of sense to Winston. Ena was such a considerate wife and never asked her husband for such things. Clara was far too demanding. He decided he would have to have a word with her. She must be made to see the logic of what his Queenie said. Queenie always had his best interests at heart and, as a devoted mother, could not bear to see her one and only son being taken advantage of like that.

He confronted Clara with her excessive demands for more pocket money. Did she really need maternity clothes? Surely she could make do with the clothes she had. She should realize that once she had the baby, those clothes would be useless. The money was needed for more important things.

Clara decided that enough was enough. Two weeks before the baby was due, she packed her bags and went home to her father's house in Diamond where Nan would take care of her until the baby was born. She was sure Winston would soon come running to her, he would not be able to bear being away from her, especially now that it was almost time for the birth of the son, he had always wanted.

Winston was surprised to say the least that Clara went home to her father. How could she do such a thing now that baby was due? "Let her be," advised his mother. "She is bound to come back to you in a day or so now that the baby is due. Who the hell does she think she is, emotionally blackmailing you like this? She is using the baby as a tool. Just leave her. You will see... she will come running. Hmm! These rich young women! They think all they have to do is snap their fingers and we jump. Where is our self-respect? Where is their respect for their husbands? Just because we do not have money does not mean we have to bow down to their whims and fancies."

Winston was totally confused. Part of him wanted to go to Clara and bring her home. A niggling thought told him it was the correct and expected thing to do. After all, she was soon to be the mother of his long-awaited son. But part of him also saw the logic in what Rookie had so gently and patiently advised. Why should he go and beg her to come home? He was the man. He was the husband. She had been the one to leave. He did not send her away; she chose to go off in a huff. She would have to come back on her own. Clara would think too highly of herself if he made the mistake of going to her first. He would never be able to live that down. Rookie was right. She was his mother and she was the only one who was truly loyal to him and had his interests at heart. Clara needed to be taught a lesson. He was curious to see how long she would stay up there on her high horse. Rookie was correct, he finally convinced himself. Well-to-do young women like Clara had too many unreasonable demands.

And so he never called or went to see Clara, and neither did he even bother to make discreet inquires about how she was doing.

Meanwhile, Clara stayed in Diamond fretting and fuming while waiting for Winston to come to her. She was sure he could not forget the happy times in her arms. The concerns for his mother surely could not replace that. He would soon come to take her home.

Dora was also pregnant and due to give birth about the same time as Clara. Larry was thrilled to finally be starting the large family he had always wanted. He was very considerate to Dora's needs. He tenderly looked after her on the days she was feeling ill from morning sickness and too lethargic to do much. He hired a maid, even though it strained their finances somewhat. He even helped with the household chores and bought all the things that she and the baby would need. Clara noted these things and kept them locked in her heart. Dora, her baby sister, was the weak one and needed that kind of attention she rationalized.

By this time, Larry had qualified as an accountant and had a very good job with Texaco, an American Oil Company. This job had good prospects. He could rise to the position of Chief Accountant if he continued the way he was going. The American management liked him and had said he would go far in the company.

He was still doing his Saturday stint at the Race Club, as well as doing the books and tax returns for a few of his own private clients. He was making a good living and had put aside enough money to buy a piece of land to build a house. He had found just the right piece of land in the better part of town. The price was right; he had enough to pay for it with some left over to begin construction. Texaco would give him a loan for the rest. He was hoping to have the house finished around the time the baby was born. Texaco had a hospital for its employees and he arranged for Dora to get the best possible medical attention for the delivery.

Two weeks had gone by since Clara had left Winston and he still had not come to see her or made arrangements for the birth of his baby. Victor was beginning to worry. Clara was agitated and nervous. What if he did not come? What if he never came back? Should she go back to him? She decided not to. It was his baby and he was bound to come once the baby was born. He would be curious to see it. It was sure to be a son. It just had to be.

Victor decided they could not to wait any longer for Winston to come by. Realizing that he would now have to arrange for the birth of Clara's baby, he spoke to Larry and arranged for Clara to have the baby at the Texaco Hospital with Dora. Since both babies were due at almost the same time, it was decided that Dora and Clara would share a double room. It would be good for the two sisters to be near each other. Clara knew Dora was afraid of giving birth and was worried about her in spite of her own confused state.

While Noman worked and studied during the day, Fifi would spend time with each of her sisters, trying to help whenever she could. She knew that Larry was very supportive of Dora. She worried about Clara. Winston was being pig-headed. She tried several times to visit him, but confronting Rookie was not a pleasant experience. A couple of times she had summoned up the courage to leave messages with Rookie, but Winston had never responded. He most likely did not get the messages.

In desperation, Fifi decided she would go to the College where he was teaching. Perhaps he would see her there and she could talk to him. She could not believe he was being so heartless at a time like this. When Fifi went to the college to talk to him, Winston refused to see her. He was sure it was some kind of trick. Rookie had warned him that they would probably try some kind of clever scheme like that.

It bothered him, though. He would like to have met with her and find out how Clara was. Rookie would be very upset if she knew he felt this way. He was confused but could not take the pressure. It was easier to deal with his conscience than listen to Rookie's constant reproaches.

Knowing in her heart that the situation was not right, Fifi kept telling Clara that for the sake of the child she should make the first move. But by now, Clara was stubbornly adamant that she would not. It was Winston's child and he would have to come to her.

On April seventeen, Clara got the first sign that the baby was coming. She was rushed to the hospital. After a long labor, a little baby girl was born on April eighteen at four thirty in the morning. Clara was alone for the birth. Although a message was sent to Winston, he did not come to the hospital. It seemed that he—or Rookie—was disappointed that the baby was not a boy.

Victor, Nan, and Fifi were on hand at the hospital but to Clara it was not the same, it was not enough. She thought of Little Sparrow and how upset and sad she would have been.

The next day Dora also went into labour. She, too, was rushed to the hospital. Both sisters were sharing the same double room. Clara had her little girl next to her when Dora was taken into the labour room. Clara was very anxious; she could hear Dora's groans and could not contain her tears. She may have been crying for Dora or for herself, perhaps both. Larry was a nervous father-to-be. He paced back and forth, unable to contain his excitement. Calra witnessed all of this with a heavy heart. She wondered what kind of man Winston was.

The next day after a long and tiresome labour Dora gave birth to a baby boy who made his entry in the world by bawling lustily. After he was washed and dressed, the little fellow was brought to Dora and Larry, who anxiously waited at Dora's side to see his son for the first time.

He had brought a bag full of toys, which of course the baby could not play with. The baby was placed in Dora's arms and Larry looked at his son for the very first time. Overcome with joy, he picked up the baby and held him to his heart.

Across the room, Clara sat crossed-legged on the bed hugging her baby girl to her. A lump rose in her throat and her eyes burned with unshed tears. She would not allow Dora and Larry to see her pain and loneliness. She looked down at her baby, who was all wrinkled and ugly with a huge nose that dominated her tiny, wizened little face.

Victor was also excited at the birth of his first male grandchild. Everyone peeped and fussed over the handsome little fellow, who took advantage of all the attention he was getting by crying nonstop.

Clara's baby girl was just the opposite; she lay quietly, never crying. She was a good baby, they said. Pity her father did not care enough to come see her. Nan looked at her and shook her head. Surely this baby was jinxed. Her own father had not come to see her. It was evident he did not want her. Had anyone ever heard of such a thing?

Both new mothers were discharged five days later. With great love and tenderness, Larry took Dora home to the new house he had built. Clara went home with her father, instead of her baby's father, to the house in Diamond.

It was three months before Winston summoned up the courage to come to Diamond to see Clara and perhaps his daughter for the first time. He brought Carla a box with three strands of the finest Japanese pearls he could afford. Rookie did not know he had bought the pearls or that he had gone to see Clara. She would have been extremely disappointed in him and would have come down with one of her now infamous heart attacks.

Winston hugged Clara and begged for her forgiveness. He promised he would work something out and that they would be together. He took little notice of the baby. It did not even register that she looked just like him. He told Clara it was a pity the baby was not a boy. Perhaps the next time around....

Clara called the baby Veena— Vee, for short. She tended her baby with the help of Victor and Nan. Winston visited from time to time, but made no plans to take Clara home with him. Whenever Clara brought up the subject, he always had an excuse. He said Clara needed to rest in Diamond. She had Nan to help her and the old mid-wife, Miss Trinity, who came to help in the house.

Winston took very little notice of Vee but could not keep away from Clara. He tried to woo her all over again. Clara could not remember if she had ever seen him pick up the baby. All he wanted to do was sit with her and put his arms around her or beg to spend part of the night. He did not dare stay all night in case Rookie got wind of the fact that he had begun to visit Clara.

This situation continued for about a year before Clara realized Winston was not being truthful when he said he wanted her to come home. It was obvious he wanted her but he did not want to upset Rookie. He never intended to take Clara home while Rookie was alive. And it was painfully obvious that he had no love for or interest in his baby daughter.

Chapter 12

When Fifi and Noman made their home in one of Victor's apart-
ments near the Law Courts, they made sure that it was close to
the law office where Noman was articled and walking distance
to the town's shopping centre.

The small wooden structure had two bedrooms, a drawing
room, a dining room with a small kitchen at the back, and a
veranda at the front with a cane rocking chair. They could not
afford much furniture so they made do with just the bare necessities. Noman was adamant that he did not want Victor to pay
for more than his education, so they lived on the small salary
he earned from his part-time teaching job. Noman was very
involved with his studies and was preparing to fly to London to
take his Bar exams at Lincoln's Inn.

Believing that she had to be Norman's right arm, Fifi waited
on him hand and foot, doing everything she possibly could so he
would be free to study and achieve the goals he had set out for
himself. This became her mission in life. Fifi always found time
for everyone and was especially conscious of her duty to her
family. She visited her sisters every day and Victor several times
during the week, making sure these visits were when Noman
was at work. She rarely told Noman when she visited her family, and always ensured she was home by the time he returned
from the office.

Peter, Noman's younger brother, went away to Teacher's Training College. Barbs stayed in the village of Piparo to look after Parpie and Joie, the brother who had been born without legs. Joie often spent time with Noman and Fifi in town. He bubbled with the enthusiasm of life, feeling neither embarrassed nor handicapped by having no legs. This had to be because Noman had instilled in him the confidence and belief that he could do anything he wanted to do.

Noman had arranged for Joie to apprentice with a jeweler. After Joie had learned the trade, Noman planned to open up a store for him. With Joie's game for anything attitude, he was sure to make a success of anything he tried to do. His handsome face and cute dimple in his chin no doubt further increased his self-confidence. He was also very charming. It was often said that his charisma more than made up for his lack of limbs.

Joie had the strongest arms we had ever seen. He would use his arms to swing on and off chairs. As kids, we often copied him because it looked like so much fun. His upper body was perfectly formed. When we were kids, he would show off his biceps and tight stomach muscles. How we loved to squeeze his massive arms and then watch the muscles pop up. He could also make one eyebrow go up and down and his ears wiggle to the left or right, together or separately.

These antics always impressed us youngsters and we pestered him to do it again and again. Joie never refused our demands and would cheerfully indulge our requests. He was also fond of doing magic tricks and was never too tired to entertain us with his varied repertoire. He was definitely one of the favourite family members and always took our side when we made unreasonable request and demands of the grown-ups. He was one of us and we loved him dearly.

Joie was quite the dandy dresser, very Beau Brummel. Everything matched perfectly. His jackets were made to measure with a matching pair of tiny pants that just covered his tiny limb. He wore flashy ties for every-day functions and black bow ties for formal wear. Over his hands he wore soft leather gloves in brown or black. This was to protect his hands as he swung himself on them to move around.

Joie loved to sing ballads about unrequited love or make up romantic poems to an elusive lost love. He kept brandy in a small hip flask, which he would very ceremoniously put to his lips, pretending to take a long swig before he began his mournful serenade.

That he was always falling in and out of love was no surprise. His love was true only until the next pretty girl came by. Amazingly, despite his physical disability, he always had many girlfriends. His cheeky, flirtatious good humour, incredible good looks, and bedroom eyes contributed to his irresistible charm.

Joie was very close to Fifi, who pampered him almost as much as she pampered Noman. But he was even closer to Carla. He would go to Diamond to sit with her to lament about his love life and tell her the latest naughty joke.

It was understandable that Joie needed to constantly prove his manhood. He had the reputation of being very wild and falling in love with several girls at the same time. Eventually, when his girlfriends found out he was cheating on them, they would dump him. He could never understand why they were so upset. He had so much love to give that none of his girlfriends could complain that he was an inconsiderate lover.

As far as he was concerned, none of them was ever left wanting for attention. He took each break-up very badly. Whenever he was ditched, he would be so heartbroken, he would drink more brandy and sing his songs more mournfully, very often with real tears running down his cheeks. It was so sad. There could be no doubt that he felt the pain every time.

One Christmas day Joie arrived in Diamond out of the blue. He was not expected to join in the family gathering, as he was supposed to be in Piparo with Barbs and Parpi. There were many whispered conversations behind closed doors and a lot of what appeared to be important phone calls. The children were all rushed out of the room while the adult members of the family who had come to Diamond for the day went into private, secret meetings.

Victor was angry and red-faced as he stormed out of the room, closely followed by Carla, who seemed to be trying to reason with him. Peeping into the room, we saw Joie sitting on the chair, his head hung low while Fifi pleaded with him.

There was not much festivity that day and we children were all rushed off to bed early that night. The next morning we discovered we had a new visitor who must have arrived very late the previous night or very early that morning. She was a somewhat plain-looking young woman, very rustic in her appearance. She sat very nervously with her head bent low and her hands limp in her lap. She must have been crying, as her eyes were red and swollen and her hair was mussed up. Her name was Elsie and it seemed she had run away from home because she was pregnant with Joie's child.

Victor was adamant that Joie do the right thing and marry the poor girl. He was welcome to stay in the house, but only after the wedding had taken place. Joie was frightened that Noman would find out. Elsie's father had already found out and was on the warpath. He had vowed he would not rest until he had "killed both Elsie and that no good son-of-a-bitch who did not have legs but still had the audacity to chase and seduce all the young, innocent girls in the village."

A hasty wedding ceremony was arranged. Victor knew the right people and was able to pull a few strings so that the marriage could take place on Boxing Day. Strangely, Elsie, the shy, nervous little county girl, suddenly became a lively, flirtatious woman minutes after her wedding ceremony. Perhaps she was relieved that her delicate condition had now been legalized. It was also shocking that she did not seem to think of her parents and the shame she had brought to them.

By the end of the ceremony, Joie, too, had undergone a change. He was his jovial self and, now, the attentive new husband. Beginning to enjoy the attention he was getting, he called out for a drink and threw his arms around his new wife. Had he forgotten that not long before he would have done anything to get out of the marriage? Did he forget that only his fear of Noman and Victor had enabled him go through with the wedding? The whole thing was very strange indeed. Was that how grownups behaved? We children were shocked.

Joie and Elsie stayed in Diamond for about two weeks before Elsie went back to visit her parents in Piparo. By then, Fifi and Clara had of course visited Elsie's parents to tell them that Joie had done the gentleman thing and that their daughter was now married. They were relieved that their daughter was finally married and lovingly welcomed their daughter and her new husband. So what if he did not have legs? He was the brother of the brilliant, young, soon-to-be lawyer and who was sure to make a name for himself. They were proud to have Joie as their new son-in-law. The fact that he had a craft and would soon have his own shop was an added bonus. Their daughter's financial security was assured.

Peter visited Piparo every weekend. On one of his visits he brought his good friend Harry to spend the weekend in the country. Barbs and Harry got on very well and before the family realized what was happening, they had decided to get married. Parpi was relieved. He had lived to see all his children do well. After the wedding, Barbs went to live in the town of San Fernando, and Joie and Elsie moved into the house in Piparo.

Elsie helped Parpi look after the small plot of farmland while Joie rode into town every day to the small jewelry store that Noman had opened up for him. Noman would soon set up his own law practice.

Peter, who seemed to have his life under control, was dating a nice girl whom Parpi expected him to marry as soon as Peter had finished with Training College. Peter eventually did marry his girl Della, and they moved to England shortly after that. Parpi then divided his time between Joie and his family in the village and Noman and Fifi in town.

Fifi was very goodhearted and cared for her in-laws with a devotion that many envied. She was especially close to Joie and his growing family. If however Noman paid attention to his family, Fifi would go into a jealous rage. She could not bear the thought of him suggesting they visit Piparo or take gifts to them. If, on the other hand, she suggested they visit Piparo and smother them with gifts and presents, then it was okay.

Fifi generally overdid everything. Noman soon caught on to this and to keep the peace let her think she was making all the decisions that had to do with his family. When Noman died a few years ago, Fifi found out that he had financially supported all of Joie's five children and had found time to visit them on many occasions. The worse part of it was that he had managed to do this for forty years without Fifi ever finding out.

Because Fifi could not bear the thought of Noman caring for his family and assumed he must be extremely jealous of the love and affection she felt for hers, she hid her visits to her

family and the presents she gave them. Many years later, Noman admitted to knowing about the many things Fifi did for her
family and the generous presents she gave them and he was
not at all upset by it.

In fact he told me he actually enjoyed the fact that he could
indirectly repay Victor for all that he had done for him. To keep
the peace, he decided it would be better if Fifi did not know how
he felt, as she would have thought he did not care enough about
her to be jealous of those she gave her affections to.

Some time after Noman had his law degree, he had set up
his own office with a staff of six people. Victor assisted by providing all the financial backing. Noman had a reputation for total
honesty and absolute fairness. Knowing what it was to be without money and struggling to exist, he was very kind and helpful
to poor people. He often gave free advice and did not charge
legal fees to people who could not afford to pay.

He also loaned out money with very low interest rates to
poor farmers. As a result, his fame grew and his practice prospered. Before long, Noman and Fifi were able to move out of the
small apartment Victor had given them and into a proper house
in a better part of town. Noman attempted to repay Victor for
the money he had spent on his education, but Victor always refused, saying it had been an investment in his daughter's future
and besides he did not need the money.

Fifi and Noman's social life began to pick up, as they were
being invited to all the elite parties in the country. Fifi learned
to entertain with panache and soon their parties were on everyone's must attend list.

Foie developed a taste for fine wines, in which she indulged
during the many trips they now made abroad. For their first
trip, we all got dressed in our best clothes and went to the

airport. When Fifi reached the top of the aircraft steps, she turned around and waved. She looked like one of those fancy, sophisticated people in a 'who's who' magazine. We were so impressed!

Despite all this, Fifi was unhappy because she had still not become pregnant. She visited one doctor after the other to see if there was any chance that she could have a baby. An operation was suggested to straighten her twisted tubes. Fifi went through the operation but she still did not get pregnant.

The old midwives told her that drinking aloe juice would help her, so Fifi drank a small glass of thick and bitter aloe juice every night for six months. Nothing happened. Then someone suggested that her tubes might be blocked or stuck together. She was advised to sit on a pot of hot water every evening so the steam would seep into her tubes and open them up. Fifi sat on a hot pot every night for four months. Nothing happened except that her genital area got red and too sore to have sex.

By now Fifi was even more depressed and turned to Clara for comfort and advice. Dora was far too busy making her own babies and coping with a very smug Larry, who was proud of his growing family, they now had two robust boys and another baby on the way.

Clara suggested that Fifi should relax forget about getting pregnant and perhaps she would get pregnant. That was known to happen, Clara predicted with authority. "The stress of trying too hard could be the problem", she diagnosed.

Fifi tried that too, but still did not get pregnant. And while Noman wanted babies and seemed fond of children, he told Fifi he had himself checked out and that he had a low sperm count, so that even if she could have had kids, it was obvious to him that he would never be able to father a child.

No one ever knew if that was true because he never produced a doctor's report to prove it. It was a wonderful generous thoughtful gesture on his part to share the blame of their childless condition and this show of sensitivity and love for Fifi endeared him even more to the family.

Fifi suffered from chronic constipation. She was always in a rush to do things for people and never found time for her morning calls of nature. On one occasion when she was particularly constipated, she broke out in a rash. All the well-known doctors were her friends by now, so she decided to call one of them for advice.

Dr. Trevor asked her when she had last passed stools. When Fifi admitted it had been five days, he laughingly told her she had the worse case of constipation he had heard of and that all she needed to do was to take a dose of caster oil.

Fifi took a large dose of caster oil, but that did not work so she called him back. He told her that perhaps a strong dose of Epsom salts was what she needed.

As it happened, Clara and I were spending the weekend with Fifi when she took a strong dose of the bitter salts. Not long afterwards, very severe pains began. She felt a sharp pain in her abdomen and a rush of wetness down her legs. Fifi rushed to the toilet and screamed for Clara.

Clara went rushing in and found Ffi her collapsed on the floor with blood everywhere. Clara was quick to see that Fifi had miscarried. She scooped up the bloody mass in a towel so she could show the doctor and then washed Fifi off and put her to bed.

The doctor confirmed that the Epsom salts had caused her to miscarry. Inconsolable, Fifi cried and cried. Noman gently consoled her, telling her that babies were not meant for them, as they had far too many foreign trips to make and other people's problems to solve. With their hectic lifestyle, he told her, they would not make ideal parents. He reminded her that she had already proven she could have a baby. She was not barren.

Noman reminded Fifi that this was yet another sign that God did not want them to have children and they should no longer try. If it happened naturally, that was fine; if not, they should just get on with their happy, busy lives and not worry about it anymore. Fifi reluctantly agreed.

When Dora's third baby was due, Fifi had an idea. If it turned out to be another boy, she announced, she would take him and love him as her own. No one, least of all Larry, thought it was a good idea, but no one had the heart to tell her.

CHAPTER 13

I often wonder how far back people can remember events in their lives because I remember my very first recollection so vividly.

It was November 16, 1952—the day my cousin Marleen was born. I was exactly two years, six months and twentyeight days old.

It was morning and I clearly remember the quiet air of expectancy. Something important was going to happen that day. Mummy was in the kitchen, which in itself was an unusual thing, as she never cooked and hated being the kitchen. Cleaning and polishing, yes, but cooking, a definite no!

Mummy was wearing a blue and white flowered sleeveless dress with large, floppy frills around the neckline and a sash tied around her tiny waist. I can still see her distinctly, as if it were only yesterday. She had an old, wet rag in her hand and she had a grim expression on her face, as she somewhat nervously wiped the top of the cupboard.

The heavy, oval-shaped mahogany kitchen table with its fruit-patterned oilskin tablecloth had already been laid out for lunch. A huge blue enamel cooking pot well worn from use was simmering gently on the old-fashioned three-burner kerosene stove. Now that I think about it, the contents had to have been our family's favourite emergency one-dish meal—Country Style Stew with lots of plump, glutinous dumplings cooked in lentils with ground provisions like potatoes, sweet potatoes, carrots etc.

This thick, soupy dish was always prepared when there were other more important things to do and no one had time to be in the kitchen "slaving over a hot stove." The aroma of the stew and the faint smell of kerosene—which we in Trinidad called 'pitch oil'—permeated the whole house. Apart from the soft, whispering breeze and the slight rattle of the windows, it was strangely silent.

Dora's and Larry's two boys, Arnie and Ricky and I huddled together outside the back bedroom door where we had a clear view of the kitchen. I always thought of the three of us as "me and the boys." Even at that tender age and despite the fact that I was older than Arnie by only two days, I knew I was the leader of the group. I knew I could take better control of a situation than Arnie could. I was the strongest, the one who could nurture and protect.

I have no idea why that day felt ominious to a child of just over two years old. I remember feeling very grown up and knowing I just had to take charge. I knew that no matter what was happening, I would handle the situation and protect the boys. It seemed like that it was the thing I just had to do, everyone else was too busy or preoccupied.

Perhaps I thought the boys would not be able to cope with whatever was in store for them. This feeling of needing to protect them, in fact, carried on throughout our childhood, into our youth, and later on into adult life.

So here I was at the head of the line in my faded rolled-up cotton shorts, loose, seersucker shirt, and bare feet, waiting for the news. Would it be the desperately wanted girl or yet another boy? If it were a boy, we had heard that Fifi, Mummy's childless middle sister, might take the baby for her own. After all, Fifi logically reasoned to herself and those around her, Auntie Dora and Uncle Larry already had two naughty, boisterous handfuls to raise.

I have often wondered if Fifi would have actually taken the baby if it had been a boy or if Uncle Larry would have even agreed to that outrageous idea. Knowing him and seeing him with his children as we grew up, I am confident he would never have agreed to hand over any of his children to anyone.

After what seemed like an eternity, we could hear rustling and movement inside the room. The silence was finally broken by the soft whimper of a baby's cry. We waited with bated breath until Uncle Larry peered out of the room a few moments later. In a quiet, emotional voice he whispered, "It is a girl! A tiny little baby girl." He beckoned us into the room. We tiptoed quietly into the room to have a look at the miracle, for that is how Uncle Larry made it seem.

The faint smell of Dettol greeted us as we pushed our way inside the room. The curtains were drawn and all three doors in the room were closed, making it quite gloomy. The huge iron bed covered with surprisingly clean, crisp white sheets took up most of the room.

Auntie May, the tall, plump, black midwife with her hair neatly tucked underneath her starched white nurse's cap, was washing the new baby in a large galvanized basin that was on a low table in a corner of the room.

We quietly moved towards the basin to see the new baby. Having confirmed that it really was a girl, Auntie May explained the difference to us. We then approached the bed where Auntie

Dora lay with her head tilted to the right and her eyes closed. She looked ever so tiny and still as she lay on the plumped-up pillows, her dark face looking drawn and gray.

I wondered if she was happy and relieved to have given birth to a girl, as she did not show any emotion at all. Perhaps she was just tired. Uncle Larry, on the other hand, had a triumphant smile on his face, as if no one had ever performed this feat before. Looming thin and very tall over the bed, he tucked the mosquito net around it protectively, keeping an eye on Auntie May and the baby.

Auntie May finished bathing the baby and swaddled her in an enormous yellow blanket. She gave her to Uncle Larry who then called the boys to him so they could have a closer look at their sister. The proud boys started to ask him questions but he shushed them quickly so as not to disturb their mother.

I think Arnie was most delighted; he beamed as though he were responsible for the happy event. Perhaps he understood the importance of the birth of a girl in the family. I suspected that Ricky, although trying to look pleased and forcing a stiff smile, would have preferred a baby brother.

I stood back a little, waiting to be asked to join the group. Then it slowly dawned on me that I was not a part of that cozy group that so obviously belonged together. Uncertain, I hung back near the door, hoping to be included. When Uncle Larry still did not call me closer, I realized sadly that I was not a part of their family of five.

I remember suddenly feeling cold. No one noticed as I quietly crept out of the room in search of my mother who was still in the kitchen. That was the first time I remember feeling cold and alone. Since then, I have always associated aloneness with feeling cold.

I threw my tiny arms around Mummy and clung to her. She, too, had a strange look in her eyes. Perhaps she understood how left out I felt and could read the pain in my eyes. She quickly hugged me back. It was a sad, lonely hug.

Some time during that hug Uncle Larry came out of the back room with the two boys in tow and held out the baby for Mummy to see. As they gazed at the tiny thing, Uncle Larry kissed the baby. Mummy then asked in a stiff, business-like tone that brought us all back to reality, "What are you going to call her?"

Uncle Larry replied that they had not thought of a name. They had not wanted to tempt fate by selecting or even thinking of a girl's name in case they got another boy. Mummy, who was always prepared for anything, had a name in mind already. Not wanting to appear pushy, she casually said, "Marleen is an easy and pretty name. It has a nice, soft ring to it and no one else in the family has that name."

"Marleen? Marleen! That is a nice name. We will call her Marleen," Uncle Larry immediately decided. So the baby girl was called Marleen. I felt a tender love swelling up inside me at that moment. I wanted so desperately to hold her. Uncle Larry again kissed Marleen and then made a solemn promise to her as he hugged her close. "This house will always be yours because you were born here. I will bury your navel string under the mango tree in the backyard."

Growing up over the years, this always remained a family joke. "Don't say anything to Marleen," we would tease. "Better not upset her. This is her house and she could turn us out anytime. Remember, her navel string is buried right there in the backyard under the mango tree."

Knowing that her navel string was buried in the backyard

gave Marleen a definite air of quiet importance, which was always very apparent. Whenever the topic of conversation came up, Marleen would hold her plump little self more erectly and look down her round little snub nose on us unfortunate mortals who had the misfortune of having their navel strings cast out with that day's hospital garbage. Oh, to have the privilege of being born at home! How we envied her!

Marleen was the cutest baby I had ever seen. Maybe this was because she was the only baby I really knew at that time. She quickly grew into a cuddly little thing with dimpled knees and soft chubby legs. She was always very quiet and didn't smile very much.

When things got too noisy and boisterous for her, she was content to sit in the rocking chair on the porch and sing to herself. She would sit there rocking away in her own little world, singing the same song over and over again in a dull monotonous tone. "Baby must play with baby, dog must play with dog, chair must play with chair" and so on. I always wondered why she sang that peculiar song. She seemed to have the need to put things into little groups or boxes and categorize them according to their kind or species.

Many, many years later when we were grown-ups, I asked Marleen if she remembered singing those little ditties. She laughed softly and said she most certainly did. In her mind, she firmly believed there was a great message in those apparently silly philosophical words. She still believes today that nature intended each person, animal, place, or thing, to belong with its own kind.

When I was younger and related the memory of the day Marleen was born, the family would wonder skeptically at my clear recollections. I too could never understand why I should have remembered the day so vividly and why the events after her birth day till I was perhaps four years old stay so dull and hazy. I have no answers except for the fact that Marleen and I are some how inexplicably bonded together. We share an intuition with each other and have very often had identical thoughts and feelings at almost the very same time.

In October 2000 I was in Sydney, Australia for the Olympic Games when amidst all the thrill and excitement of the Games I felt a sudden deep loneliness and a yearning to visit the old Inca city of Machu Picchu in Peru. The closest I could get to Machu Picchu then was to listen to the haunting pipe music of the indigenous Inca people.

I desperately searched in all the music shops but I could not find the music anywhere. This feeling lasted several days and then slowly passed away.

A few months later I was visiting Trinidad and just happened to mention to Marleen about the compulsion that I had felt to visit Machu Picchu. Marleen stopped dead in her tracks and told me that she too at that very time, had the same sudden urge to go there. She said that she immediately made plans and was surprised that she was able to get tickets and hotels at short notice and so she had actually visited the city and had brought back several CDs of the pipe Andean music that I had longed to lose myself in. Needless to say she shared some of that music with me.

Chapter 14

Over the long months after my birth, Clara reconciled herself to the fact that Winston was content to let her remain in Diamond and visit her whenever he felt the need. Victor was not happy with this situation; he felt Winston should take Clara back to their home so they could be a real family. He tried on several occasions to talk to both of them, but they did not seem to understand what he was trying to say. Not being a man to impose his will on anyone, he just kept silent after that. He was afraid that if he kept on talking about Clara returning to her husband their home, Clara might misunderstand his motive and think he was trying to get rid of her and the baby.

Nan was still as physically fit as ever, but inside she was heartbroken. After the death of Little Sparrow, she continued to look after the house and take charge of the family. Ramsey, who was living with them while he attended college, had recently gone to the north of the island to attend Teachers Training College. Occasionally, Nass would come to spend a few weeks with Nan.

Ismat, Nan's other daughter, rarely came over. She had her hands full with her two daughters and two sons. Her husband did not like her going away for long. Her elder daughter Dori had gotten married, but her husband had left her with their baby boy and she had come back home to live with her parents. Savi, the younger daughter, was still at school but her two boys were troublesome. They did not want to study and showed no interest in a career. All they seemed to do was run around in bad company. Too gentle and quiet to properly control her family, Ismat spoiled her sons and was forever making excuses for their behaviour. Her husband was no better. He was a weak man who was only happy when he was doing things with and for her. He could not cope with any major problems. Both Ismat and her husband owned a general dry goods store in the small town of Princes Town and made just enough money to provide the family with the necessities of life.

Victor kept busy doing things that gave him pleasure. He played cricket with his team twice a week and became more involved in the community, encouraging people to make and set up more schools. The village people still turned to him for help and advice. If he was lonely, he did not show it. And he certainly did not do anything to make the village women gossip. Several of the older ladies tried to catch his eye, but he remained aloof. He was not at all interested in settling down with anyone after Little Sparrow. She was the love of his life.

The Chand family lived across the street from Victor. Chand, was a very quiet and gentle man who made a decent living running his battered old taxi back and forth from Diamond into town. It was an easy but boring job. The only way he could make it big was to expand his taxi business. But he was cautious and not very ambitious. He made enough money for his family and did not want to run the risk of expanding his business and losing what little money he did have.

Chand had a wife, Rachel and two children, a daughter Merle and a son Kelvin. Rachel, who was very ambitious, was very frustrated that Chand did not want to make the effort to expand his taxi service and make a better life for his family.

Rachel, a tall, imposing woman, was not what one would call beautiful. She was only five years older than Clara was and although these two women lived across from each other for many years, they never became friends. In fact, they did not like each other at all; each had an uncomfortable feeling about the other. The dislike was so strong that they did not even greet each other for many months at a time. Rachel had a nasty habit of dropping taunting remarks whenever she knew Clara was around and could hear her. This became worse after Clara came back to Diamond to live.

Rachel was from the north of the island. 'Northerners' always considered themselves to be the fast smart city people who knew the best way to do everything and set the latest fashion trends. They believed that people from the south were like country cousins. Being a show-off by nature, Rachel would hang her new dresses, lacy underwear, and other personal garments in the sun to air. Clara could not take that competition, she knew she was better looking, better dressed, and certainly had more privileges than Rachel had. She believed Rachel did these things to hide her inferiority complex. Clara was convinced Rachel was jealous of her.

Whatever Clara may have believed, Rachel's sights were set elsewhere. Clara was merely an irritation that could prevent her from getting what she wanted. One day Rachel came boldly over to the house to talk to Victor about her problems. She told him how terrible her life was, how Chand beat her and did not give her money to buy food, and that she and the children would starve if it were not for the fact that her family sent her money.

She cried and begged Victor not to say anything to Chand because she was sure he would take revenge on her and beat her even more. Victor was very upset for this poor woman and spoke to her about having courage. He reminded her that her son Kelvin was fast growing up and soon she would have someone to stand up for her. Rachel listened carefully. When she left she told him how much relief it gave her to be able to talk about it to someone who she could trust. She would now go home and face her dismal situation with new courage.

When Clara found out that Rachel had come over to the house to talk to Victor, she was livid. She asked Victor what cock and bull story Rachel had come over to discuss. Victor would not elaborate on the details. All he said was that the poor woman had a lot of problems and that Clara should be more sympathetic to her and not jump to her own conclusions. Clara tried to persuade Victor to tell her about Rachel's problems so that she would understand, but he said he had promised not to talk about it to anyone. Clara lashed out at Victor. Could he not see what Rachel was doing? Was he blind? Victor was shocked at Clara's reaction. All he had done was listen to an unfortunate person's problems and try to help as best he could.

A few weeks later when Clara was out, Rachel made another visit to the house to talk to Victor. This time she was crying hysterically. Between loud sobs she told Victor that the night before Chand had behaved worse than ever. He had come home drunk and beaten her so badly that Kelvin was forced to intervene. This led to a major confrontation between father and son and Chand ended up beating Kelvin mercilessly. Kelvin was so badly hurt and bruised that she had to send him to live with her mother in the north because she was afraid that from now on the two of them would not be able to live together.

She felt she could no longer stay with Chand. How could he beat his own flesh and blood so badly? She was now scared for her own life and that of her daughter Merle. She believed Chand was crazy and had now become impossible to live with. She should leave him but had no choice but to stay in that hellhole because she had nowhere else to go. She could not go back to her family, as her father was very ill and would not be able to handle the physical nor the financial strain of her separation. If he knew of her plight, it would be enough to kill him.

Victor had empathy for what she said and could understand what she was going through. His daughter Clara had had her share of problems. Thank God she had him and that he had the means to help her. This poor suffering woman had no one to turn to. He would have to help. It was his duty to assist another helpless human being.

He had an idea. He had an apartment in another village that was empty at that time. He would allow Rachel to stay there rent-free until she sorted out her life. He gave her the keys and told her she could stay there. Rachel rushed back home to pack up and left with Merle before Chand returned home that evening.

When Clara came home later that day, Nan told her that Rachel had come over in a highly emotional state. Nan had no idea what had gone on. All she knew was that Victor had spent a long time talking to her before she had left in a calmer mood. Clara confronted Victor. She wanted to know exactly what that bitch had wanted from him and what he had said to her. Trying to remain calm, he told Clara what Rachel had told him and that he had given her a place to stay until she got her back on her feet.

Clara was not at all happy about what she had heard; she knew this was the beginning of trouble. How could she explain to him that he was sure to get trapped into the web Rachel had made to snare him? It was difficult to explain those kinds of things to her father. Clara voiced her fears to Nan, who also had suspicions about Rachel and her recent antics. She was sure Rachel had devised a clever plan. Perhaps she wanted money, Nan speculated. After what Clara had told her, she was sure Clara was right. No decent woman would play those tricks if she had not set her eyes on a man.

Nan decided she would have a serious talk with Victor. He must be made to understand that this was not right. Rachel was a conniving wretch who was out for his money and his name. She spent the whole evening explaining the situation to him, but Victor did not see it that way. He was sure they were mistaken. They had misjudged the poor defenseless woman. Did they really believe he was so stupid he could be taken in like that? Is that what they thought of the man who loved Little Sparrow with all his heart? He still thought of her every day and missed her desperately. He could never betray or tarnish her memory.

Relieved, Nan was now convinced that Victor was just being kind. He had no interest in Rachel and would be able to handle anything she may have in store for him. She chuckled at the thought that Rachel was in for a big shock. She hoped she would be around to see Rachel's face when she found out that Victor was not going to fall for her jezebel-style trap. Nan told Clara there was nothing to worry about, but Clara was not convinced, she knew the wily ways of a woman who desperately wanted a man with money. She kept quiet and waited to see how it would turn out.

The next day Chand came over to talk to Clara. Too much in awe of Victor, he was more at ease talking to Clara. He wanted to know what had happened to Rachel. Had they seen her? He told her that Rachel had sent Kelvin to her mother's in the north of the island to live while he attended a good school in the big city, and now she had taken Merle and just disappeared. Clara did not know what to say. She could not ask if they had had a fight or if he had beaten Kelvin and Rachel. Chand looked like such a harmless, quiet person. Instead, she said she was sure Rachel would turn up after a few days. She suggested that perhaps Rachel had needed some time alone. Chand went away none the wiser, still confused and very worried.

When several days had gone by and Rachel still had not come home, Chand decided he now had to ask around. Someone told him they had heard rumours that she had left him and was now living in another village a few miles away. He went looking for her in every village in the vicinity. When he eventually found her, she made it very clear that she did not intend to return to him and she now had a man of means who was supporting her. Chand left, disappointed and distraught. He could not understand why she would want to leave him. He stopped off at the rum shop for a drink. One drink led to another. By the time he was ready to drive home, he was well and truly inebriated.

The next morning Clara and Victor heard the news that Chand had died in a terrible car accident. It seems he was very drunk and was driving so fast he lost control of the car and crashed into a tree. He had died instantly. Clara was convinced he had deliberately killed himself. Victor, however, was convinced that this proved exactly what Rachel had always said—that Chand was a drunkard who was capable of irrational, impulsive, and thoughtless behaviour.

Rachel did not go to the funeral, but her family did attend. Kelvin was heartbroken. He could not understand how this could have happened or why his mother did not come to the funeral. He held her responsible for the tragedy and became estranged from her from then on. A very subdued Merle was there, but she did not give any reasons why her mother was not there. Victor, Clara, and Nan were part of the sad little procession that went to the graveyard on that wet and rainy day.

A few days later Victor went to visit Rachel. He had to find out the truth about what had happened. He did not come home that night. Clara and Nan were worried sick. What could have happened? They did not know for sure that he had gone to see Rachel, but they had a good idea that that was where he was. He had never done this before.

Victor did not return home till 9.00 a.m. the next morning. He came in very quietly, not saying a word for several minutes. Then he very softly and almost ashamedly told Nan that Rachel would be moving into the house the next day. Clara immediately stormed out and locked herself in her bedroom. Victor was subdued. He did not eat a thing and spent the rest of day alone in his bedroom.

The following day Rachel arrived at about three o'clock in the afternoon. She walked brazenly and confidently into the house with an air of ownership, that even I as a young child picked up on. Clara and Victor were nowhere to be found, so poor Nan was left to cope with the intruder on her own. Nan sat quietly on the steps of the back veranda while Rachel busily unpacked some pots and pans that she had brought along with a bundle of clothes and bedding. I went up to her, looked at the ugly, dented, blackened pots, and asked innocently, "Why have you brought these ugly, dirty pots into our home?" Maybe that was one reason Rachel never took a liking to me in those early years.

And so Rachel entered our lives. She did not take kindly to Nan living there. In her mind Nan's rightful place in that house had ended when Little Sparrow died. But Victor set some firm rules for Rachel right at the beginning. She was not to do the cooking; that was Nan's job. She was not to say one word about Nan; she must treat her as though she were his mother. And most importantly, she must realize that whatever money he had was for his three daughters. She would get only the pocket money he would give her. If anything were to happen to him, she would get a monthly allowance to live on and would have no claim whatsoever to his property. Rachel agreed to that proposal without any argument. She was prepared to bide her time.

Years later when I was older, Victor in one of our quiet moments, explained to me what had actually happened when he visited Rachel that eventful day so many years ago and why he had had no choice but to bring Rachel home.

He said that when he arrived at the apartment, Rachel was apparently sick and in bed. She was too sick to get up, she said, and he had to go into the bedroom to talk to her. Then the inevitable happened. He had sex with her. Afterwards he was angry with himself. How could he have allowed that to happen? He had loved his wife and had vowed to stay true to her memory. Now he would have no choice but to do the honourable thing: take her into his home and make her his wife.

And so he brought her home. He could not bring himself to actually marry her, so he kept her as his common law wife. He admitted that, as a man, he did need companionship but he would live with the painful shame of what he had done for the rest of his life. It was many years before he took Rachel around with him and introduced her as his wife.

Rachel adjusted to the big house very quickly and with incredible ease. She tried to assume the role of the squire's wife and earn the trust of the people as Little Sparrow had, but it was no use. Initially she was not liked. Most of the village people knew what she was all about and how she had gotten to her elevated position. They were disappointed that Victor had fallen for her tricks. It was several years before they began to give her any kind of respect. Even then it was because she had worked hard to earn it, making a point of visiting the sick, sending presents for weddings, attending funerals, and so on. It did not matter to her that people talked about her and disliked her. She had thick skin and knew they would eventually forget where she had come from and accept her as Victor's wife. In the meantime, she would continue her role as supporter and do-gooder of the poor and needy just as Little Sparrow had done.

When Rachel moved into the house, she sent Merle to stay with Kelvin up north in her mother's house. But after she had spent a few months in the house, Rachel started bringing Merle to visit. In the beginning she stayed for a few weeks, then a few months, and then she stayed for good.

Merle was a nice girl with a pleasant, easygoing nature. She began to go to the village school. She got on very well with Nan and Clara. She liked to draw. She once sketched a picture of me, which hung in the village school for several years.

During the first few years, Kelvin never visited, still maintaining his cool distance from his mother, and Rachel never went to see her family. We heard that her brothers were very angry with her and had forbidden her to visit them.

Rachel never liked me during those first years. Maybe it was because Victor, my dear Papa, gave me some attention. He would bring me a bar of Nestle's fruit and nut chocolate every day when he returned from his business trips downtown. Her eyes followed us and I could feel her dislike for me, so I stayed far away from her and avoided him when she was around.

Rachel and Mom had many rows. At times it was difficult to know who started the rows, but they were always so violent and loud I would run and hide. Victor was seldom at home when these rows occurred, but the few times he was there he would get upset and frustrated that they were fighting. In the beginning he would always take Nan's and Clara's side, reminding Rachel that she knew what she had gotten into and that she had to live with it. But as the years went by, he started taking Rachel's side more and more, which would irk Clara so much she would not speak to either of them for days and weeks and at times even months. Clara grew more and more bitter because of the house situation and her personal problems with Winston.

Chapter 15

Although the house in Diamond was the only home I knew, I never felt I belonged there. During my early years Rachel always made a point of telling me that my real home was in my father's house. Since Winston had never made a home for Clara and me, I did not have anywhere else to go but wherever my mother was.

For as long as I can remember I have longed for my own home where I could hold my head up high. I never wanted to stay in someone else's home. I did not want to be an intruder or stay somewhere out of charity, which is how Rachel made me feel. I later developed a fiercely independent streak because of this experience.

I kept these feelings locked up in my heart. I knew I could not—or dare not—share these emotions with Clara my mom, so I did not tell her. I learned when I was very young what I could talk to Clara about and what I could not. I would look at her face to know if it was going to be a good day for me or not. A good day meant that she would hug me; a bad day meant that I had to be very careful; otherwise, I would get badly beaten. I had gotten used to Mom taking out her pent-up rage and frustration over Winston, Rachel, or the unfairness of the world on me.

Victor, Nan, Clara, Rachel, Merle, and I lived in the house. The environment was not at all harmonious due to the tension that existed after Rachel moved in. There was resentment on both sides. Added to this was my peculiar, stressful relationship with Mom.

Now old and getting senile, Nan began to do strange things. She became a hoarder and refused to throw out empty bottles, old tins, used wrapping paper, etc., saying she would likely need them in the future. She was always losing things and then accusing "someone" of deliberating hiding them just to annoy her. We all knew who that some one was and that added to the tensions. She would forget where she had put things and was becoming irritable and irritated by all her little aches and pains.

Rachel did everything she could to aggravate Nan's condition. When Victor was not home, she would say things to get Nan started. When Victor came home, she would tearfully and innocently exaggerate Nan's antics. Desperately wanting Victor to understand her point of view, Nan would try to explain what had actually happened. But all Victor could see was Rachel's effort to be accommodating in the face of Nan and Clara's negativity. He believed that although Nan was a problem he did owe her a lot and genuinely wanted the best for her, as she was the only mother he could remember. To keep the peace, he told Nan that it was time for her to sit back and let Rachel run the house and do all the cooking.

That was just what Rachel wanted—total control of the household. But Mom continued to do her best to ensure that not everything went Rachel's way. While Rachel ruled the kitchen, Mom took control of the house itself, looking after the cleaning, polishing, and the all-important task of choosing new curtains and furnishing every year. Mom let Merle help because she was such a "fair" person. She wanted Merle to feel at home, as "Merle was a sweet, harmless child who was there through no fault of her own". It also made Mom feel self-righteous to be kind to her enemy's child.

Major spring-cleaning was a most important event in our calendar when preparing for the Christmas, Easter, Eid, and Diwali seasons. Everything had to be absolutely spick and span for these special occasions. I loved to help. Those three or four days of cleaning were always a jolly time for me at home. I took great pleasure in the hustle and bustle.

We scraped, scrubbed, dusted, and polished the furniture and the floors until they shone so brightly we could see ourselves in the wood. To this day, the smell of Mansion Polish reminds me of those times.

During those cleaning days, we ate delicious one-dish meals. We had a choice of Pillau, a dish of rice and meat, then there was 'kitchery', a sticky mixture of rice cooked with lentils and pickles to go with it, or our favourite Country style soup, that cook up of all the vegetables and ground provisions we had in the house, cooked with lentils and dumplings and served piping hot.

Another reason why spring-cleaning was a happy time for me was that Mom was so busy being busy and full of her own importance that she was less critical of me and did not notice my many bad habits and shortcomings. How I relished those three or four days!

With very little to do now, Nan was not very happy, she became miserable. She moped around the house complaining that the food Rachel cooked was not up to the high standard we were used to. In truth, Rachel cooked very much like Nan; she had learned by watching Nan every day. Nan also complained that Victor did not sit with her as often as he used to, which caused her much stress and strain.

One day Nan got up with chronic pains in her chest. We

quickly called the doctor, who told us she had suffered a mild heart attack. Thankfully, Nan recovered soon enough. After that, all the events in her life dated either "before mey heart'tak" or "after mey heart'tak."

It was during this time that I learned a lot about my family's history. I spent a lot of time listening to Nan as she related stories about the old family and how they had come from India so many years ago. I was very curious to know each and every detail. Eager to keep me with her for as long as possible, Nan gladly told me everything she knew. She filled me in on the gossip and news of all those we knew or had heard about.

As I listened intently, my imagination created vivid pictures of crowded cites and villages in India, rough sea voyages, and romantic images of my ancestors. I shared their suffering, took pleasure in their achievements, and was shocked by the scandalous, outrageous behaviour of some of the black sheep in the family. This was an important part of my heritage that helped me to feel like I belonged to this long line of people, some of whom I admired greatly.

By this time Mom had began to work in Noman's office. This gave her something to do and provided her with some extra pocket money. Most importantly, it kept her out of the house and the environment she hated. With Mom going to work every day, I found Diamond very lonely. There were no other children in the house to play with and I was not allowed to go to other children's homes to play. The closeness that Victor and I shared in my early years had also disappeared. He now seemed preoccupied and embarrassed to even look at me. Rachel made sure that he was so busy sorting out little jobs and situations she had created for him that he no longer had any time for me.

I understood. I knew I had no place there anyway, as it was not my father's house. Merle was busy with her mother and school. Rachel made sure Merle was always on hand when Victor needed his slippers or his hat or whatever it was he could not find. He found her to be a very helpful and thoughtful child. I stayed in my little eight-by-seven foot playroom.

When I was about four, Mom decided I should start play school at a nice place about three miles away. I remember the first day I went. Mom had packed a flask of chocolate milk and a snack of cheese and jam sandwiches, which I hated but she insisted on giving me. She had arranged for Milo, a young man who ran a taxi service, to pick me up and drop me off at the play school every morning, and then take me home when school finished at 12.30 p.m. everyday.

The school was under a house built on stilts. We sat on long, wooden benches beside long, brightly colored matching tables. I don't recall much about my play school except that on one occasion, the teacher whom we called Auntie, took us for a nature walk in the semi-jungle area behind her house. I found it very interesting. I walked beside Auntie, holding her hand and listening to her very attentively as she pointed out various things. When we came upon a mossy tree Auntie signaled us to be quiet and look closely at the bark of the tree trunk. There we saw a lizard unlike any lizard I had ever seen before. Its colour was changing from the green mossy shade of the tree bark to the bright colours in Auntie's dress.

I was fascinated. It was the first time I had seen a chameleon. I stooped and peered at it closely. Then I overheard one of the children whisper that now our Auntie would die because the lizard had stolen her life when it took her colours. I got a sudden sharp pain in my stomach and had to be taken back to school. I was frightened that Auntie would die. I could not tell anyone how badly I felt, so I just kept quiet and prayed hard that it would not happen. Of course Auntie never did die and I was sure that God had answered my prayers, as He knew how much I loved her.

Shortly after that it was time for me to go to 'big' school. Mom wanted me to go to the government school in the town. Arnie, who was only two days younger than me, had already been admitted to that school, thanks to Larry's influence. They were also living quite close to the school and it made sense that Arnie go there.

Mom had no such influence and Winston was not concerned enough to ask if my school admission had been arranged. Victor took it upon himself to go to the village school and admit me there so that is where I began my first year of formal schooling.

All the schools followed the very same syllabus so the village school was a very good school. The headmaster at that time was a highly educated man who had been to the same training college that Winston had attended. He was very helpful and sympathetic to Mom and her situation. Victor's position of respect in the village gave me a certain edge; everyone treated me gently and kindly. Merle was also going to the same school, so we would walk to school together every day. She looked after me that first year.

I was in Standard I, the first class, and I did pretty well. I very quickly learned to read and developed a love of storybooks. Perhaps it was an escape but I would lose myself in a wonderful fairyland world. When I read the story of the Princess and the Pea, I placed a pea under my mattress and was very sad that I did not feel the pea that night as I slept. I was painfully aware that I was just an ordinary person and not a real princess at all.

Still, in my secret fantasies I was a poor princess who had somehow got lost and ended up living in a nasty, cruel world.

My prince charming would come and rescue me from the empty loneliness I felt. I dreamed about the comfort of having someone love me, give me my own home, and not beat or hurt me. I longed for that happy-ever-after world.

Pamela was my best friend in those early days. Her mother, who was big, dark-skinned whom, I thought, quite ugly. She was a mixture of African as well as European blood. Pamela's father was a handsome man of Indian descent. These two people had produced a daughter who was extremely beautiful. Pamela seemed to have inherited the best of all her ethnic roots. She was lovely and I admired her beauty so much as she did not have a big nose

Pamela and I were in the same class at school. We often sat together for our recess break, sharing our lunch and playing skipping or hopscotch.

I felt sorry for Pamela because she always looked so sad. Her parents had split up and she was living with her mother, grandmother, and numerous children from her uncle's and auntie's liaisons with different women and men. Her brothers lived with their father and his new wife. Pamela did not have nice clothes or shoes and had never tasted chocolate, never had toys nor been to the cinema.

One day, Pamela came over to the house to play with me. It was the first time she had ever come over. I was thrilled. I did not know what to give her to eat or drink and wanted to do something special to make her happy for the time she was with me.

Mom had gone to work, so I had no one to ask. Then I remembered that Victor had some special throat pastilles he had got from England. I rushed upstairs and got one for her and one for me. Rachel must have seen me because the next thing I knew, Victor came thundering downstairs with a belt in his hand and began beating me. I don't know why he did that; I can only guess that he was so fed up with Rachel's constant complaining about me that he had to do something.

I could not believe he would do this to me. I was too ashamed to cry out loud with Pamela standing there. Thank God she quickly ran home, scared of Victor's fury. Then I screamed out loud from the burning lashes of the belt. Nan hearing my screams came down stairs and somehow got in between Victor and me.

She must have taken a few lashes with the belt before she managed to grab hold of it. Victor dropped the belt and went upstairs.

Nan held me close and told me I should not have done what I did and that I had to understand the situation and act accordingly. I looked up to see Rachel turn away with a look of satisfaction on her face. I know Victor was angry with himself for hitting me. I knew that he knew I did not deserve the beating he had given me. That was the only time he ever hit me, but I have never forgotten it, nor did I trusted him or his love again, even though all throughout his later life he shared many things with me that he shared with no one else.

When Mom came home that evening, I did not tell her what had happened because I knew from experience that she would not believe anything I said. She would have gotten angry with me and told me the same thing Nan did—that I must not forget my place, that I should not touch anything that was not mine, that I must learn to realize I had no home of my own. And with great satisfaction she would remind me that my father was a no good so-and-so who had denied me a home of my own.

Mom would repeat this to me over and over again. It was a

terrible feeling deep inside to know that I still did not belong and had no right to anything.

I also had the unforgiveable misfortune to look like Winston. Mom would tell me about 'Baby' and what a beautiful baby she had been with her delicate pretty features. If she had grown up, she would have looked just like Mom. I sadly looked at my reflection in the mirror and saw this huge nose and small, slanted orential eyes with sad lips that rarely smiled.

Mom said that when I smiled, my nose widened and spread out and that made it look even bigger. I decided I would look less ugly if I remained serious. After that I never smiled when I had my picture taken.

Being "a chip off the old block," I was apt to make many errors and do many things that would make Mom angry, like forgetting to dust behind the radio or be outside playing when she got home. The most unforgivable and worst sin, however, was to be caught talking to Rachel.

When Mom got angry, there was only one way to ease that anger and that was to straighten me out. Running and stomping like a wild woman, she would search for a belt in Victor's wardrobe. I got beaten for lying, which Mom accused me of doing most of the time. Lying was the one thing she could not stand. My father was a liar; therefore, I had to be a liar too because I was a 'chip off the old block.' I could not help it. Because I looked like him, Mom believed I was him. She never failed to remind me of the many failings I had or was sure to have one day soon. On average I received a beating five days a week.

Apart from the one beating that Victor gave me, no one else ever hit me. But they all called me a 'chip off the old block' and 'big nose.' Once when we visited Noman, I overheard him telling Mom that he could never have any sympathy or feel love for me because whenever he looked at me, he saw my father's face.

I felt just as badly when I went to stay at Auntie Dora's. Her family appeared to be a happy one with a father, a mother, and three children who sat down together for meals. I wanted so desperately to be a part of a family like that.

Whenever I visited, though, my cousins were polite and friendly, they would not allow me to be a member of their clique. They would cruelly remind me that I was just a cousin, not a brother or sister. Uncle Larry would give me the same treatment. If we were all together, he would fix his children's laces, tie their kites, comb their hair, and give them a hug as they crowded around him. I stayed back, afraid that if I went forward I would be rebuffed. It had happened before and I promised myself I would never be embarrassed like that again.

I always wondered what it must feel like to be hugged by a father. Were hugs from a man different from those from a mother?

I did not think it was fair that I was judged by my physical appearance. I always liked me. I had a soft, kind nature. I just wished somebody, anybody, would have see it. I also wished they could see the beauty of my heart and not judge me by my unfortunate looks. So I did not have a pretty face but I wanted so much to be liked and recognized for who I really was and not what I looked like.

I learned to read before Arnie did. Ricky and Marleen were both too young to read, so I read to them all the time. The first book I read by myself was "The Water Babies" by Charles Kingsley. I remember because it had the most wonderful pictures and it was the first book I ever received. Victor had bought it for me for Christmas. The story also appealed to me because of the happy ending. I hoped I too would have a happy ending to my life. The story gave me hope.

When I ran out of books to read, I would make up stories. In my favourite made-up story, I would go into a large, dark forest and find a big, beautiful tree with lots of branches and leaves. I would climb up the tree and find a tiny door in the middle of the trunk. I would open the door and climb down some stairs into a beautiful, perfect world. I would make up many tales and adventures inside that tree. Every night when I lay down to sleep, I would pray that I would find that warm, cozy, happy place where no one suffered and love was everywhere.

Books were the only presents that I was allowed to have around me, because Mom said reading was a good habit. All my other beautiful and expensive toys and Christmas presents that Victor who I called Papa had bought me were locked away in Mom's cupboards so that I would not ruin them.

On rare the occasions they were taken out. The dolls and my collections of stuffed animals were for display on the bed and not to be played with. At times I was allowed to play with the other toys if I had been good or if the cousins were coming. I did get to keep the broken and worn toys however and these I kept in a box in my little study to play with when my not so important friends came over.

Heaven forbid if I played with them at any other time. That would be another reason to get a beating for wasting my time playing childish make believe games.

By the time I was ready for Standard II, Mom had had enough of the village school. I had to be in the same school that Arnie and Ricky were now attending. She went to the inspector of schools and told them who she was and what connections she had. By now Winston had risen to the rank of Principal at one of the top colleges. Noman was a top lawyer in the country and

Victor was a well-known philanthropist.

I was accepted. Mom decided that I would now spend week-days with Auntie Dora's family and go home to Diamond on weekends. I hated feeling like a rolling stone, never living in my own home, always in someone else's house. I don't think Uncle Larry approved of the idea, but once Mom makes a decision, it was difficult to dissuade her. She would have been offended. So Larry and Dora kept their feelings to themselves and put up with their unwanted guest. It was worth it to keep the peace. From then on I stayed with Larry and Dora from Sunday evenings to Friday evenings and went home to Diamond every weekend.

Winston continued his visits to Diamond. He always visited on a Sunday or on a public holiday. Mom secretly looked for-ward to these visits. I think I did too because Mom would then be occupied and not focused on my bad deeds. I could breathe more easily. I would wait outside on the veranda from the early morning.

When he arrived, I would wave and call out to Mom, "He's come." I never called him Dad or Papa or whatever it is that chil-dren call their fathers. He would run up the stairs. Mom would be waiting in the drawing room or on the veranda, pretending to be cool and aloof.

Winston would always sit at her feet. I would take my place on the arm of the chair she was sitting on, not wanting to be left out of the cozy meeting and desperately wanting to be included. Winston would hardly notice me. He would tease Mom, telling her that he loved no other. Mom would be coyly flirtatious, chas-tising him for making promises of love but not following through on them.

While their banter continued, Winston's hand would creep up Mom's skirt. He was always touching and caressing her. If I tried to intervene for attention, Winston would remind me that he had come to see Mom and not me. I soon learned not to disturb them when they were like that.

I had my few moments with him after he had lunch and when he went to lie down for a short afternoon siesta while he waited for mom to come back from the kitchen. It was then that he would tell me stories of the ancient Greek gods and goddesses. I enjoyed those brief moments. Mom would not be seen lying down next to him in the middle of the day because people would talk. I recall him spending a few nights with us when I was about five years old. I would be surprised when I woke up in the morning to see him still asleep in our bed.

Shortly after that one of those times, Mom got sick. Miss Trinity, our washerwoman and the local midwife, was called over in the middle of the night. Mom had miscarried. Mom was convinced that that was her son, her salvation. Winston's visits became fewer after that. Years later when I asked Mom about the incident, she told me that Winston was very happy to visit her and spend the night with her at her father's home. When she found out she was pregnant, she told him it was time for them make their own home. Winston told her he could not take her to the same home as Rookie and he could not leave Rookie to make a home with her. He calmly reassured her that when Rookie died, he would come for her.

When I was six years old, Mom noticed a lump on the right side of my chest and took me to the doctor straight away. The doctor said it could be a tumor and that it should be removed before my breast began to develop. Mom decided to get another opinion, but the diagnosis was the same. Still unsure, she took me to several more doctors, who all recommended the lump be removed in case it should turn into breast cancer. There was no mention of taking a biopsy. Perhaps there was no such thing then.

Mom was in a state of panic. She arranged for me to go into the hospital the next day. That night Mom could not sleep. When morning came, she remembered that Fifi's friend, Dr. Trevor, had just returned from a trip abroad. Perhaps she should ask him.

That morning we stopped at Dr. Trevor's clinic on the way to the hospital. After examining me, Dr. Trevor told Mom he was very sure the lump was not a tumor but that my breast was beginning to develop prematurely. Mom was relieved to hear that. She had had a gut feeling that it was my breast, but was six not too young to be sprouting breasts? Anyway she was glad we had not gone to the hospital. I might have ended up with only one breast, she said.

Victor was surprised to see us return home so quickly. He was not entirely sure about Dr. Trevor's conclusion. What if it was a malignant tumor?

The next day, while Mom was at work, he decided to take me to see an old doctor friend of his that none of the family had ever visited because he was so old and doddery. This old doctor was very scary with his long gray hair and bushy eyebrows and beard. After Victor explained my problem, the doctor examined me. Without saying a word, he picked up a big, thick syringe and came towards me. As he began to give me a painful injection, he announced to Victor that it was my breast beginning to grow and that since the whole family seemed so disturbed by that fact, he was giving me an injection to delay the growth of the breast for a few years.

By the time I got home I had begun to feel ill. I was afraid to say anything because I had seen the amount of tension and worry this lump had caused everyone, so I quietly went to my bed to lie down. By the time Mom came home that evening, there was a large, red, hard lump where I had received the injection. My whole body was beginning to swell up and I had developed an itchy rash. Victor, Nan, and Mom began to panic. What could have happened? It had to have been a reaction to the injection.

I was once again rushed to the doctor. I had indeed reacted to the injection, which we then found out was some kind of hormone. I was quickly given a course of treatment and recovered quite quickly.

But the irony of it all was that despite the injection, my breasts continued to grow. By the time I was seven years old, I had budding breasts while all my school friends remained as flat as pancakes. I don't remember how I felt about my premature breasts, but I realized that Mom found it very embarrassing. She made me wear very loose clothing so people would not notice breasts on a seven-year-old.

I hated the loose clothes. They seemed unfashionable when all the girls my age were wearing nicely fitting clothes. Mom would proudly say to people, "Vee wants to wear loose clothes. She hates fitted clothes." I was too scared to contradict her.

I suddenly began to grow tall and soon towered over all my classmates. I now hated that my breasts, my height, and my big nose made me stand out. I felt sad and ugly. Everyone else was so sweet, pretty, cute and dainty. In our class picture that year I stood at the back of the line as usual and scowled into the camera so my nose would not spread out and look bigger than it was.

When I took the picture home, no one recognized me. I don't know why that depressed me. I was only seven years old.

Chapter 16

Mom dressed me up whenever we went out. Because she wanted me to have curly hair, she would wind my wet hair very tightly around thick strips of newspaper and leave it to dry. It would hurt a lot, especially when it was time to unwind the tightly wound hair that was now dry. If I cried or complained, she would tug, pull, or slap. I dreaded this beauty treatment. I think she wanted me to look acceptable when I was around her and felt she had to make these efforts because I was not a natural beauty. I might embarrass her with my ordinary looks and big nose. I must admit though that the result was excellent and it pleased Mom very much. Seeing her so happy with my looks made the pain worth it.

Mom made most of my everyday clothes from the fabric that Papa bought for me on his once-a-year shopping trips, usually during the Christmas shopping season. For special occasions I would wear either of the two pretty dresses that Fifi had bought for me on one of her many trips abroad.

Once we were dressed and ready to go out, Mom would insist that I walk arm in arm with her. This made me very uncomfortable because more often than not, just before we stepped out, she had just given me a beating. How could she behave like nothing had happened? I would wonder. I always went out with a heavy heart, embarrassed for her more than for myself, as I knew she did it all for show. I don't ever remember smiling or feeling elated during these outings. I also knew that everyone in the village knew what was really going on in our lives.

By the time I was nine years old, I was quite well developed and Mom had bought me my first bra. I was ashamed to wear it because all my classmates would now know that my breasts were big enough to fill a bra. Oh, the shame of it! I was afraid to go to school. Mom was quick to point out that since my shirts were suitably loose, no one would realize I was wearing a bra.

About the same time I started wearing a bra, we had our annual school field trip. School trips were always something I enjoyed. We went on long drives and got to stop at interesting places. As long as I had a nice friendly and gentle person sitting next to me for company on the long ride, I was fine. I looked forward to that year's trip with the same enthusiasm I always had.

As usual, I had potato salad and fried chicken for lunch, and a pile of delicious sandwiches, my favourite orange cake, and lots of fruit to snack on and share with my schoolmates. Mom was careful that I had nice things to eat on these trips so my friends could see how much she cared for me.

All went well during the first part of the outing. On the way home, though, I noticed that some of the loud, naughty girls in the class were looking at me and whispering. When they called me over to sit with them, I became wary. I knew they were up to something. I politely refused and sat back in my seat. But these girls would not give up. How could anyone refuse their overtures? They were only being friendly, they insisted, as they sweet-talked and pleaded with me to come up and join their group. They just wanted to chat, they said. I knew they were laying a trap, but was too polite or scared to offend them. Unable to refuse, I decided to sit with them for a little while and then return to my own seat.

When I went up to them, they asked me if I was wearing a bra. I told them I wasn't. They pulled me over their laps and began to pull at the back straps of my bra, making jokes about me, singing "Vee's wearing a bra-ah.....Vee's wearing a bra-ah" over and over again and laughing loudly. When the teacher at the front of the bus called out to find what the ruckus was all about, I managed to pull myself away and return to my seat, my face crimson and burning with embarrassment. The boys at the back of the bus were laughing and making crude jokes about the fact that I was the Trinidad and Tobago Bus(t) Company. Everyone thought that was funny and burst out laughing, especially the girls who had started the cruel game.

When the teacher came over, she reprimanded the girls for misbehaving and asked them to apologize. They promised to do so. The teacher then left, taking it for granted that the apology would be made. But no apology was forthcoming. One of the girls, who knew my family and my history, told the others there was no point in apologizing to me because my parents were separated and my father did not want me. She said this loud enough for me to hear, which started another round of whispering and snickering. I was the only one in the class whose parents were separated and, therefore, a curiosity. I knew I would have to face these same girls and boys in school the following Monday, so I steeled myself. I would pretend they did not exist and learn to ignore people like them. I prayed that God would help me to be strong. "Please, dear God, don't make me cry." I pleaded.

Since I was "so well developed," Mom thought she should tell me about the facts of life and the monthly periods that women got. Apart from the biological details, which were very interesting, Mom went into great graphic details about what I should and should not do. It sounded quite worrying and difficult, especially when she talked about staying away from boys. She said if

I let a boy touch me, I could get to 'the point of no return' and that would be the end of my virginity. I would be labeled a bad girl with a loose reputation like my father's mother. I was both afraid of and very curious about that 'point of no return.' What would it be like? How did one feel or know when one got to the point of no return?

I decided it would be better if I stopped talking to boys in case one of them accidentally touched me and I got to the point of no return before I even knew it. I would surely be in for big trouble. I decided I would distance myself from that sort of thing.

As Mom had predicted, my periods arrived early. I had just turned ten when I woke up to find that I was now a "young lady," a most important yet difficult thing to be. This was a lot for a child of ten to cope with. Worrying about being a young lady and trying to protect myself from getting to that point of no return was more than I could take. I did not know how I would manage such a heavy burden. I told Mom I could not go to school. She kept me home for the full eight days of that first period. When I returned to school, many of my classmates asked where I had been for so long. I made some silly excuse that I had a fever, but I think some of the more astute girls figured it out.

A few months later Susan, one of my friends, asked me if I would go with her into the school toilets, as she wanted to show me something. I was the only one she could trust, she added. We quickly went into the toilet. She raised her skirt and pulled down her panties to show me the sanitary napkin neatly tucked in her panties. She told me her period had come that morning and that she was scared to tell her mother. I asked her how she knew what to do. She said she had seen her older sister use a sanitary napkin. I advised her to go straight home that day and tell her sister.

How relieved I was to find out that I was not the only one who was having her period. The next time I got my period, I confidently announced to all my girlfriends that I, too, had just started my period. I was surprised to find out that there were quite a few of them who had already started their periods. My burden was suddenly lifted and I no longer felt different.

For entry into high school, all children had to take the Common Entrance Exam after they had turned eleven. This exam was often referred to as the Eleven Plus. From the time children were about nine years old, the strain and stress would begin, as parents frantically prepared their children for this all important exam so they would be guaranteed a place in one of the top high schools.

Uncle Larry took great pains with Arnie, working with him long hours every day. Uncle Larry was very good at arithmetic and algebra and knew where to get the best practice books. Mom nagged me to ask him for help. She thought that if I asked him, he would not—could not—refuse. Against my better judgment, I asked him. He politely refused, as I knew he would. His excuse was that he had no idea what was being done or what was required and was sorry he was unable to help me. I did not believe him. Devastated and disappointed, Mom took his refusal very badly. She kept asking, "How could he refuse to help a poor, helpless, fatherless child?"

Mom now took on my exam preparation as her most important mission. Since I was staying at Auntie Dora's, she decided she would also stay there during the week so she could coach me. She would show Larry.

I was not looking forward to this new turn of events. Mom was a very impatient teacher. She would bring her face close to mine and in a loud, clear voice, with perfect diction and enunciation, repeat the question again and again and again, demanding an immediate answer. I would get confused and not be able to answer immediately. Every time I missed an answer, I would get a hard slap or the book across my face or head. The more she hit me, the less I remembered. The less I remembered the more she hit me. It became a vicious cycle.

While teaching me, Mom noticed everything. If she saw that I had a broken nail or thought I had bitten them, I would get beaten. Mom thought my fingernails had a strange way of growing. She insisted I had a habit of digging down into the nails, which made them look ugly and offensive. Holding a heavy wooden ruler in her hands, ready for action, she would summon me to examine my hands. When she saw how my nails were growing, she would put my hand down on the table and hit my fingers and fingernails with the edge of the ruler with all her strength until I promised to never do it again.

Even though I begged and promised to not do it again, she continued to hit my fingers, saying I was deliberately digging my nails just to make her upset and angry. She accused me of having no consideration for her feelings or for the fact that she loved me too much to see me disfigure myself.

Mom was very strong. I hurt so much. My heart was aching. As I gently hugged my bruised, painful fingers, I would curl up and cry, feeling cold and alone. Looking at my hands today, I see how ugly they are, with flat fingers, out-of-shape nails, and crooked joints. Ironically, even today, some forty-five years later, my nails still grow as if they had been dug under. They grow that way naturally. Mom never believed anything I said, so she did not believe that I had never touched or disfigured my nails. What she didn't realize was that by hitting my nails, she disfigured them even more by breaking the inner root of the nails and the tiny bones that affected their growth. Even at that tender age, I knew this but could not tell her.

With these frequent vicious beatings, I became nervous whenever Mom was around. Mom would scream for the belt, which more often than not she would ask me to fetch. Then she would stomp around in a frenzied rage and use all her strength to lash out at me with the belt, her hair flying and sticking to her face as she broke out in a heavy sweat. Mom was ugly when she was like that. When Mom beat me she would not stop until she had administered at least thirty good strokes. It did not matter where the blows struck.

Mom used not only belts but also broom handles, clothes hangers, or whatever else was handy. Mom would also bite and pinch until my skin peeled off and blood was drawn. In her mad craze, she did not know what she was doing.

By the time Mom had finished, my hands and body were covered with blue-black bruises from the belt, bite marks, and pinch marks. When Mom was particularly enraged, she would throw me on the bed and smother my face with the pillow, screaming, "Why don't you die? I hate you, I hate you! You should never have been born. You are your father's child. I hate the day I gave birth to you, I curse you, I curse you, if it was not for you my life would be different!"

At our home in Diamond Mom had a long piece of rope that she kept in the dirty clothesbasket. On many occasions after beating me she would go to the basket and pull out the rope. She would hold it and twist in her hands to form a noose and look at me with lowered eyes. Then in a very soft and quiet but menacing tone, she would ask me to get her some water. I knew what was going to happen next. It was always the same.

When I went to get the water, she would quickly lock all three doors that led into the room. She did this to make me think she was going to kill herself. I would sit outside the door, crying and begging. "Mummy, please don't do it. Please don't kill yourself. I promise I will be good." This would go on for a couple of hours while I went from door to door pleading with her to open up so I could tell her how sorry I was for being so bad and so she would not kill herself.

After a long while, I would find one door open. Mom would be lying on the bed with her eyes closed and her arms and body limp. I would sit on the floor next to her and beg her not to die. A part of me knew she would never kill herself, but the child in me did not want to take a chance that she might hurt herself in a fit of rage.

It was only natural that Auntie Dora and Uncle Larry would be very upset when Mom demonstrated this hysterical madwoman behaviour in their home. They were embarrassed. What would their neighbors think? Uncle Larry told Auntie Dora that she had better explain to Mom that we had to leave their house. Now that her husband had spoken, Auntie Dora had no choice but to tell Mom she could not behave that way in Larry's house.

Of course, Mom took this very badly. She got even angrier and reminded Auntie Dora about all the things she had done for her. She quickly collected our belongings and we went home to Diamond. In the end, though, it was my fault. If I had not been so bad and pushed her like that, things would not have reached that stage. I was relieved and thankful that I was at least in the place where I felt most at home. Mom sulked about Uncle Larry for many few weeks, blaming him for what Auntie Dora had said. But she could not maintain that distance for long, though, since her sisters were the only close family she had and she needed them.

As Mom continued to supervise my studies, my academic performance dropped and the more she beat me the more they dropped. Everyone knew how much Mom beat, me but no one ever stood up to her except frail old little Nan occassionally, she would beg her not to hit me but Mom never listened.

The time came for my Common Entrance Exam. Mom was very nervous. If I failed, what would people think? I was not worried at all. I had so many other issues to deal with that failing an exam did not seem to be the end of the world.

Although I was young, I knew Mom really did want the best for me. I never doubted that. I understood that she was a single mother coping the only way she knew how. She had to take out her frustrations on someone and I understood that that some-one had to be me. There was no one else. I was the closest thing to her, the only one who would put up her tantrums.

But even at that age, I felt no love for Mom, only great sad-ness and pity. In my heart, I understood she was mentally unwell. I tried to do the things she wanted of me and never wanted to upset her in any way. I tried very hard to please her. I brought things for her and made her little gifts. I tried very hard to make her smile. When she did smile, I would breathe a sigh of relief and sleep well. When she beat me and behaved in that awful manner, I took it and accepted it as just one hazard of being her child. I learned to live with her as I would live with a handicap like blindness or having only one leg. I did not like it, but I coped with the situation. I had no other choice.

Mom told me she could no longer put up with my badness and had decided to send me to live with my father because I was a 'chip off the old block' and so we deserved each other. I guess she was doing this to hurt me and punish me for being me.

I knew I was not that bad, certainly no worse than any other child my age, and I had tried so hard to please her. She called up Winston and told him that by the end of the month she was going to send me to live with him for good. She had done her bit and now it was his turn.

Mom began to prepare for my departure. She made me new pajamas and a few new dresses. While getting ready to send me to live with Winston, Mom would occasionally glance at me to see if I was upset or hurting. I stayed calm and did not beg her to let me stay with her. I was quiet and behaved normally. Mom packed my suitcases well in advance and we both waited patiently for the end of the month.

I began secretly to look forward to the move. I had had enough of the beatings and the constant tirade of insults and abuse. I was physically tired. Perhaps my father would learn to love me and I could make a new start.

On moving day I got up early and felt a spark of excitement. A quiet and solemn Winston arrived at the appointed hour. Without a tear or backward glance, I drove off with him. When I got to his house, Rookie took control. She put my case down and went to get me something to eat. I followed her to the kitchen. As she took out some food for me, she warned me that they were not as well off as my grandfather in Diamond and that the flat was very small and I would have to share a bed with her. That did not bother me, as I was used to sharing a bed with Mom.

I went to bed early that night but could not sleep. I kept thinking about Mom and wondering what I had done to make her want to send me away. Why did my father not seem very happy to have me? I realized I had no one. I recalled that no one had ever tried to talk Mom out of doing those terrible, cruel things to me. They had all watched her treat me that way and had never said anything or stuck up for me. I felt all alone and very cold. I remember pulling up my legs and curling up to keep warm before finally falling into an exhausted sleep.

The next morning Rookie woke me up very early. Winston told me I could not stay there and he was going to take me back home to Daimond. The drive back to Diamond was long and quiet. Winston and I were deep in our own thoughts. When we arrived, I got out of the car with my suitcase in my hand. I walked towards Nan and she hugged me. Then Mom came and took the suitcase. She told me that she hoped I had learned my lesson. Perhaps I would now realize that I must be cursed because if my own father did not want me, no one would ever want me. I hoped she might hug me and tell me she was glad to have me back, but she did not.

If I had had any other place to go at that moment, I would have gone. Since I had nowhere else to go, I decided to be thick-skinned and just bide my time. One day I would find my way. I felt sad and unloved and thought of killing myself, but I knew in my heart I would never be able to actually commit the act.

I continued to talk to my God often. He was my friend. He would open a door for me one day. Until then I would be patient and wait. At times, though, I would get confused and wonder why I was having a harder time than the other children around me.

As my Common Entrance Exam drew near, I did not feel nervous or worried. I knew I had a deeper perception of things. I did not need an exam to prove how bright I was. I had always thought of myself as being very intelligent. I took the exam and never thought about the results.

About one month later Mom got a call from a friend of hers, who was one of the teachers compiling the results. She called Mom to tell her that she had seen my papers. While my English paper was good, my arithmetic paper was full of careless errors.

My intelligence test paper was outstanding and well above average. Mom was relieved. I had saved her face. Thank God she had supervised my work. Her hard work had paid off. I passed the exam and was accepted at the high school Mom, Auntie Dora, and Fifi had attended.

Every August Uncle Larry, always ready to do anything for his family, would rent a large house in one of the beach resorts. They felt oblidged to take me so I always went along with them for the first week.

Uncle Ramsey, his wife Auntie Lucille and their daughter Camille Anne also rented a house nearby and we would meet on the beach early in the mornings. It was fun helping the fishermen pull in their nets brimming with slippery, wriggling fish. The fishermen would give fresh fish to everyone who had helped, so we always had fresh fried fish with avocado and hot hops bread from the nearby bakery for breakfast. The rest of the day was spent lazing around, swimming, and playing cricket or catch.

At night we would go for long walks on the beach and tell each other ghost stories. We played a lot of card games too. The losers had to drink large glasses of water, so there was always a mad rush for the bathroom during the night. The balmy nights were beautiful with the full moon peeping through the fronds of the coconut palms. The sounds of the waves crashing on the shore lulled us to deep, restful sleep. The week away from Mom was peaceful and happy for me. Mom would join us on the first weekend and then I would return to Diamond with her.

While growing up, I believed I had an intuitive understanding of life and its demands of me. At a very tender age, I began to question and read as much as I could on spirituality. There had to be a reason why life was the way it was for some and not for others. I would look around me and see the pain and suffering of others. I wanted so badly to take it away, make it all better for everyone.

I knew there had to be a supreme force of energy called God, for want of a name. I was sure of this because I would not have these strong feelings and depth of understanding and insight unless a great Being had given them to me.

When I was young and alone in the house in Diamond, I would sometimes hear someone calling me gently from somewhere over my right shoulder. The voice was neither male nor female. I would search in vain for the caller but would never discover whom it was. The voice continued for many years. Then one day I suddenly realized I had not heard my voice for a long time. It had stopped. I never knew what it was or what happened to it, but I missed it.

I had a fear of blood. Just the sight of it made me feel very depressed and so ill that I would get a terrible pain in my stomach and have the need to throw up and cry. Even the sight of an injection needle would stir up these feelings. I could not understand it. One day, on my way home from school, I passed a lonely part of the road where there was a small church. Coming toward me was an open truck full of happy carnival revelers dressed up like bloody warriors with war paint on. I rushed behind the church to hide. I threw up and felt very ill.

It was some time before I could gather the courage to get out from behind the church and go home. I felt an overwhelming sense of dread, gloom, and sadness. I could not tell anyone about how I felt, so I went to bed quietly. That night I ran a very high fever for no apparent reason.

Throughout the first 29 years of my life I have had strange dreams. These dreams began when I was very young and would occur regularly about three or four times a year until 1979, the year my son was born.

In all my dreams I always looked the same: I was a young woman, very slender, about six feet tall with long limbs and bronze skin. I had silky, golden brown, shoulder-length hair that was slightly curled under. My face was long with high, arched eyebrows, large light brown eyes, and a nose that was thin and straight, lips that were wide and full, and a firm chin. It was a beautiful face, serene and refined.

The dreams seemed to be a continuation of each other or part of a serial with scenes of a life I may have had a long long time ago perhaps in anotherlife time. I was always running and hiding. Sometimes I was alone and sometimes I had my man with me. He had the same kind of colouring I had. We wore torn clothes in dull colours and we were either bare-footed or wore sandals. We seemed to be running from enemies who were trying to kill us. We would hide in bombed-out, dilapidated buildings.

In one dream, I was hiding inside a large cooling machine while the enemy was looking for me outside. I could hardly breathe. Then I would wake up with a start. In another dream, I went through actual birth pains as I gave birth to a baby boy. In yet another dream, I saw my man and me running. We were carrying our child, sometimes on my hips, sometimes on his shoulders. These dreams left me feeling far removed from reality for several days afterwards. I never understood the meaning of these dreams, but I was always curious to know if there was such a thing as reincarnation. A lot of religions say no, some say yes. I began to look for books on the topic and read arguments for and against.

I am still not a hundred percent sure, but the thought of it does give me some comfort, as it explains why some people have lives that are so much harder than others. Perhaps there is hope that life will be better the next time around.

Reading and studying up on more than one religious doctrines left me seeking an answer as to why some people choose to label themselves as belonging to one particular religion. At that time of my life, my limited research taught me that all religions had the same teachings, the only difference being the name of the prophet who had an insight to the reality of the Divine. Each prophet would teach his people the same philosophy of goodness, kindness, love, and brotherliness.

At the age of eleven I promised myself I would never label or align myself with any religious group. Too many wars and pain were caused in the name of religion. I would believe in what I instinctively knew was 'real' religion. I would try to practice good ethics, show gentleness and kindness, help whenever I could, and love everyone and everything. I made a promise to make a difference to the lives of everyone I met. I saw my life as a ship sailing by, meeting people, and then moving on, never looking back, living for the each moment. Life was where one was at a given time.

I wanted a life away from the cruelty of the world. I yearned for a life of quiet serenity. I decided to become a nun. I would find my silent moments in the cloisters of the church. Everyone discouraged me. It was a very drastic decision to make and I was told to think very seriously about it. I thought about it for a long while and then I got my answer. I would not run away and shut myself away from the world. To be a complete human being, I would have to experience childhood, feel pain, and know love, passion, and motherhood. Only then could I be the person I was meant to be. I believed I had to live my life fully, coping with all the challenges that God saw fit to give me. If I were worthwhile, I would end up being the person I wanted to be. I prayed to my God, my Divine, of whom I was sure I was a part, to help me.

I was not yet twelve years old.

Chapter 17

Clara worked in Noman's office for about two years. She had not been trained for any kind of office job after she left school, as she was expected to get married and live the life of a happy, contented housewife. During these two years, Clara learned how to type and to run an office. Being intelligent and quick to study and learn, she soon became an efficient law clerk. Clara was charismatic, witty, and charming when she wanted to be, and she wanted to be so at the office. She greeted all who came in for help or advice, be they rich or poor, with a bright smile and a warm welcome.

Noman had encouraged Clara to work with him to stop her from moping about her broken marriage and get her away from the tense situation at the house in Diamond. Noman also hoped that she would meet some new people and have some kind of a social life. Before long she made friends with and met quite a few people in the office and had begun socializing at Fifi's dinner parties.

When Clara joined the office, Noman did not pay her a very high salary, as she was quite inexperienced and he never thought she needed the money. When Clara had learned all she could about office work, she was astute enough to realize her worth. Her attractiveness and style increased her market value. She was soon being offered lucrative job opportunities with larger firms, some of which she refused outright because it was obvious the jobs would require more than just her office skills. When she was offered a management position in a large organization, however, she was intrigued and challenged. Noman was very happy for her and encouraged her to take the job, especially since the salary was nearly double what he was paying her.

This new job had the advantage of being close to where Auntie Dora lived, so Clara could go there for lunch every day and, therefore, be able to check up on me. This was particularly important, as I was still staying at Auntie Dora's during the week to go to school. It was at this time that Clara decided that she was going to help me with my studies in preparation for the Common Entrance Exam.

Mom met many new people at this office, quite a few of whom still remain her friends up to this day. The office staff arranged outings and picnics where everyone had a good time and got to know each other. I was included in one or two of these outings. Most times I was not. Mom went on beach trips, to the Carnival Queen Shows and other such grown up evening outings. I did not mind, I enjoyed the peace and quiet away from Mom's watchful accusing eyes and taunts and happily spent those evenings reading.

There were many young men working at the office. One in particular, Brian, a young bachelor, was very much a lady's man who tried his best to seduce all the women who worked there. Rumour had it that he usually succeeded. There were about eight women on staff. If I recall correctly, Mom was the only one who was without a male companion. Brian started hanging around Mom and asking her out. Mom refused. Then he began to buy her presents. Mom returned them. The more she resisted him, the more he pursued her. The other women on staff soon noticed and some got quite catty. Could they have been his previous lovers, mom wondered?

The boss, Mr. Hart, also noticed the attention that Brian was giving Mom. Mr. Hart was about sixty years old and had been making subtle advances to Mom from the very first day she had worked there. When he thought Mom was taking this Brian thing too seriously, he started to give her a rough time. She was given more work to do, tighter schedules to meet, and with no extra allowances or benefits. In this day and age, this would be called sexual harassment, but in those days it was just part of the job.

While all this was going on, Brian began to act like a long-suffering, lovesick Romeo. He wrote Mom love notes and left them on her desk. Mom would bring the notes home, read them very carefully, and lock them away in her wardrobe. I knew what was going on even though she did not tell me much. I observed her and listened when she talked to Auntie Dora and Fifi. I still can't understand why Mom brought the notes home when Brian supposedly meant nothing to her. I think she was very flattered and kept the notes as proof that someone loved her. The notes boosted her ego. I recall that while Mom feigned utter distress and confusion about Brian, she in fact dressed more carefully and made herself more attractive, knowing that he was bound to notice.

Even in my childish innocence, I could see through Mom and knew she was giving him conflicting signals, that said she might be available; and that she was a principled woman who would never stoop so low as to have an affair.

This situation added strain and stress to her already tense life and the women at work resented the attention Brian was lavishing on her. The fact that she had not succumbed to him made them wonder who she thought she was. Mom did have a very "I am above that" attitude. She flaunted her wonderfully perfect, self-righteous self in a way that irritated everyone. They might lower themselves to sleep with any muck that came their way, but she was certainly not prepared to do that, her attitude implied. A few of the women hated her with a vengeance and made her life uncomfortable with their loud gibes and jokes at her expense.

Then fresh old Mr. Hart asked Mom to work late one day. That evening when she went to his office, he tried to pressure her into having sex with him. He groped and fumbled and tried to kiss and touch her while pushing her down on the office settee. Mom was horrified that this old man would be so bold and shameless as to approach anyone for sex at his age. She shoved and pushed him. It was not difficult for her to fend him off then she hurriedly stalked out of the office, never to return.

Mom remained in contact with two of the nicer women who worked there. They continued to meet for picnics, afternoon teas, and to participate in their children's birthday parties. Brian also remained in touch with her after she left. He continued to send Mom little notes through the mail and made a point of calling her several times a day. I have a very, very strong feeling that when Mom went to the cinema, as was her habit most Sundays, Brian somehow managed to turn up there too. They were on a date but not on a date. I remember seeing them once, as I happened to be passing near the cinema with Papa one evening. We thought we would meet Mom after the show. I noted Mom's acute embarrassment at being 'caught.' I never referred to the incident to Mom, I did not want to remind her of something she was no doubt embarrassed about and would wish to deny.

To this day Brian stays in touch with Mom. He has never married, remaining very much the footloose and fancy-free old bachelor. Of course, age has slowed him down. He lives with his sister's children and looks back on his unrequited relationship with Mom as tarnish on his otherwise successful romantic life. In many ways Brian never grew up. He remained a young man right up until mid-life, still trying to conduct cheap, silly affairs and too afraid to settle down with responsibilities.

Mom was miserable, having been out of a job for about two months. She was used to going out to work every day and never taking a day off. The excitement of keeping busy must have been ego boosting. She loved meeting people and socializing, even though she denied that. Mom also enjoyed her burgeoning bank balance. The best part of working, though, was that it got her out of the house. She could not bear spending time at home with Rachel and her show off ways around.

One day she got a call from Silvia, an old acquaintance, who was moving to England for her children's education. Silvia had a very good job as office manager at an insurance company. As the head office of the insurance company was in the U.S., she was more or less her own boss. All that was required was a smart, well-spoken person to represent the company in Trinidad and a place for its agents to contact the head office.

This suited Mom perfectly. It was just want she wanted—to 'be her own boss' and not have to answer to any sick old perverted supervisor or colleague. She immediately took the job and worked happily there for many, many years.

While Mom's working career was now stable and very much the way she wanted it, things in Diamond got decidedly worse when Rachel got up one morning with a great show of morning sickness.

Nan took this new turn of events in her stride. She was wise enough to realize that since Victor and Rachel were sharing a bedroom, they were obviously living as husband and wife. Mom, on the other hand, took the news very badly. She stopped talking to Victor and was thoroughly aggravated by Rachel's exaggerated morning sickness, her ever-present, desperate cravings that had to be satisfied immediately, and her deliberate pregnant stance.

The more aggravated Mom became, the more Rachel put on airs and graces. Rachel proudly announced to all that she would give Victor the son that had been denied him. This provocative statement drove Mom insane. There was little she could do except take out her frustration on whomever she could. Sadly, that turned out to be me. I was beaten up and screamed at even more than before, but I got used to it and understood.

Victor also got caught up in the drama of the situation and began to believe Rachel's hype that he would soon have a son. Clever Mom realized that if there were to be a son, she would have to cope with a smug Rachel and an ecstatic Victor. She could not afford to be estranged from her father, so towards the end of Rachel's pregnancy, Mom decided she would be gracious and magnanimous and mend fences to show Victor that she had no malice for Rachel or the child that she was carrying.

She swallowed the foul tasting, hard lump in her throat and said to Rachel, "For the sake of everyone, we must learn to live together. It is not good to bring an innocent child into a house that has so much bad feeling." Victor was proud of Mom then and even more so when she accompanied Rachel to the hospital when it was time for the baby to be born. Mom's pride was killing her inside, but she refused to show it. She would not give Rachel that satisfaction.

To Mom's and Nan's delight and relief, and to the utter disappointment of Victor and Rachel, a baby girl was born. They called her Dawn, a name most appropriate, as this was no doubt a new day for us all.

I was very curious about this new addition to the family. I felt as if I had been relegated to an even lower status with less right to stay in that house. The baby's father was the head of the house and that gave her precedence over me. Rachel had warned me about that several times when we had our quiet talks before the baby was born. I think Merle and I were in the same boat, both feeling anxious and uneasy and wondering how this new baby would affect our lives and our positions in the house.

Dawn was not a particularly cute baby. She had inherited her mother's broad face and looked more like a bland oriental baby doll. She did all the things that little babies did and all at the right time. Merle helped to look after her, but I did not have much to do with her until she began to toddle around. It was then that she became my little playmate, at least as much as her mother would allow.

Mom did not have much time for her until she got older. In time, both of Rachel's children, Merle and Dawn were drawn to Mom and me and spent more time with us than they did with their mother. Rachel kept herself busy being important to Victor and being his rock and support and anxious to be there to supervise the finances.

By now Mom, Fifi, and Auntie Dora had begun to accept Merle as a sister. She was nice, easy to be with, and like us, had nowhere else to go. As she grew older, Dawn was also included in the little group as our little sister. Fifi however maintained her "us and them" attitude. When Fifi gave them attention, it was okay but when Mom or Auntie Dora gave either of them attention, Fifi got very jealous. Typical Fifi behaviour.

Mom and Rachel maintained a polite façade but continued to dislike each other so their relationship settled down into something that was bearable if not comfortable. As he got older, Victor spent a lot more time talking to me. He was tired of the bickering in the house and enjoyed my quiet, soft-spoken company.

Even at that young age, I was interested in deep, philosophical things, so we often discussed religious thought and philosophy.

Victor had a good collection of books, some of which he had had specially sent from England. He always told me that his books were for me when he died. He also told me that since I had no father to look after me, he wanted me to have the old house in Diamond. He said he would not have this written in his will for fear of upsetting Auntie Dora, who would then expect her children to receive some inheritance from him. He would instead leave the house in Mom's name, knowing she would leave it to me. He wanted me to eventually have the house, because he thought of me as another daughter.

He also desperately needed to tell someone the truth about what had happened between him and Rachel all those years ago. He had kept it buried in his heart because there was no one who would understand. He explained to me how torn he was between his love for his children and the situation he had gotten himself in with Rachel. He did feel some loyalty to Rachel because she turned out to be a good and caring wife. Victor said it was because of Little Sparrow that he owned all his property and, therefore, it must all be given to his first three daughters, Little Sparrow's children. He said he would build a house for Dawn next door to the family home in Diamond, and that Rachel would be given the right to live there for as long as she lived. Victor took this precaution so that Rachel could not take what was not hers by right and give it to her two other children, Merle and Kelvin.

In time, Kelvin somewhat reconciled with his mother, but he was still not entirely comfortable with her and hardly ever came to visit. Merle however was very much a part of our family, never indicating that she was or felt different from Dawn or me. Mom was positive Rachel was pilfering money from Victor. He often kept money in an iron safe at home in case of an emergency and was always replacing huge sums that somehow got depleted.

Victor never said anything or complained, so perhaps he chose to turn a blind eye, knowing that Rachel would want something for her own security when he was gone. We found out much later that Rachel did buy a large piece of land in another part of the island. No one ever knew where she had obtained the money and no questions were asked.

Mom was enjoying her new job and meeting many new people. Although Mom never indulged in any affairs, she enjoyed the fact that men noticed her. She lapped up the attention, even though she pretended to find it cheap, distasteful, and beneath her dignity. In her own way she encouraged and responded to that attention. She deliberately teased men with her low-cut, well- fitting dresses that showed off her voluptuous figure. It was obvious to any intelligent person that Mom was very aware of and flattered by the attention she received.

I found this affected coy behavior very embarrassing and would turn away in shame. Occasionally Mom would pick up on my disapproval and invent a lame excuse. If I, at the age of twelve, could see through her, surely other people would too I reasoned. I got sick of hearing Mom boast about men who found her attractive or told her what a sexy figure she had and how young she looked for her age. Mom has also forbidden me to tell people how old I was.

Mom's actions were contrary to everything she preached. She would boast about her physical attributes and her goodness and how everyone liked and admired her and then turn around and beat me, looking crazed and ugly in her frenzied, violent rage. It was at that point that I realized my mother was really crazy. She could go from being angry, wild, and vicious to being mild, coy, giggly, and flirtatious in a matter of minutes. I did not like the person I saw.

I came to understand that children do not have to love or even like their grown-up relatives just because they are family. I knew that God would not punish me for feeling this way. Children have a natural ability to judge fairly without bias. They observe and then decide if they would respect or like the grown-ups they meet. Their basic instinct is rarely wrong. Grown-ups seem to forget how they felt as children once they had children of their own.

While on one of our summer trips to the beach, I developed abdominal pains and had to have surgery to remove my appendix. It was a simple, easy operation and there were no complications. As was my way, I never complained and recovered fast and was running around not many days later.

Also during that same year, I began to have severe pains in my joints and would run a low-grade fever. After many tests, I was eventually diagnosed with having Rheumatic Fever. Complete bed rest was advised and I had to have a very painful injection every month and take up to eighteen aspirins a day. The doctor thought some deep-seated worry or stress might have brought on my Rheumatic Fever.

Mom was shocked and horrified that the doctor would dare suggest such a thing. "Vee is a happy child. She has a good life and a mother who has made many sacrifices for her." I knew better than to say anything to the contrary.

Victor would always buy my monthly supply of aspirin. Sometimes when things with Mom got too much, I would look at the bottle of aspirin and wonder what it would be like to end it all. I would take out the tablets, count them, hold them in my hand, and wish I had the courage to take them. I didn't.

Boys were beginning to notice me now, but I would get very embarrassed when any attention was paid to me. I could not believe that anyone would want to look at ugly me with my big nose. Besides, that 'point of no return' still hung like the sword of Damocles over my head.

When I look back now, I realize how silly I was. Poor Billy, one of my first admirers lived near Auntie Dora and used to walk to school with us every day. One day someone dared him to tell me he loved me, which he did in a loud voice. I ran away and never walked to school with that group again. I became an outsider.

Another time I got a love letter from another boy, this also upset me, so I hid whenever I saw him. My friend Jan had a brother named Len, who once asked me for a kiss. I never spoke to him again until the day he got married ten years later. By then I was mature enough to look at him, and we both had a quiet laugh at our youth and my naïve behaviour.

Mom did not take too kindly to my looking more grown-up and pretty enough to attract boys. Whatever I did to annoy her always came down to the fact that I was "man hungry" or that I was "wanting a man." Being a 'chip off the old block' was a very hard burden to bear. I did not know or understand why I should be paying for my father's uncontrollable, passionate libido. Mom would fly into a rage and her beatings became more frequent and violent. She would twist my breasts so hard they were sore for days. Her biting also worsened. She had very sharp teeth and I would be covered with bite marks so deep they bled.

The worse part, though, was the verbal abuse that now accompanied the beatings and left me feeling so low and depressed I could feel my spirit slowly draining away. An intense, cold feeling would creep over me after these sessions, and I would huddle in a corner and cuddle myself to sleep.

The whole of Diamond Village knew I received regular beatings, so it was very embarrassing to go out and face the village afterward. It was so much worse having to face the boys who were sending me love letters or flowers. My face would turn red and my mouth would get dry. I wanted to run away from everyone and die.

Although Mom was earning a decent salary and Victor was paying for all our expenses, Mom never spent any money on me. Every year she would tell me to go to Victor and tell him I needed new clothes and shoes. I found this very embarrassing and dreaded that time of year. I would be very depressed, but Mom would not understand. "Go ask your Papa," she would command. It would take days of her constant nagging before I would go to ask. Even today the thought of it makes me want to bury my face and scream in overwhelming embarrassment.

Mom never even gave me pocket money. I only went out when someone else took me. It was so embarrassing that I mostly refused when anyone asked me. I believed it was my mother's duty to take me, after all she was the one responsible for me. She said it was my father's.

Winston never bothered with me, but that never stopped Mom from insisting I ask him as well. When I would eventually ask him, he always told me he had no money. I hated myself for not standing up to Mom and telling her I would not do these kinds of demeaning things, but I was afraid of what she would do to me. I was in a lose-lose situation. I learned not to ask anyone for anything. It was easier to go without.

From time to time Mom would want me to get to know my father and grandmother. She would insist I go and visit them in their flat, which was about one kilometer from Auntie Dora's home. I hated doing this because it was always a prelude for me to ask Winston for something.

To make matters worse, on my return from these visits, Mom would get very upset with me because she would have assumed I enjoyed the visit. She would taunt me by saying I was an ungrateful child because even though she had done so much for me, I was being disloyal to her because I had love for my father and his mother.

It was illogical that she should send me and then shout at me for going and having a "good" time. I hated those visits because neither Rookie nor Winston ever made me feel at ease. In all my vists there I was never offered even a glass of water. But there was no point in telling that to Mom because she would only understand what she wanted to understand.

On one occasion when I was visiting Winston, one of his 'lodge' friends was there. I was introduced to him and he extended his arm to shake my hand. I was not expecting to shake hands with him, so when he held my hand my fingers were curled in.

I tried to straighten out my finders but he held my hand too tightly. I did not think anything of it at the time, but it seems he complained to Winston, who in turn, told Mom that I had tried to tickle his hand suggestively. I did not understand what he was trying to say or why Mom felt she had to tell me about it and throw it in my face during her violent rages. This was yet another reason for me to pull back and mistrust the grown ups in my life.

Winston started to visit us in Diamond more often during that time. Although Mom was friendly enough with him, she did not encourage him to stay overnight. By then I had realized he was not there to see me, but I hung around them anyway. Mom decided she would begin this new phase with him by laying down some ground rules about her rights as his wife and me as his child. Of course it would all be about money.

She had heard there was a piece of land in the town that was selling for a reasonable price and she suggested he buy it for me. Thinking that if he bought the land, Mom might let him into her bed again, he purchased the property.

The land was registered in both their names. Mom relaxed. Perhaps he was beginning to change and would one day make a home for her. A few months later Mom decided the time was right for her to raise the issue of building a house for 'Vee' on the land and she suggested that perhaps we could be a family in the true sense of the word. The thought of having my home with my parents filled me with hope that I would be like most people I knew.

But Mom and I were in for another disappointment. This time he told her there was no way they could ever live together while his mother was alive and that she must understand that once and for all. That was the last time they ever talked about reconciliation.

Winston's sister Ena had a lot to do with this decision. She now had five children and needed Winston's financial support even though her husband's trucking business had picked up and they were doing quite well. Ena, who was the controlling factor in Rookie's life, had a strong hold on Winston, he was unable to break away from his mother to be his own independent person.

To score points with Mom, Winston once took me to see a movie. On the way back he dropped in to see Ena for some reason. When we got there we went inside the house to wait for her. Almost immediately she came up to me and asked me to wait outside while she spoke to Winston in private. This was the height of rudeness but no one there took notice or said anything. I sat on the doorstep outside and waited for about an hour until the meeting was over. Ena's children—my cousins – had come out to peer at me but I pretended not to notice. I felt sick inside.

Winston finally came out of the house to take me home. I knew he was afraid of his sister, but I could not believe he would allow her to treat his only child like that. It was obvious that Ena did not want Winston to develop any love for me. She was afraid that if he did, it might affect the hold she had on him. It was a shame that Winston was not mature enough to balance his life the way a grown man should.

Chapter 18

The times I spent with Auntie Dora and her family was always interesting and very eventful. I suppose my young mind was grateful that I could stay there, so I tried to help out and would not be an unwelcome burden. Marleen was younger and stayed pretty much to herself in the early stages, so I took control of our day-to-day activities.

I became the leader of "the children", as I called them, since I could handle situations well, read better, and felt responsible for all of them. I am sure it was only my childish arrogance, but I truly believed I was the only one among the four of us who was best qualified to take charge. Seeming to agree with me, Auntie Dora assumed I would be in charge and gave me instructions whenever she had to go out.

Both Auntie Dora and Fifi treated me like a grown-up. I can't remember them ever speaking down to me, even when I was a little girl. Perhaps that is why I assumed the role of leader with the children.

When I lived with Auntie Dora so I could go to school, I shared a room with Marleen. The two boys stayed in the back room, the room where Marleen was born. We all got along as well as children do.

I told them many stories and kept them out of the way of the grown-ups. We had the usual childish fights, but nothing serious. I was still just a cousin though, and keenly aware that I was not one of the siblings. They had a special closeness of which I was acutely aware. This was particularly obvious when we had fights, as they would band together against me. To maintain my somewhat precarious place in their family, I did my best to avoid overstepping their boundaries.

When Uncle Larry came home in the evenings, I made myself scarce and left the children with him until they came to look for me or call me. I think it was during those moments that I missed having a father in my life, but I did not make a big deal about it.

In fact, I appeared to cope so well that people commented on how well adjusted I was and how I never seemed to miss having the comfort and security of a father. Mom took that as a compliment about her parenting skills. The truth was I was too proud to let anyone know I longed for a father. I was determined to show them all that even though my father had deserted and forsaken me—as Mom would remind me every so often—I could still manage. I vowed never to make his absence my excuse for being an emotional failure.

We all walked to school together, holding hands in case one of us began to lag, particularly when crossing roads. I took special care of Marleen because she was quiet and little. The only problem was Ricky, who was always running off when he saw his friends or breaking away to kick an old tin on the road. He was also the one who questioned everything we did and argued over everything.

Auntie Dora had a tough time coping with him over the years. He always wanted to know why we had to follow that same road every day, why we could not take a different road sometimes, and why we had to go straight home and not stop off at any friends' houses on the way home. We would end up in the most terrible fights. He would not listen, always wanting to do his own thing. I would stand up to him and tell him that what he was doing was forbidden, and Arnie would warn him that he "would tell Mummy."

But it was all pointless. Ricky pleased only himself and would calmly retort that we could do whatever we liked and he would do whatever he wanted, as long as he got to school on time, which he always did. I never tattled on him, but Arnie always did. Arnie enjoyed it when Ricky or any of us for that matter got into trouble at home.

Sometimes when there weren't enough of the boys' friends around to play cricket, Ricky and Arnie would suggest I join them. In the beginning I was very happy and proud to be given the very important tasks of bowling and fielding, but I soon realized their plan. Curiously, whenever it was my turn to bat, I would called out on the very first ball...L.B.W. I would vehemently deny that I was out, but Ricky would explain that I was most certainly out because the ball he bowled was going straight to the wicket and my leg was blocking it. Couldn't I see that?

His tone of voice told me I was very stupid for not seeing what was obvious to all the boys on the team. There was no point arguing with him. His only concession was to give me one more chance to bat when I threatened to tell. But I would once more be out L.B.W. on the very next ball. This was very frustrating for me, especially when they did the same to little Marleen. She would cry and cry but they never made allowances for her. We both decided to stop playing cricket with them. We had fun playing 'school school' instead and I got to be the teacher every time. Ricky laughed at us for playing such sissy games, but I was sure that Arnie would have liked to play with us some of the time.

In the evenings we played many different card games, some of which I have not seen played anywhere else in the world like 'Pedra and All Fours'. We also played board games like Monopoly and Ludo. The hot favourite however was Snakes and Ladders. Marleen loved it, so we played it again and again. It was always a treat when the grown-ups also joined in.

Ricky loved to wrestle with me. He never bothered with Marleen because she was quiet and cried easily. I endured many arm locks, throws, and other holds in a wrestler's repertoire. Ricky teased me the most and was extremely irritating. He kicked me under the table, threw water on me from upstairs, sprang out from behind the door, sprayed me with a water gun, frightened me, tickled me until I begged him to stop, and generally did all the naught things that mischievous little boys do.

Ricky had a bad habit of taking apart all the appliances and equipment in the house. It was unbelievable how many clocks and watches he ruined, irons he wrecked, screwdrivers he lost, and toys he took apart and could never fix back. When he took the Hoover apart and could not put it together again, Uncle Larry was livid and he was grounded for a week.

Uncle Ramsey was very close to Auntie Dora. They were the same age and got along very well. He and his wife Lucille lived a few streets away and he would often drop in for a cup of tea or to give Dora some new plants he had bought or grew especially for her.

Uncle Ramsey was another favourite with us children. He was such fun. He always wore his gardening clothes, which consisted of dirt-soiled shorts, a string vest, muddy slippers, and a floppy hat. His face was creased, sunburned, and damp from sweat. He also had many playful dogs that he spoiled. He would bring his daughter Camille Anne over to play with us. In the beginning, Camille Anne remained aloof. Our parents said this was because of her mother's influence.

Marleen left Camille Anne alone not bothered to make the effort as Camille Anne thought she was too good for us. Both Arnie and I tried to be nice and went out of our way to include her in our games and Ricky teased her nonstop. But strange as it may seem Camille Anne preferred the rough teasing that Ricky dished out.

They became very, very close and stayed that way till Ricky got married years later. We all knew that Camille Anne had more than a cousin feeling for Ricky and that perhaps Ricky also had that feeling for Camille Anne but his attachment for Uncle Ramsey stopped him from taking their relationship down that road. We all knew that kissing cousins was taboo and definitely not something our family would have tolerated.

Uncle Ramsey would load us up in his big battered old car and take us for long drives to the beach or fishing villages, flower shows, dog shows and the like. It took a long time for Auntie Lucille to warm up to us, but that was because she did not get on well with Uncle Ramsey's mother Nass and we were part of the family. Later we developed a very warm and comfortable relationship that has lasted to this day.

Mom, Auntie Dora, and Fifi lamented over the fact that Uncle Ramsey, the closest thing they had for a brother, appeared to be so dirty. He reeked from a mixture of dog, manure, dust, and wood from his woodshed. He would pick ticks off the dog and then eat cake with the same hand "without washing!." We didn't mind one bit. He was so much fun to be with. He let us do things our parents did not let us do, like going far out to sea, eating things from dirty wayside stalls, watching the dogs give birth, and bringing us home well after the time he said he would, which caused mad panic with our parents. We knew we were safe with him and used him as our shield against the dull, staid grown-ups and their boring over cautious ways.

We were told that Arnie was a very greedy baby who cried a lot. Auntie Dora said she was totally frazzled and could not cope with him, especially when she became pregnant with Ricky very soon after his birth and had to stop feeding him. Arnie screamed and screamed during his first year, keeping quiet only when he was being fed or was asleep. Mom was breast feeding me at the time. Since I did not need much, she always had a surplus of milk, which Arnie was only too eager to have, so he was in effect 'my milk brother'.

Arnie loved to sing. He attributed his beautiful singing voice to the fact that he had well-exercised lungs caused by his yelling and screaming as a baby. Arnie and I used to sing the latest musical numbers from popular movies. We would practice simple operatic arias just to hear the sound of our voices. We also talked in song occasionally to see who could carry the notes the longest or the highest. Everyone said Arnie had a beautiful voice, a Trinidadian Mario Lanza no less his parents boasted.

So Arnie loved to show off his voice. We children were all embarrassed when he offered to sing at other people's weddings, receptions, or at school. He even started attending church so he could show off his voice. We were mortified when he would break off from the choir and start singing a loud solo over and above the voices of the choir. The other members of the choir did not like it, but the old ladies in the congregation certainly did. When they told him how much they enjoyed his singing, his head would swell and he would sing even louder the following Sunday.

Arnie decided he would be an opera star, not just an opera *singer*. When Uncle Larry discovered this, he had a long talk with him and made him see that he was never going to become an "Opera Singer" and that he had to have a real profession, like a doctor, lawyer or chartered accountant. Something proper!

Uncle Larry took great interest in his children's studies. Every evening he would sit with them while they completed their homework and explain whatever they had not understood at school that day. I thought I could also ask him for help when I did not understand something but stopped when I realized he was not keen on helping me. I suppose he thought it would take time away from his own children. When it was time for lessons, they would all gather up their books and head straight for the dining table. Uncle Larry would sit at the head of the table during those long study sessions.

I headed for the table in the kitchen and seemed to finish my work very quickly. Mom was convinced I was doing a shoddy job and that was why I finished so fast. I understood everything, though, and thought they were stupid to take learning so seriously. I enjoyed discovering and learning about the wonderful things around me—the way things worked, the day and night, how the earth evolved, the wind blew, what caused the waves in the sea or the stars to shine and people to love. I did not want to be restricted to the limited books we had at school, but no one understood how I felt. I would spend long hours thinking about things and wondering how they worked and how it all came about.

Auntie Dora hired a maid, Mrs. Howard, to do the washing and ironing, and any additional help when there was extra cleaning to be done during holiday season. The rest of the time she coped with the housework on her own. Since Mom had never really asked Auntie Dora or Uncle Larry if it was okay for me to stay with them—she had just sent me there—I felt like an uninvited guest who had overstayed her welcome. Not that anyone ever said anything to me. I just felt out of place.

Knowing that Auntie Dora did not usually have help, I tried

to help her all I could. I took it upon myself to help with the dishes, set the table, and tidy up. It was nice to be able to help her, particularly in the evenings after dinner when she was tired. Auntie Dora was prone to colds and I felt sorry for her. I was glad she liked what I did to make things easier for her. I would overhear her tell the children how helpful I was. I glowed from her praise. I was finally not as useless or a burden as I was led to believe by my mother.

Auntie Dora baked bread on Wednesdays and Saturdays. On Saturdays, I would be in Diamond, but I looked forward to Wednesdays. The smell of freshly baked bread would greet us as we entered the gate on our way home from school. We would rush upstairs and have hot rolls dripping with butter and melted cheese. Auntie Dora also baked the lightest orange cakes I have ever tasted and always had a fresh cake on the cupboard for the children when we came home from school. It was cake with chocolate milk for the boys and Marleen, and my favorite, ice-cold milk, for me.

Auntie Dora was a very gentle mother. She had a quiet de-meanor and spent her time quietly tending the family of which Uncle Larry was so proud. She cooked, cleaned, tidied up, and waited for her family to come home in the afternoon. They were a very closely-knit family. All activities revolved around the children and their devoted father and mother cared deeply for them. I guess most families were like that, but I had never seen or been with any other family.

Uncle Larry and Auntie Dora were not as social as Fifi and Uncle Noman, but they did have a small circle of friends. Uncle Larry enjoyed a social drink and so during the Christmas Season between Christmas and New Year, there would be rounds of cocktail parties when friends and neighbours would visit them and vice versa.

Whenever Uncle Larry had his drink, usually scotch and soda, he would give us all a tiny sip. "Good for the worms," he would always say. Auntie Dora had not developed a taste for alcohol. On rare occasions when she did have a glass of sherry or wine, she would fall asleep. We teased her a lot about that.

Fifi as was her habit would often drop in during the day when Uncle Noman was at work It was a big thing for us when she got the chance to run away for a quick visit on evenings when Uncle Noman was busy with his seminars or meetings. She would come over, full of infectious excitement. When Fifi came over, we knew we would hear some interesting news or receive a treat. She would ask us what we wanted to eat and no matter what time of the night it was she would somehow get it for us. Crispy fried prawn Won Ton followed by rum and raisin ice was always the favourite.

Mom wanted me to take piano lessons. She found out that a good piano teacher lived not far from school and arranged for me to take lessons three times a week. When Auntie Dora heard that I was to take piano lessons, she thought it would nice if Arnie also took piano lessons. Uncle Larry decided that if Arnie was taking piano lessons, he should have a piano to practice on, so he went out and bought one for him.

Mom knew it was important for me to have a piano also, so she told me to talk to Winston about it. I stubbornly refused to ask him. I knew it was an expensive item and did not want to put myself in the position where he would refuse me, which he always did, and put me in my place. Mom had already mentioned to the teacher that I was going to ask my father to buy a piano for me.

One day Winston was walking by the music teacher's house. She called out to him and told him I needed to practice the piano several hours every day in preparation for my practical music exam. Winston apparently told her that I did not need a piano to practice on and that I could use the table as a keyboard and practice my finger exercises that way. The music teacher thought this was very funny and related the story in front of all the other students. That was the last time I went for piano lessons.

After that episode Mom wanted me to begin violin lessons. Before she could arrange for me to begin, Auntie Dora decided that Arnie should also have violin lessons since he was "so musical." I could not handle the continuous competition, so I refused to even think of it. Arnie, of course, did take violin classes and did brilliantly, as everyone knew he would.

Ricky also began piano lessons but soon decided the guitar was his passion. He said that piano playing was for sissies. He also contemplated learning to play the drums, but Auntie Dora put her foot down. Marleen also took piano lessons but gave up because of her studies, saying she could not excel at both. All this pleased Arnie, as he wanted to be the only one good at something. He had to be the centre of attention and get all the praise because he deserved it.

That year Auntie Dora became pregnant. We were all excited about having another baby in the family. Everyone except for Ricky hoped it would be a girl. Ricky wanted a younger brother and said he would run away from home if he got another sister. The excitement was unbearable as the time drew near. The joy that heralded Viv's birth was unbelievable. Uncle Larry was as pleased as if he had won a million dollars. Auntie Dora was relieved that now Marleen had a sister. Her family was complete. Ricky never did run away from home. Everyone told him his new sister looked just like him, so he decided it would be all right after all.

Viv was a beautiful, sweet-natured baby. With all of us to

look after her, she was the centre of attention and never cried. Viv was everybody's darling and the apple of her dad's eye. She soon learned that she could get her way by being charming and would flutter her beautiful eyes, which were just like Auntie Dora's. I realised then that baby girls knew instinctively how to flirt.

As Viv became more precocious, Marleen became even more withdrawn. I loved Marleen very much and wanted to comfort her, but she would not usually allow me to get as close to her as I wanted to.

Everyone said Marleen was a "funny" child. By this they meant 'peculiar.' She was extremely quiet, read her books, and rocked in her rocking chair singing her little ditty of a song over and over again. She did not get along well with Ricky, as he was too rough for her. Arnie was good to her, but she found his theatrics too embarrassing. Marleen and I became close when she realized we shared the same interest in books. We would sit together for hours, discussing our thoughts and sharing our books. We were of like minds, made from the same mould. I understood her and knew that beneath her wall of shyness was a passionate, loving person.

Although Marleen looked like her father's sister and I looked like my father, there was something very similar about our looks. Although our faces were the same shape, the real similarity was in our eyes. We had that same lost, sad look. The only difference was that I could see her. She could not yet see me and was not aware of the instinctive affinity we shared. In time she would.

Chapter 19

Fifi eventually came to terms with not ever having children. While it still hurt her deeply inside, she now kept busy by being an integral and indispensable part of all of Noman's activities. Fifi became the perfect legal assistant, making a point of getting to know all the clients and their cases. It was no surprise they welcomed her involvement, as they appreciated her personal touch and warmth. Fifi's effective participation was therefore an important part of Noman's business. Fifi instinctively knew exactly what to say and when to say it, which endeared her to those people who needed sympathy and understanding as much as they needed legal advice.

Fifi also conducted much of Noman's research work. She made numerous trips back and forth to Port of Spain, the capital, to check out the archives of the Red House, home of all the legal documents on the island. Fifi knew every case and every reference and was Noman's sounding board for all his seminars, meetings, and forums. With all the research she did for Noman and her attentive devotion to him, Fifi was as accomplished as any qualified lawyer on the island. She kept her knowledge well hidden, though, and never spoke about law in public

Fifi accompanied Noman on many of his conferences and would wait in the car for hours on end in case he needed her. Fifi epitomized the loyal wife and Noman thoroughly enjoyed this devotion. He would look at her with soft, indulgent eyes and wonder about her selfless love for him. He knew he was lucky to have her in every way.

Noman was now so involved with the farmers and their many problems with the large landowners and government policies that he decided to form a Farmers Association so that the farmers would have a formal and legal platform to fight for their causes. From its inception in Trinidad, the Association was so successful in helping local farmers that sister organizations were then formed in the other agricultural farmers of the British West Indian Islands.

These organizations sent their representatives to the United Kingdom to discuss and demand better prices for the West Indian Agricultural Market. Over the years this association led the way for the formation of a worldwide organization on agricultural matters. Later it combined with the then newly formed Farmers Association in Europe to form an international organization to help poor farmers to negotiate better trade policies, prices and to open up new markets for their produce all over the world. The head office of this organization was based in Geneva, Switzerland. Noman was elected chairman of this Organization.

With this additional commitment and involvement, Noman was now traveling to many more places. From the West Indies, he found his way across the continents to Japan, Australia, New Zealand, and to the exotic agricultural islands of the Pacific Ocean. Fifi accompanied him on most of these trips, which enabled them to see the world and meet important people.

Fifi often related stories about what this or that President said to her or how a particular First Lady admired her clothes and other silly nonsense. We lapped these stories up in wide-eyed awe. We had never met anyone who had traveled so far or met so many important leaders. We were very proud of Fifi and Noman. They added colour to our otherwise boring, unimportant lives.

The two major political parties in Trinidad and Tobago tried to persuade Noman to join their parties and stand for election. He abhorred 'the political game' as he called it, and preferred to remain apolitical. He was, however, an advisor to the government on economic and farm matters and traveled on many states visits with the Prime Minister.

As the wife of such an esteemed and respected personality, Fifi received her share of the limelight and loved every moment of it, reveling in all the attention. She took to socializing, rubbing shoulders with the rich and famous, and meeting important people and heads of state as if she were born to it. She knew exactly how to handle each and every one. Noman enjoyed her popularity with the delegates and showed her off to his advantage. She was a definite asset, a beautiful compliment to his expertise and wit. Hearing all the exciting details of Fifi's high life made us feel like we were on the fringes of her elevated world.

Although he had risen from the humblest of beginnings, Noman never boasted about his meteoric rise to the top. He thought it was arrogant and in bad taste to talk about one's rise in position or remind people how well one had done despite one's struggles and handicaps. But he did indulge himself when he traveled, by flying first class, staying in the best hotels, drinking the best champagne and brandy, and eating the finest food. He also enjoyed wearing the finest Savile Row suits along with the gold Rolex watch he presented himself on his fiftieth birthday and the huge diamond signet ring Fifi gave him. When he was at home, he was content to lounge around in old, baggy shorts and eat a simple TV dinner of grilled cheese on toast with a huge mug of a milky frappe.

By this time Fifi had joined many of the local ladies charitable organizations and was busy raising funds and helping with charity bazaars, lunches, dinner dances, and so on. Fifi entertained often and we were always included either as invited guests or as helpers during formal events.

Some members of the family did not see the importance of meeting people or entertaining to promote oneself or one's causes. Auntie Dora was introverted and could not cope with making conversation with highflying, well-traveled socialites. "What would I say?" she would ask. Her children poked fun at me because I enjoyed it.

Clara, my Mom, had her own reason for not enjoying Fifi's social evenings. She said it was a waste of time, money, and effort and that she only helped Fifi out because Fifi needed her and she could not let her down. But everyone could see that she wanted to be the centre of attention and was envious of the lifestyle that lucky Fifi and her husband enjoyed. "Of course, Fifi has no children to hold her back and she has a husband who supports her as she indulges herself in these frivolous activities. Poor Fifi also does need to get involved in these things to pass the time and can she well afford it," Mom was often heard to patiently explain to anyone willing to listen.

Of all us children, I had the most understanding affinity with Fifi and spent much of my holidays with her, helping wherever and whenever I could. Concerned that she was lonely for her own child, I tried to fill that space. I could not bear for her to feel that pain. I wanted her to be happy and enjoyed being a part of her busy life. She gave a lot of herself to the people who needed her and expected nothing in return. I admired this quality very much. One of the ways she demonstrated her generosity was by paying for children's school fees and books. Of course, Fifi had the financial resources to donate and share with the less fortunate but not many people who had the resources shared it with the needy as Fifi did.

Shopping was another one of Fifi's obsessions. If she liked a particular pair of shoes, she would buy all the available colours in that style. If she liked the design of a particular piece of material, she would buy it in all the colours as well. My Mom—the sister who had "taste"—advised Fifi on how to style her hair, what make-up to use, and how to dress to suit the image she now had.

Of course, Mom would also very kindly and subtly point out the flaws Fifi had in her skin and hairstyle and give advice on how to fix or cover them. Mom could not help but remind us all that we were not perfect. She had a special knack of doing this just when we were feeling happy and content with ourselves.

Fifi now had refined tastes, having bought expensive, fancy things like the finest crystal, English crockery, silver cutlery, and Irish linen. Her cupboards and storeroom were full of every imaginable household item and appliance. Fifi could not stop buying things and often ended up with several of the same items. When she realized this, she would give away the extras. Fifi had a tendency to waste a lot and spend her money foolishly. Noman knew what was going on, but indulged her wasteful extravagances. "Let her play" was his attitude.

Noman wanted and needed to move to the best part of town. So for Fifi's birthday he secretly bought her a beautiful house she had always admired in a very exclusive part of town. He presented it to her when he took her for a drive after lunch on her birthday.

He stopped in front of the house and told her he had brought her to visit the owner of the house. As they walked up the driveway, Noman called out to the watchman who opened the door. Fifi was a little surprised at that, but did not say anything. As they entered Noman turned to her and said, "Welcome home." Fifi could not believe it and shrieked in delight. A lot of champagne flowed that evening, as we toasted their good fortune.

Mom said the right things and then felt it was her duty to point out the 'few' problems she spotted. "Fifi, you will need to fix that up" and "I wonder what made them paint that wall that particular colour. Fifi, you will have to do something about that too."

Noman, who was always drawn to literary pursuits, began to write books. He wrote several on the angricultural economy, which was expected, since he was so intimately involved with it. Surprisingly, he also began writing books of poetry. Altogether he wrote five books of poems, all of which he dedicated to "Tuk Tuk, the perfect wife." "Tuk Tuk" never knew when he was writing his poems, as he always did it in the quiet of the early morning when she was still asleep. She would only come to know of each book when he presented a copy to her after the book was printed.

Noman loved surprising Fifi. She would read each dedication as if for the first time and would be moved and flattered. I know for sure that Fifi never read any of Noman's poems, as she never had the patience or the incline for poetry. But she did keep the books in a very special place and would often run her hands over the covers and stroke the books as she walked past. Noman never minded that she did not read his poems; he understood her limitations.

When Noman's law practice was twenty-five years old, he decided he would hold a large dinner to honour the people who had been with him through all those years. During the speeches, Noman paid tribute to and thanked everyone for their support, including his father and Victor. Then with great emotion he went on about the love and support that Fifi had given him, going into detail about the sacrifices she had made and the time she had devoted to him, how she never complained and was always at his side.

After receiving tremendous applause for his emotional speech, everyone pushed Fifi into making a speech in reply to her husband's heartfelt accolades. Fifi, who was quite tipsy from champagne, graciously stood up and with the utmost confidence, poise and dignity, announced, "I totally agree with my husband" and sat down. Later, after she realized what she had said, Fifi was quite embarrassed. To this day, her friends still tease her about this.

Noman loved big, comfortable cars and changed his car whenever a new model came out. He hardly ever drove his car, though. He did not like driving and preferred to be driven so he could spend the time reading and relaxing. Fifi did all the driving. Tiny as she was, she maneuvered the car with the assurance and ease of a racecar driver.

When Noman suggested they get a driver, Fifi blew a fuse. There were two reasons why Fifi did not want a driver. Firstly, she liked having their precious moments alone together in the car when Noman would go over his cases and discuss other office work with her. She felt it brought them closer together.

The other reason was a more personal one. Fifi did not want to lose her independence. "A driver would know too much about what I do. I would lose my privacy," she protested confidentially to her sisters. Fifi always said she would not like to have some strange man in the tiny confines of the car.

The real reason must have been her fear that a driver would report back to Noman about all the times she ran away to see her family, the many places she went, and what she did. As harmless as her activities were, she did not want a driver on her hands that might turn out to be a spy and report her silly doings to anyone and everyone.

Noman and Fifi's frequently had visitors from abroad stay in their home. During these visits, Fifi would be the official tour guide. I was often invited to accompany them on excursions to the mountains for picnics beside little waterfalls hidden in the cocoa plantations or to the old farmhouse in Piparo. Norman had purchased extra land around the house and the property was now a substantial farm with a comfortable country house.

My favorite trip was going for long, slow drives around the island. It would take a whole day, as we would stop for lunch, tea, and dinner breaks or for a quick dip in the sea.

It was breath taking for me to see the scenery change. From the lush green mountainous terrain on the northern coast to sandy, coconut-fringed beaches on the east coast then to grassy marshland on the southern and western coasts of Trinidad, which I assumed from my atlas, formed part of the Orinico Delta, one of the largest rivers in South America.

We would sometimes go for boat rides to the tiny, rocky islands on the western tip of the island, where schools of flying fish and dolphins playfully jumped over the waves like exuberant children. On balmy, tropical evenings we would enjoy barbeque parties on the beach and everyone would drink too much, eat too much, and laugh too loudly. It was a wonderful time for me, and a respite from the sad and emotionally traumatic periods I spent in Diamond with Mom.

While I was with Fifi and Noman, I met some interesting people. The most impressive of these was the son of one of the leading Shakespearean actors of all time. This handsome young man had the same personality and aura as his internationally acclaimed actor father but chose to study economics instead of following in his father's footsteps. Young as I was, I think I had quite a crush on him. Fifi was careful to keep me close to her in case I embarrass myself.

We were constantly reminded of the soft spot Victor had for Fifi, even though he vehemently denied it. It became obvious, however, when Fifi would drop in to the house in Diamond for one of her runaway visits. He would get very excited and flustered and call out for Rachel to quickly prepare Fifi's favorite snack, a Trinidad-style kedgeree—leftover rice, stir fried with tinned Canadian red salmon, onions, hot West Indian Congo pepper, and local herbs like French mint and subtle flavoured spices. A bottle of wine would make it a perfect evening, as we all shared in this unusual but delicious treat.

Because Fifi and Noman did not have children, they tended to baby each other. This would sometimes mean talking in baby talk to each other. Noman's nickname for Fifi, "Tuk-Tuk," came from some childish game they played. They bought cute toys for each other at Christmas and ceremoniously placed them under an elaborately decorated Christmas tree.

Fifi's Christmas tree and Christmas garden decorations were famous or perhaps infamous, all over the island. People would drive past the house just to see or admire her seasonal setting.

Santa Clause's enormous herd of blinking reindeer was positioned on her rooftop beside Santa himself, who was poised to enter the make-believe plastic chimney erected especially for the season. All the trees around the garden were lit up with tiny fairy lights that blinked and flashed until the early hours of the morning. Fifi would hang tiny lights along the eves of the house. When they were lit, they resembled snowy icicles. The garden was laid out like a miniature winter wonderland with sleds, plastic snowmen, gnomes, and elves.

Christmas decorating became an obsession with Fifi and she felt she had to outdo everyone else. While her Christmas display may not have been the best, it was certainly the most elaborate and expensive.

Dora and Mom found the whole exercise unspeakably embarrassing. They said it looked like she was showing off and flaunting her wealth. Fifi did not agree. She believed she had created a wonderful Christmas fantasy for her and Noman. Noman was content if Fifi was happy.

Chapter 20

I was thankful I was no longer staying with Auntie Dora while going to school. Even though I had a thirty minute commute to school by taxi every day, I felt far more comfortable being in Diamond, the only place I felt I had any right to be.

I loved the fresh air in Diamond. The house was on Papourie Road, which was the main link between San Fernando and the southeast portion of the island. At the back of the house the land sloped down about thirty feet, just enough to preserve the back view all the way to the horizon and allow the air to flow through the house even when other houses were eventually built at the back.

It was cool relaxing and refreshing to see the lacy, white curtains billowing in the breeze. At about six o'clock in the morning, Mom would throw open all the doors and windows of the house so the fresh dawn air could blow through the house and clean out all the stale smells and negativity lingering from the previous day. It was almost ritualistic, this early morning routine of purifying the house.

How beautiful it was to watch the sun creep out from under the horizon little by little, impressing us with its magnificence. It was such a pleasure to wake up early and see the warm, yellow hues of the early morning sky. I could so understand why people in olden times worshiped the sun and felt compelled to

make some offering to its majestic splendor. The house cap-
tured that golden glow of the early morning sun and the rooms
inside came alive.

I had a simple but rigid schedule to follow. When I turned
thirteen, I was given specific chores to do. Before leaving the
house for school every day I had to make up my bed and tidy up
my room. On weekends I hand-washed all my school blouses.
Socks and underwear were washed every evening when I had
my shower before going to bed. I also helped with the cleaning on weekends. Mom thought this would be good training
for when I grew up and went abroad to study. I enjoyed doing
these chores. I would turn up the radio and sing loudly to all
the latest pop music while I dusted, tidied up cupboards, and
so on.

At 7.15 a.m. on weekdays I would leave for school by taxi
and return by 3.30 p.m. in the afternoon. Then it was study
time until bedtime. At that time there were no distractions like
television in Trinidad. The radio offered some entertainment in
the way of pop music programmes from London. There were
also some plays and some very exciting science fiction serials. I
never missed these radio shows. I particularly liked the science
fiction ones, my favourite being "Captain Miracle." Captain Miracle and his crew took me far across the galaxies into new, exciting worlds. This aroused my imagination not only because these
worlds were so different and dangerous but also because there
were also stories about perfect, Utopia-like worlds to which I so
wanted to escape. Another favourite of mine was "The Shadow,"
who caught mischiefmakers and saw that justice was done. In
all these stories, good always triumphed over evil.

Music touched me very deeply. I did not have the need or
compulsion to play an instrument, but I longed to listen to and
get swept away by the rhythm and harmony of the music. I
don't know why I would cry when I heard the earthy throb

of folk music or the haunting melodies of some island beat or robust classic. Music made me want to dance, to reach up to the sky with my arms outstretched and embrace the whole universe. Every part of my body vibrated to each unique blend of notes. My imagination was swept away by the intricacy of every chord.

For me music was the harmony and rhythm that kept the cosmos in perfect balance and I could not keep myself from responding to it. I was touched by the power of my Divine and would experience a deep, indescribable euphoria that often made me weep. In each style of music I could see and feel different aspects of the universe—the hum of spinning worlds, the clashing of colliding planets, the spiraling of deep black holes, the explosions of hot, fiery novas. When I listened to music I felt I understood creation and had no choice but to respond.

Mom, of course, was not be able to comprehend or relate to my deep, spiritual response to music and viewed it as another one of the wanton traits I had inherited from Winston. I learned to hide my enjoyment of music when Mom and other people were around.

I used to love sitting on the back veranda of the house with my book, looking out at the soft, green sugar cane grasses swaying gently in the breeze on the undulating hills. I could feel the soft breeze cooling my body as I imagined rolling down these hills and looking up at the woolly cotton clouds as they sailed slowly across the sky, wondering how freeing it would be to fly away.

Sometimes, while sitting on the veranda, I would get the urge to rush down and lie on the naked earth. So I would dash downstairs and out to the back garden, where I would lie down under a pigeon peas bush, gaze up at the clouds, and feel the earth spin. When I would put my ear to the damp ground, I could almost feel and hear the earth's heartbeat.

I loved looking up at the leaves of the trees as they shimmered and shone in the sunlight. I would wonder at the miracle of creation and know that my Divine was sharing some of its "knowing" with me. I knew It had given me this wonderful gift of awareness and that there was nothing anyone one could do to take that away from me.

Sometimes while gazing out at the beauty around me, I would feel myself getting lighter and disintegrating into tiny atoms. Then I would float away and become part of nature. I would feel I had been 'chosen' and would pity those around me who did not see the world as I saw it. Mom could beat me and hurt me physically, but she could not take away the wonderful insight that my Divine had given me. I was sorry that she could neither see it nor feel it.

High School was uneventful for me. I did what was expected of me reasonably well. But I was not the brilliant, outstanding student Mom was hoping I would be. The only reason I did not excel was because I was bored with some of the subjects and the way they were taught.

I was not interested in conjugating monotonous, boring Latin verbs day after day, or cramming long lists of French words. I wanted to study subjects like Archaeology, Anthropology, old religious beliefs, and the ways and customs of tribal people. Since these were not taught at school, I borrowed books on these topics from the library. I also managed to get some of these books as presents when I would exaggerate the importance of them as "research" books for the exams I had to take.

I would pour over these wonderfully interesting books when I was supposed to be studying. It was no surprise, therefore, when my school progress reports always emphasized that despite being a good, well-behaved student, I needed to work harder to realize my true potential. Little did my teachers know where my true talents really lay.

This kind of progress report infuriated Mom. She would go wild, beating and biting me until she got tired. Then she would pretend to tear up my books and set them on fire.

I would promise to study harder and beg her to stop because I knew it was expected of me. I had to tell Mom exactly what she wanted to hear so she would stop her crazy, disgusting behavior and I could carry on doing what I wanted to do.

Not that I ever failed any exams. I did quite well and scored very high marks in the subjects I found interesting. But I made careless mistakes, particularly in arithmetic and algebra where I would transpose numbers or symbols, add when I should have subtracted, and so on. I always got good marks in geometry, but Mom could not appreciate that. I really outdid myself in history, geography and biology, and sometimes even received an award for my efforts. I got engrossed in those subjects when I studied them.

Literature was another subject I loved. I must have inherited this fascination from my father who from the little I knew of him seemed to live and breathe literature. I truly loved the sound of words and was convinced that its origin was a mystical science yet to be fully explored. I did not discuss this theory with anyone, as they would likely think I was mad or something, but I enjoyed thinking and wondering about it for many long hours.

Perhaps this is why I became an avid reader. Books became by best friend. Failing to conform to the accepted way of getting an education did not bother me. I thought the whole school system was out of touch with real education. Learning should be fun and I was having fun learning about the things I was interested in.

No one seemed to understand me or my way of thinking. If I could understand and appreciate other people's ways and idiosyncrasies, so why could they not appreciate me and mine? So I was very lonely and sad. Victor was the only one who came close to understanding me. Rachel and Dawn did not allow him much time to sit and talk to me.

I knew I was different and that I would have to conform somewhat so I was not left out. I knew I needed to be around people sometimes, so I would pretend to be "normal." I made some friends at school and would chat to them about the things they were interested in. I found it quite easy to blend in. We had music in common; they all loved the new groups and I could identify with that. They also loved to dance, I could identify with that too. I loved nice clothes enough to be able to talk about that as well.

But after a period of time these frivolous pursuits became tiresome and I would have a desperate need to run back to books, nature, and other things that nurtured my soul and 're-generated my batteries.'

Mom allowed me to go to dance parties. All the cousins would go together and be allowed to stay out late provided we stayed together and came back together. That suited us just fine.

We had a good time dancing. Ricky, of course, would disappear into dark corners and we would have to search for him before we went home. This bothered Marleen, especially since the girls he disappeared with were usually some of her friends. I am still not sure if she was disappointed in him for his wildness or with her friends for allowing him to get away with it.

The rest of us were quite 'well behaved.' We did not get into trouble or have to deal with fresh, young boys. I did have one close call when one boy held my hand a little too long after a dance. I ran away. The scary part was that his mother was my mother's good friend. I was afraid he would say something to his mother and my mother would find out.

Cheryl was a good friend of mine or so I thought. From time to time she would come over and spend the weekend with me. Her mother and Mom were in high school together and remained close. It was her mother who had seen my Common Entrance paper and told Mom I had done so well.

Our friendship continued until I realized she was only friendly with me because she wanted to get closer to Arnie. Arnie was not interested in her at all. He said she was too loud and flirtatious, so he ignored her. She then tried to get through to Ricky and succeeded, but he quickly dropped her when he found her younger sister more attractive. Cheryl cooled toward me after that; it seemed she no longer needed my friendship. I never trusted Cheryl after that; I always saw her as clever, conniving, and willing to use people to get what she wanted.

I don't remember ever making a deliberate decision to befriend someone. I did not need to pass my time in other's company when I had so many of my own interesting things to think and read about.

But Niala was bound and determined to have me as her friend. She sat with me during breaks, shared my lunch, and insisted I share hers. She visited me and insisted I visit her. Niala's mother had died and she was living with her four older sisters and her father, a successful businessman. Niala was pampered and got everything she wanted but was not spoiled. She was just a sweet girl longing for a friend her own age. We remained friends all throughout high school.

During high school Niala found a boyfriend. She shared this news with me, swearing me to secrecy. She even offered to fix me up with his friend. Of course I politely refused. I was scared, but Niala could not understand why. Niala showed me her smooth legs and neat eyebrows. She told me to shave my legs and pluck my eyebrows and explained how to do it. I shaved my legs, cutting and scratching myself in the process until my legs were a sorry mess. I plucked my eyebrows, pulling bits of skin off as well.

Mom could not help but notice and had her usual violent reaction. Mom must have forgotten her own youth, when she shaved off her eyebrows. I thought of reminding her but then decided to drop it; she would have just gotten angrier. As it was, I was beaten sore and grounded for a month.

Niala then told me that it was now fashionable to have short hair and that my hair was too long. When I asked Mom if I could cut my hair, she was non-committal and did not say much. I knew better than to push it at that point. The next day Niala reminded me again that I should cut my hair. She said I would look so much prettier. "Your nose would not be so big on your face." It was easy for Niala to talk. She never had to ask permission to do anything; she just went ahead and did it. How could I explain that I could not do that?

I so wanted to have short hair. As I listened to her I made up my mind to cut my thigh-length hair that very day. I would discuss it with Mom and make her see reason. I had a tough time combing it every morning for school and it was a problem during sports and games. I waited anxiously for Mom to come home from work that evening. She was late. I paced back and forth. I decided to talk it over with Nan.

Nan agreed that it was far too long and troublesome. She said, "Yu mus cut it, it too too long" she insisted. Good! I thought. I now have Nan on my side. Mom would have to agree. But Mom still had not come home. I asked Nan how much she thought I should cut and she said I should cut it to my shoulders. She suggested that I snip off the braids and Mom would fix it up for me when she got home.

I thought that was a good idea, so I snipped off my braids and waited excitedly for Mom to come home. A little while later I heard the car and rushed out to show her my new hair.

When Mom saw my hair she went crazy. It was a miracle I survived that beating. It was the worse torture I had ever endured. Victor could not eat and threw his food out the window. Nan screamed out loudly but Mom was beyond hearing and understanding.

She kicked, pinched, punched, cuffed, picked up the broom and broke it across my back, as she frantically looked for the belt that would bring her the satisfaction she needed. I huddled behind the door and covered my face with my hands, trying to make my body as small as possible. The belt slapped me again and again, burning my skin. In exasperation Mom threw the belt away. She dragged me by the hair and began hitting my head repeatedly against the wall. I think I must have blacked out for a little while because the next thing I knew, she was lying down on the bed, once again playing her old tricks with the rope she kept in the dirty clothes basket.

My face was swollen and bruised and my hands cut and bleeding from the belt buckle. My head throbbed and I began to throw up. Nan came and helped me wash up. I changed my torn clothes and went to bed, my sore body stiff and aching. The next day I had a high fever and, thankfully, could not go to school with the marks of my beating.

The fever continued for four days. I could not go to the doctor because of the bruises on my body. Apart from Nan, who helped me to get changed, no one else had come to my aid and explain to Mom that she should not treat me like that. I suppose they were afraid of Mom.

I think that was the lowest point in my life. I wanted to die. I could no longer take the beatings Mom gave me. I talked to God, my Divine One, and prayed for Him to take me. I begged Him to give me the courage to take my own life since He was not taking it for me. I stayed in bed, hugged my pillow, and wept. I did not eat for those four days and no one came to give me food.

Mom went to work as usual, all dressed up and looking beautiful, and when she came home she did not speak to me. On the fifth day, I got up, weak with hunger. I went to get something to eat. No one had bothered with me. I knew no one would take care of me or be brave enough to love me. No one cared if I lived or died. I would have to manage by myself. I promised I would be brave and never let anyone see how much I hurt.

My bruises healed and I decided I had to go to school. My hair was all jagged and out of shape, so I tied it up in a ponytail. I put on a smile, held my head high, and told everyone I had cut my hair myself and would have it shaped in the latest style as soon as I got used to having it short. Niala was very proud of me. If my friends guessed how things really were, they were too polite to tell me. I pretended everything was just fine.

Mom did not speak to me for a month. Rachel snickered whenever she looked at my hair. Nan shook her head whenever she saw me. Victor never looked me in the eye. I kept my head up and helped myself to food from the kitchen whenever I was hungry. I would survive this. Let them look at me. What did they know of real life and how to survive with a mother like mine?

One morning three months later, Mom told me I was going to the hairdresser to have my hair shaped. She took me to her friend, who gave me a stylish cut. It looked good, so Mom could now allow herself to forgive me.

Chapter 21

My rheumatic fever symptoms continued despite the heavy medication I was taking, so the doctor decided I should spend most of my summer vacation in the hospital on complete bed rest and the doctors would be able to monitor my condition. Mom visited me every day on her way home from work. Those summer days in the hospital were peaceful and I was able to indulge my passion for reading.

Although I was supposed to be on complete bed rest while in hospital, every mid morning I would quickly run down the corridor to the nursery in the pediatric department of the hospital to spend a few hours playing with the babies and sick children. Seeing their tiny little bodies attached to tubes and other types of medical paraphernalia made me feel sorry for them, so I would keep going to see them.

Sometimes I got caught sneaking off to the nursery. I would solemnly promise not to do it again, but as soon as the nurse who had caught me disappeared, I would once again dash out of my room and head for the nursery. I enjoyed reading stories to the little children and sometimes I sang songs and nursery rhymes to them. It made my day when I got to hold the babies. I was thrilled that I could bring some comfort to these little people.

One incident that has stayed with me was when a little five-year-old black girl asked me to help her comb her hair. At first I was taken aback, as I did not how to do it. I took the comb in my hand and paused. I wondered where to start and how I should hold the short, tight curls so I could begin to braid her hair in the distinctive style that was typical of her race at that time. The little girl spun around, looked deep into my eyes, and asked me if I was hesitating to comb her hair because I was afraid to touch it. I felt ashamed and hurt for this little girl, who was eight years my junior yet already aware that some people felt prejudice or revulsion for her race and were afraid to touch her because she looked different. Over forty years later, I still wonder if she believed me when I told her I had hesitated because I had never braided hair like hers before and was not sure how to do it.

From my own personal experience I knew that children were experts at hiding their pain and heartache. As I sat with the little children and looked at their beautiful, innocent faces, I wondered if they were happy with their homes and parents. I wondered if their faces hid a life of pain and hurt, as mine did. I hoped and silently prayed they would always be happy, understood, and surrounded by love.

Winston visited me a few times while I was in hospital. Each time he would tell me that Mom had put me in hospital for the summer so she could go out and have a good time with her boyfriends. I knew Mom better than that. She may have fantasized about having a boyfriend, but she was much too afraid to have one, so I never believed him.

When I told Mom what he had said, she stopped him from coming to see me. That did not bother me. I was used to their fighting and using me to hurt each other. It sickened me that they played these childish games and were not grown up enough to handle the situation without involving me.

While in hospital I met an Irish Catholic priest, who would come around every evening after dinner to visit and give spiritual comfort to patients. He somehow singled me out and would spend a few more minutes chatting with me. I found him very calming and comforting. He had a kind, peaceful face and looked like a priest should. Father would tell me wonderful stories about the biblical days, stressing the miracles and goodness of Christ, "the Son of God," who was conceived without sin and born pure. The part about being conceived without sin confused me, as Mom had already told me the facts of life in detail. Despite this, I still listened attentively because I enjoyed the pictures he painted about life during those ancient times.

I felt the pain that Christ felt and the sadness his mother must have felt to see her son suffer so much. I remember asking Father why God felt he had to make "His Son" suffer to make people believe in Him. I wanted to know why God did not just make us all good from the moment we were born and why God did not stop grown-ups from being cruel to little children. Father never did give me satisfactory answers. He just rambled on about having faith and believing. I could not understand the notion of blind faith but I kept quiet, I did not want to upset my friend.

Father mistook my interest in his stories for deep, religious fervor and gently tried to convert me to the Catholic faith. Even though I enjoyed his discourses, I knew that the Catholic Church—or any other church for that matter—was not the right path for me.

Some time later when he began to pressure me to be baptized in the Catholic faith, I explained to him about my inner thoughts. I told him I did not want to follow any religious doctrine. I pointed out that if I was a good human being, I could be a good Catholic, Presbyterian, Muslim, Hindu, or Jew. I told him that too many wars were fought because of religion and I did not want to be a part of anything that caused war rather than love. Father smiled quietly, patted my head, and never visited me again, although I heard he was still making his evenings rounds. I really missed his visits and the stories he shared with me.

Even at that young age I knew what I believed in. After having been a part of Trinidad's wonderful, multi-religious culture, I could not see myself accepting what I believed was the limited view of the Catholic Church or any church for that matter, even though I still longed for the serenity and peace of the cloisters.

Several weeks later I left the hospital feeling rested. I didn't know if my Rheumatic Fever was any better, as I still had swelling and pain in my joints. I returned home to Diamond for what was left of my summer vacation. I could now look forward to having the neighbours around for company and for entertainment. As I observed the neighbours with intense interest, I wondered how they coped with the complicated challenges in their lives.

The most interesting of our neighbours was Tante Ella and her large brood of children. They lived next door in the house that Victor had built for Dora. Tantie Ella was a widow with four sons and three daughters. We had a close relationship with that family primarily because we all felt sorry for them. Tantie Ella was a very sweet natured, gentle lady who coped as best she could with her menagerie of rather strange offspring.

Tantie Ella's two older sons gave her money when they had it or their wives allowed it. The younger ones, however, always looked to her for help, demanding pocket money for cigarettes or booze. Tantie Ella was too soft with her children. She could not say no to them and let them walk all over her.

Against his brothers' advice, the eldest brother Paul married Percil, a mulatto divorcee three years his senior. They had three children. They lived four or five houses away and threw loud, wild parties that went on late into the night, much to the distress of the quieter neighbors around. There was a lot of gossip and speculation about what went on at those parties.

Frankie, the second son and his neurotic, alcoholic wife Sandra had three daughters and lived with Tantie Ella. Sandra screamed and shouted at her in-laws on most days. I don't know why they took her verbal abuse and put up with her at all.

Plump, pretty Rhea married someone we had never seen before and lived in Table-Land, a village ten miles away. Rhea often came to visit her mother, forever crying and complaining about not being able to get pregnant. Tante Ella often quoted Fifi's example of how to cope, but Rhea continued to lament her sad fate loudly to everyone who would listen. Most people tried to avoid her as much as possible.

Sam, son number three, was free-spirited and constantly in and out of jobs, or perhaps jail if the rumours were true. He was always looking for freebies and 'loose change.' When Tante Ella was unable to help him get out of a situation, Mom would feel obliged to bail him out. Everyone said Sam was headed for trouble. He wanted a life of idle fun with lots of money to spend without having to work for it.

At twenty-six, Molly, the second daughter, was considered well past marrying age. Gossip had it that she was wild and would do anything to get herself a man or the money she needed. Molly drifted in and out of our lives. When she visited us we made sure she was never left alone because she had a bad habit of stealing. She was the village kleptomaniac.

Many times we would find things we had lost hidden amongst her belongings. Molly would calmly hand the items over and continue to pick up our things whenever she got the chance.

Mom insisted it was an illness. Molly was desperate to get married and move out of that house and its many problems, but with her reputation of stealing and sleeping around, no one wanted to marry her.

When she came over to cry on Mom's shoulder, we kept a watchful eye on her just in case she "accidentally" picked up something. Mom tried very hard to fix her up with suitable older men, but nothing worked out. Molly's reputation had spread far and wide.

Lennox, also known as Bello, was still in high school trying desperately to make something of himself. He was a good student and a keen football player. Bello had an eye for the pretty girls in the village and could be seen chatting them up and huddling with them in bushy shrubs or in dark corners of closed shops in the late evening. Mom repeatedly warned me about him.

Janet, the youngest of them all, was three years older than me. I felt sorry for her and would share my chocolates and fancy imported sweets with her and give her my old, broken toys. I "allowed" her to come over and help me play with my wonderful array of toys, picture books, and fancy nick-knacks whenever my mother would allow me to play with them. Janet did not have any toys and I felt sorry for her. I may not get to play with my toys often but at least I owned them, I reasoned.

Janet was also very happy to get my old clothes for even though she was older than me she was shorted than me so when I out grew my dresses she made full use of them. I felt so good that I could help her.

Janet knew that Mom was a violent mother and that she hit me mercilessly. But Mom was very kind to her and her family and was always trying to get jobs for the boys and help Molly whenever she got into trouble. Janet never forgot that. She remained very loyal to Mom and never criticized her. I admired her for that. Unlike some of my other so-called friends, she never questioned me about my father or the beatings I received.

By this time Merle had left school and had taken a secretarial course. Always wanting to help the family in any way he could, Noman immediately hired her to work in his law office. He thought it would make Victor happy to know that Merle was okay. While working in the office Merle had the opportunity to meet many young, eligible men and was constantly falling in and out of love with every new young man who came to the office.

The family was quietly worried that she might do something that would bring them shame, for although she was not "blood," she lived with us in Diamond like a real sister. Everyone heaved a huge sigh of relief when she finally fell in love with a long-time client's son, who was prepared to marry her. Her wedding was quickly arranged, as everyone was anxious for her to be married off. Victor was relieved that he would no longer be responsible for her. He had done his duty to Chand's daughter. Perhaps God would now forgive him for what had happened those years before.

I was looking forward to Merle's wedding. Victor bought me some genuine Chinese silk to make new clothes for the wedding. It was the first time I had worn silk. The feel of it next to my skin was so wonderful that I felt beautiful, despite my ugly nose.

It was a wonderful wedding and I was sad when it came time for Merle to go. Over the years we had shared lonely times together, each of us painfully aware of our insecurities and sadness. We also had fun singing songs and trying out new fancy recipes. I remembered the time we tried to make marshmallows. We tasted the mixture so much as we beat up the egg whites and castor sugar that there was little left to turn into marshmallows.

Then there was the time we went guava hunting so we could make guava cheese, and bees stung us. Merle took me to summer classes at the "Y" so I could learn how to sew, something I hated, and decorate cakes, which I loved. I would miss Merle. She was like an older sister. Dawn did not figure much in our activities, as she was so much younger and Rachel kept her close to Victor, hoping to forge a strong father daughter bond. Rachel had a lot to gain if that happened.

Shortly after the wedding, Mom and I spent the weekend with Fifi while Noman was out of the country on one of his seminars. We were awakened at about 2.30 a.m. by a phone call informing us that the extension of the old wooden house in Diamond had caught fire and had burned down.

We were in a state of shock. Victor had kept all his important papers and money in the cupboard in that section of the house. Mom began pacing back and forth and bawling. She was sure Rachel had done this to them. It was an act of retribution for the sin Victor had committed by bringing Rachel into their home. Fifi hushed her, saying there was no time for such talk. She shoved us into the car to go to Diamond. Fifi had phoned Auntie Dora and Uncle Larry, who would meet us there.

The noise and confusion in Diamond was heartbreaking and unbelievable. It seemed the whole village had come out to see Victor's humiliation. People were talking and gossiping about Rachel. The disaster had reawakened the past. The whole village appeared to share Mom's view that Rachel was in some way responsible for the tragedy. "God does have a way of making people pay," they whispered. "Rachel go have to learn she lesson now. If money is for yu, yu go get it. If it not for yu, no matter what yu do, it ain't gonna come yu way. Look at what bad luck she gone and bring on de man. An he such a good nice man, always helpin' the poor people."

I was upset for Victor, who stood to one side silently looking at the ashen remains. I did not know what was going through his mind, but I'm sure he viewed it as a cleansing. He had now paid for his foolish act years ago and everything would now be okay. I went up to him and slipped my hand in his, as we both quietly surveyed the gray, wet, depressing scene. He sighed deeply and then turned away from the melee to return to the house and the quiet of his library.

Auntie Dora and Uncle Larry had now arrived. Not knowing what to do, they joined Fifi and Mom. Mom went to calm Nan, who was crying hysterically and talking about Little Sparrow, who she seemed to think had been burned in the fire. Auntie Dora went in search of Rachel, she found her sitting quietly with Dawn huddled by her side, wide-eyed and scared.

One could not imagine what was going on in Rachel's mind, but it was most certainly not a time for reproach or recrimination. Auntie Dora held her and in a show of togetherness, brought her out to join the family.

Ramsey and Lucille arrived. Ramsay took control of the situation. Getting back to normal was top priority. The fire brigade had long gone and it was time to get things cleaned up and have something to eat. Fortunately, the main part of the house was undamaged. Except for some water damage and the smoky smell, it was quite habitable.

Ramsey had brought a doctor friend with him and all the grown-ups were given shots to calm them. Victor refused the shot and stayed alone in the library with his thoughts.

An investigation later determined that someone had left the

iron on in Rachel's workroom and a nearby curtain had caught fire. We all knew who that someone was, but no one said a word.

It was surprising how quickly our lives got back to normal after the fire. Although Victor had lost a fair amount of cash and some important items of sentimental value, no one else had lost anything. Both Fifi and Ramsey took it upon themselves to make sure we were not taking this setback too hard or worrying too much, and that Victor, in particular, realized he still had many wonderful things in his life. Many family get-togethers were organized in Diamond in the days and weeks following the fire. In fact, the experience brought the family closer together.

Rachel, who was very subdued for the first few days after the fire, had a long talk with Mom, Dora, and Fifi. They were somehow able to clear the air of all the years of hard feelings and nastiness. A close, warm friendliness began to develop. Nan's relationship with Rachel also improved. Rachel finally began to regard her as Victor's mother and, therefore, her mother-in-law. Rachel began to mix more with Nan's daughters, Ismat and Nass, and their children. She became an active member at all family gatherings, helping out and acting as though she were part of the family. Everybody finally accepted her as one of them. The fire was a symbolic death and burial of the ugly past and there was an unspoken agreement to never talk about it again.

Victor had no animosity towards Rachel, as he wasn't that kind of man. But deep inside he must have worried because he collapsed with a heart attack not more than three months after the fire. Fortunately, it was a mild attack and he came out of hospital after only two weeks. The doctor said he could carry on a normal life, which he did—with the exception of his New Year's tradition of shooting away the old Year with his gun at the stroke of midnight. Victor never held or shot his rifle again.

We missed that tradition because it was part of the Christmas and New Year celebrations. The holiday season was always an exciting time in Diamond. Everything was cleaned and polished. The Christmas tree, which took a whole week to decorate, was finally completed on Christmas Eve just before we sat down to a late dinner of fried chicken and potato salad. We kids drank Pepsi while the grown-ups opened up a bottle of red wine.

Both Dawn and I tried to stay up to wait for Santa Clause but we always fell asleep, only to wake up at the crack of dawn to open the numerous presents that were miraculously laid out under the tree. We carried on with the tradition even though we were older now and knew that Santa Clause was none other than Victor, our Papa.

Christmastime was a time for eating. It was the only time of the year when Trinidadians got the best Canadian British Columbia apples, the best California grapes and pears, and a wonderful array of dried fruits and nuts like walnuts, almonds, brazilian, hazel, and pecan.

Christmas lunch was an odd but delicious mixture of a delightful variety of treats. We enjoyed Scottish or Canadian red salmon blended with the local traditional seasonal fare that included pastels - a corn meal steamed patty stuffed with minced chicken and raisins, roast chicken filled with the traditional minced liver and herbs, cauliflower cheese, macaroni pie, and curried goat. All this was followed by lots of imported fresh and dry fruit, pone, black Trinidadian Christmas cake, and mince pies. For dessert, the children helped to make homemade ice cream in an old-fashioned wooden ice cream maker with crushed ice and salt packed all around it. We all took turns winding the tub around and around. We thought ice cream made this way was by far the tastiest. By late afternoon we would all be stuffed, certain that we had gorged ourselves enough to last until next Christmas.

Shortly after that first Christmas after the fire, Ismat died. Nan was heartbroken. She had now seen two of her daughters pass away. She would cry endlessly, asking God to take her too. She said the worse thing any mother could face was the death of her child. Nan's health started to decline. She decided she would spend her last years with Nass, her only remaining child. Nass was quite happy to have Nan stay with her, but she liked to travel and having Nan in the house would curtail her expeditions. Mom came up with a compromise. Whenever Nass had to travel, Nan would come back to Diamond. This did not please Nan very much until Victor insisted she stay with him, now that he was a heart patient. Nan agreed, as Victor was still very close to her heart, the son she always wanted.

Diamond did not feel the same to me after Nan left. Nan was my friend and always had time for me. Nan was the one to tell me stories and listen to my accounts of school activities. She praised me for the jobs I did. I could never do wrong by her. She loved me to comb her sparse hair and I would rub balms on her aching joints while she chatted on and on, many times repeating stories she had already told me time and time again.

Meanwhile, my mundane life continued at school and home. I studied as little as possible just to get the grades I needed. I read anything and everything I could lay my hands on, and continued to dream of a perfect world where there was love for all, music, and dance. Everything else seemed unimportant.

During each term of the school year there were the usual parent teacher meetings. I dreaded these meetings. I wasn't afraid of what the teachers would report; the worse thing they could say was that I was capable of doing much better. I dreaded the meetings because I was ashamed when Mom came to school all dressed up and looking beautiful, not like the simple, dowdy, down-to-earth mothers of my friends.

Everyone's eyes would immediately be riveted to Mom when she walked in. I knew my friends and classmates would remark to me later how beautiful my mother was. Mom was womanly and sexy and she carried herself well. Even children could pick up on that. I was afraid everyone would ask me why I was so ugly and wonder how such an attractive mother could produce such an ugly offspring. I was worried that Mom was ashamed of me.

When I was in the Forth Form, the year before my "O" levels examination, I discovered the Beatles and the pop music coming out of London. I loved it. It seemed to unlock feelings I had buried in my heart. It touched the deep, lonely depths of my soul and gave me a release from the pain I was suffering. Mom did not like my newfound passion and did her best to discourage it by stopping me from listening to the radio. But my need to listen to that kind of music and get caught up in its frenzy was too strong. I could not stop myself from listening to it, even if it meant I had to put up with the punishment I got.

Around this time I began to take notice of how I looked. I looked closely at myself in the mirror and saw a soft, gentle face with a budding, voluptuous figure. Maybe there was some potential in that face I mused. But then again, I recalled my mother saying my nose was big like my father's. Perhaps people looking at me would see only the nose on my face and not the dark, almond- shaped eyes fringed with long lashes or the soft full lips on my smooth, oval-shaped face.

I noticed that a few of the smart "with it" girls were coming to school with mascara on their eyelashes. I thought it made their eyes look beautiful. I, too, wanted to have thick, black lashes.

One day I decided I would try it out. I went through Mom's

make-up bag and found the mascara compact. I was afraid to put it on in the house, as I knew that that would make Mom mad, so I hid it in my school bag. When I got to school, I rushed to the washroom. I wet the cake of mascara, rubbed the brush on the wet cake, loaded the brush with mascara, and proceeded to plaster it on my eyelashes.

I carefully layered coat after coat, waiting patiently for each coat to dry. Finally I looked in the mirror. I did not recognize myself! There was this thin, pale face with huge, wide eyes and the thickest, longest eyelashes I had ever seen. I was very pleased with the results, even though my eyelids felt extremely heavy from all the layers of sticky black stuff. Soon the school bell rang and I went to my class.

As I entered the classroom, I noticed that all the girls were looking at me and whispering. The smart girls began to snicker, which started the whole class laughing. They called me copycat and other silly names, but it did not bother me very much. I knew my eyes looked much better than theirs and that they were just jealous.

All that day the teachers looked at me as though something was wrong with me, but they could not quite place what it was. I did not mind one bit because I now had the most beautiful eyes in the class. My friend, Niala, stood by me and was the only one to compliment me on my new look. That was enough to encourage me to fix myself up even more during the break I went back to the washroom, this time to restyle my hair. I wet my hair and combed it in the Beatles' hairstyle that was the craze in England. I felt cool and trendy. This was the wildest thing I had ever done and it felt good, albeit a little scary.

I strutted around the school for the rest of the day holding myself erect with my shoulders back, chin up, and full of confidence. I looked up and met everyone straight in the eye.

I smiled more often. For the first time in my life I felt beautiful. Maybe I was not so ugly after all, I secretly thought, wondering if a little light lipstick might add that final touch to complete my new look.

School finished at 3.00 a.m. every afternoon. By 2.30 p.m. that day I realized I would have to wash off the mascara before I went home or face the consequences. As soon as the last bell rang, I again rushed to the washroom, this time to wash my eyes clean.

There was so much stuff on my eyelashes that the more I washed the blacker my eyes and the area around them got. I washed and washed, but the blackness kept spreading more and more over my face. My eyes were also becoming red and sore. What should I do? It was getting late, nearly 4:00 p.m. I always arrived home by 3.30 p.m. I knew I would get into trouble when I got home.

I prayed to God to help me out of the mess I was in, promising that if He helped me out I would never get into this kind of mischief again. By about 4.15 p.m., my eyes looked a little less black and I decided I had better go home and face the music. By the time I got home, it was nearly 5.00 p.m. The whole household was worried. They were standing in the veranda, anxiously watching every taxi that pulled up.

Mom had also arrived home by then and was worried I had been kidnapped and raped. When she saw my red, swollen eyes, she was convinced I had been hurt. I decided to come clean. I told her about the mascara episode.

Surprisingly, she listened without saying a word. For a change I did not get the beating I was expecting. All she said was that I must not do it again. What a relief that was!

Another surprising thing that came out of that incident was that the smart and fast bunch of girls in school now all wanted to be my friends. We did become friends, but I was always careful to mind my own ways. I did not approve of their loose, loud behavior and the fact that all they talked about was boys. It is strange that of all my supposedly close friends, they are the ones who still call up Mom to ask about me, even after all these years.

The most important topic of conversation now was 'boys.' Everyone seemed obsessed with their boyfriend or was looking for a boyfriend. If one did not have a boyfriend, one was considered a failure. No one admitted to not having a boyfriend except me.

My friends were always trying to fix me up. I was not interested in finding a boyfriend. I was hoping my Mr. Right would one day find me and take me away from the cruelty in the world. I knew I would immediately know him when I saw him. He would be someone so special I would just look into his eyes and he would recognize me as his soul mate. He would understand my very thoughts and feelings and love me forever. He would love me so much he would wipe all my hurt, fears and cares away. I was going to wait for him. He was sure to come, my gentle, kind, loving knight in shining armor.

At the many parties I attended I danced with everyone who asked me, but I never sat alone with anyone, held hands, or accepted any dates. One day Niala invited me to go to the cinema to see the latest movie. Mom agreed to let me go, so I was very excited. She never liked me going to the cinema.

Naila and I agreed to meet outside the cinema at exactly 4.15 p.m., as the movie started at 4.30 p.m. When I arrived there Niala was waiting with her boyfriend and another boy. She had brought a blind date for me. I was furious. How dare she lie to me! How dare she put me in that position! What if Mom saw me? What if Victor saw me? What if anyone I knew saw me and told Mom? Mom would kill me. She would never believe this was not my doing. I could have died right there and then.

Anyway I reluctantly went into the movie, feeling very nervous and self-conscious. That was the last time I ever went out with Niala or any other friend for that matter. When I returned home later that evening I told Mom what had happened. Fortunately, she believed me and never mentioned it again.

At the beginning of my last year at school I was chosen as prefect for my class. This was an unexpected gift of importance and authority. I had never imagined being chosen for such an exalted position at school. I always thought my teachers never really noticed me and that I was just a name on the exam paper or report card at the end of the term.

I enjoyed the privilege, and by the end of the year realized that my teachers respected me and appreciated that I was a good prefect and a decent person. I came to know then that my teachers did know who I was and liked me. Years later I would sometimes bump into some of my teachers while shopping. They still remembered me by name. Even Polly, my Latin teacher, who made me conjugate those silly Latin verbs I hated so much, still asks about me when she meets my mother. I was not the non-entity I thought I was.

Chapter 22

With so many religious beliefs and traditions, it was no wonder that we Trinidadians were such a superstitious lot. The mystical "jadoo" of the east and the voodoo magic of Africa ruled our everyday lives.

Fifi was the most superstitious of all of us. If she was in the kitchen and a spoon fell on the floor, she would immediately announce that guests were expected shortly. If the house was clean and tidy, she would arrange for tea, cold drinks or whatever was suitable for refreshment at that time of day, and wait expectantly. If, however, she thought it was not a convenient time to entertain guests, she would run around turning up all the brooms in the house. This was supposed to stop guests from arriving.

There were many other rules. You could never make the mistake of handing a sharp instrument like a knife or scissors to anyone, or you would be sure to have a disagreement. If you passed chilly sauce or hot pepper directly to someone, this, too, would lead to a most heated argument. If you happened to spill salt, you had to throw some over your left shoulder. If you did not do that right then and there, the witches will follow you around and when you died, you would have to pick up all the grains you spilled with your eyelashes.

Sweeping after dusk was strictly forbidden. It was considered very rude and an insult to the goddess of light, who you had just welcomed into your home when you switched on the lights. Sitting under a tree after dark would surely tempt the tree spirits to take you away with them to their dark underworld. You should not comb your hair outside, nor throw pieces of hair out, in case the birds found them and built their nests with it. You were bound to go stark raving mad and wail like a banshee.

Never make the mistake of coming into the house with an open umbrella; you would never marry. Neither should you eat from a pot; it would definitely rain buckets on your wedding day. A light drizzle on your wedding day, however, meant good luck. Wearing a hat indoors was also unlucky for you and was bound to bring you ill health. If you mistakenly put your clothes on inside out, you had to continue wearing them that way, as it would be unlucky to change it back.

Once we left the house, we were reminded that under no circumstances must we turn around and go back for anything we may have forgotten or we would surely have a terrible accident, most probably fatal.

Walking under a ladder was asking for big trouble. And you should be very careful that you never made an ugly face, lest your face stay that way. This particular superstition was reserved for children. Never point at the stars or you would most definitely get a wart on your finger. Always flush your nail clippings down the toilet because if the Obeah man got hold of them, he could use them to put a black magic spell on you.

Trimming your hair on a full moon would ensure thick, lustrous growth, but if you cut it on the new moon, your hair would grow very long. I suppose this meant you should cut your hair first on the full moon and then on the new moon to ensure thick, long hair. Mom totally believed that particular superstition; she even cut my eyelashes on those days so they would grow to be long and thick.

A baby's fingernails should not be clipped with scissors; it was best to bite them off. If you put mother's milk into a baby's eyes, the baby was guaranteed to have the most beautiful eyes. Mom said she tried that on me. I am not so sure it worked on me, but it surely did for Viv. Under Mom's instructions, Dora squeezed lots of milk into Viv's eyes when she was a baby. Girls must never wear black until they are over twenty-five. And we should never touch ourselves anywhere on our body, as those places would become terribly ugly and deformed.

We must always remove the Christmas decorations and all the seasonal paraphernalia before the 6th of January; otherwise, we would have a whole year's bad luck. Should you break a mirror, this would mean seven years of bad luck. But if you buried every single piece of the broken mirror in different places, then you may avert that bad luck.

Despite all these "do's and don'ts", we managed the day-to-day job of living, growing up, and graduating from high school. When I graduated, I decided that since I was only seventeen years old, I would spend a year working before I announced my chosen career.

Uncle Noman had by now gotten over his warped idea that because I was Winston's daughter, I was unacceptable and he suggested I join his law firm to see if I liked law as a profession. He was hoping I might develop a liking for law and follow in his footsteps, since he had no children.

So that first summer after I graduated from high school, I spent a month in Uncle Noman's office. I did not enjoy the atmosphere. The older men who worked there had dry, scaly skin and balding hair and dressed in formal black suits that were shiny with age and had flakes of dandruff like snow on their shoulders. They smelled as old as the musty books and files that were piled high on top of their desks, on the old dented steel cabinets, and in the dark wooden cupboards.

My job was to be useful and help wherever I was needed. I was mostly relegated to digging out old deeds, contacts, letters, and other item that could not be easily found amongst those dusty piles of legal papers. The office was situated behind the law courts in an archaic Victorian building. It reminded me of scenes from Charles Dickens' Pickwick Papers or David Copperfield. I did not enjoy reading the lengthy, confusing jargon ever-present in legal documents. I did, however, enjoy answering the telephone, so I managed to stick it out for the summer.

During the latter part of the summer, I heard that trainee teachers were being sought for underprivileged schools in the smaller towns and villages as part of their training. I was considering that option when Uncle Noman suggested I join the bank where he was a director. Mom, who was finally beginning to realize I was now grown up, gave me the choice of where I wanted to go.

I insisted the school environment was what I wanted. The thought of being with the poor children of the village, teaching them, and sharing their lives was something I felt compelled to do. Mom was not happy with my decision; she preferred the dignified atmosphere of the bank. She was disappointed that I was going into the same field as Winston. I had reverted to being a 'chip off the old block.' I lived with Mom's verbal ridicule for several days, but my mind was already made up. I did not care what she said. I had the support of Victor, who knew the people on the school's Board of Governors. He felt I would be safe and sheltered in the teaching profession and would not have to deal with nasty men or the rude public. Mom dared not argue with Victor, so I got my way.

Victor had heard that a nice, middle-aged man named Mr. Carlos was the principal of the school. When Victor spoke to him on the telephone, he sounded like a good, responsible person. I joined the school as a trainee teacher.

Every morning Mr. Carlos drove past our house on the way to the school, which was five miles away. He offered to take me to school every day. How convenient this was. Everyone was relieved that I would be in safe hands and not at the mercy of the public bus or taxi schedules.

On the first day of school I was very excited and looked forward to helping the poor, young children. I saw myself as some kind of beacon, bringing a shining light of knowledge and the desire to learn into their little forlorn lives. I was going to be the best teacher because I knew I had the ability to understand and teach.

I firmly believed that teaching was the noblest of professions. A teacher guided and inspired budding leaders, scientists, and doctors. I had found a way to contribute to society until I went off to university to follow my true vocation.

Mr. Carlos came to pick me up at about 7.30 a.m. He was a short, rotund, middle-aged man with sparse gray hair that was neatly oiled and combed across his balding pate. He had a dark, bloated complexion, red eyes, and a gold tooth. I did not take to him at first, but since everyone said he was a nice man and old enough to be my father, I decided to bury my discomfort.

The drive to school took us through the undulating hills with sugarcane fields on both sides. In between the fields were private roads for the trailers to collect the sugarcane that had been burned and cut down by labourers. The drive to school along twisted roads was peaceful and scenic and punctuated with a few small, sleepy villages.

The school was one of three schools in the small town of Barrakpore. Barrakpore was a pretty town with a population of about five thousand people. Most of the inhabitants were labourers who worked on the large Government owned sugar-cane plantations surrounding the town. Most of the people lived in little huts surrounded by small parcels of land on which they planted the vegetables and fruit they ate. Most of them kept small herds of goats, chickens, and a cow for milk. They were quite self-sufficient as far as their food was concerned, and oc-casionally sold surplus fruits and vegetables in the larger town of San Fernando.

The women in the village worked the fields, looked after the house, cooked the food, and minded the children. The men worked the fields as well, but often drank too much potent rum and in many cases beat their wives and children. The young boys, seeing only this male example, usually followed in their father's footsteps.

The school was built on the cleared section of a small hill. It had only one storey and was about one hundred metres long. It had no windows, but there were a total of ten doors—five on each side of the building—and lots of latticed bricks for ventila-tion.

Although there were no lights or fans, the classrooms were bright, airy, and comfortable. There were eight classes from Standard 1 to Standard 8. Large soft boards used to display charts, etc. and movable black boards separated the class-rooms. At the far end of the school there was an elevated stage upon which were the Principal's desk, his oversized chair, and two chairs for visitors. From this high position, he could look down over the whole school and survey the activities.

Behind the school, the land sloped down to a huge, seven-acre field that was used for playing cricket, football, netball, and other games.

In most villages children began school at any age and left whenever they or their parents thought they had had enough schooling and were needed to work the land. Because of this, the age of the students in the classes varied somewhat, with the oldest being about sixteen. All three hundred students in the school wore the mandatory school uniform of navy blue pants or skirts with white shirts or blouses. Although students were required to wear white canvas tennis shoes with while socks, many of them came to school barefoot or wore slippers.

By the time most of the boys came to school in the morning they had already worked a couple of hours in the fields, so they would be tired and in no mood to study. They looked upon school as a fun pastime, a place to play and relax away from the hard fieldwork and nagging of parents. As a result they did not take lessons and learning very seriously.

My entry into the school aroused many curious stares. I was the only female among the eleven male teachers. I was also very young, being barely a year older than the eldest students. I could tell that many of the teachers doubted I would last the summer. The looks of amusement on the faces of some of the mature students told me they were wondering what they could do to get under my skin, to get me to lose my cool. My life experience had taught me how to cope without showing emotion and how to be strong. I was up for the challenge.

Mr. Carlos decided I should be given Standard Four as my class. The children were between ten and twelve years old. I was to teach all subjects including art and games. Working with those children was a wonderful experience and I soon developed a good rapport with them.

My students realized that I had flare for teaching. They quickly adjusted to having a young, female teacher and learned to respect me. I found myself becoming emotionally involved with the children and their home lives and tried to help by collecting clothes, books, and toys for the poor families. I was often invited to their homes to share their humble meals. I would sit with them on the floor of their small huts and eat off the banana leaves they used as plates. I held their snotty-nosed babies in my arms and comforted them. Before long I had endeared myself to the people in the village. Knowing that my small human gestures seemed to bring some joy and happiness to their simple lives filled me with humility and gratitude.

The school had many wasps nesting in the eaves. One morning as I was walking into school, something had disturbed a nest and a swarm of them swooped down and stung me all over my face. Mr. Carlos rushed me home and I was put to bed. My face swelled up to three times its normal size. The doctor was called in and I was given injections to ease the pain and counteract any toxins or reactions that I might have. It took me a week to recover from the episode and I returned to school the following week.

As usual, Mr. Carlos picked me up that morning. On the way to school he told me he had visited me when I was sick but I had been sleeping. He told me that he had some strange stirrings when he saw me lying in bed and that he was falling in love with me. Of course I was shocked, and I told him that he was like a father to me. He did not say much to me that day, but I could feel his eyes on me from his desk on the stage.

I was nervous about going home with him that evening but I had no choice. I did not know how to go home by taxi without causing speculation as to why I had not gone home with Mr. Carlos. I sat as close to the door of the car as I could, thinking I would jump out if he tried anything. As we drove home, he kept touching my knee and telling me how he felt about me and what he wanted to do to me. I was sickened, embarrassed, and too scared to even breathe. It was a long drive home. His parting words were that I should not be scared and that I should think about it. "We will have good times," he promised.

I wanted to tell Mom about it, but I was afraid she might misunderstand what I was trying to say. She might even think I had imagined the whole conversation or that I was responsible for him talking like that to me. I did not say anything to her and dreaded the next morning when he would arrive to take me to school.

The next morning he came unusually early to collect me and then had the nerve to come out of the car to chat with Victor until it was time for us to go. I was so nervous I could not drink my usual glass of milk. I tried to linger and delay the departure, but Victor called out for me to hurry, as Mr. Carlos was waiting. I nervously got into the car. Mr. Carlos was in high spirits as he called a cheery good-bye to Victor and hummed a silly tune as we drove off.

I huddled close to the door as I had done the day before. Mr. Carlos told me how easy it would be for us to be friends. He said he would take care of everything and I would have nothing to worry about. He took out what I assumed was a condom and waved it at me. As he was talking to me, I kept quiet. He again touched my knee and moved his hand up and down over my skirt. I knew he would not try anything on the way to school because we had to be there for the morning assembly. The fifteen-minute ride seemed more like an hour.

When we got to school, I quickly rushed out of the car and went to my class. The other teachers must have suspected something was not quite right. Two of them came up to me to ask what was wrong. I did not say anything, but I could see Mr.

Carlos looking at me. As I carried on with my class, Mr. Carlos kept making rounds. He stood at the back of the class and kept asking me questions pertaining to the lesson I was teaching. Thankfully, the recess bell rang. I was relieved, thinking he would leave me alone when some of the other teachers came over to chat.

He did leave when Rupert, another teacher, came over to talk. Just as Rupert was asking me what the problem was and why I looked so worried and ill at ease, I got a message saying that the Principal wanted to see me immediately. I looked up at the stage where he was sitting and I saw him glaring at me. I hurried over. When I got there, he asked me to sit. As I sat down I saw a tissue with the imprint of my lips on it. At another time I must have put on my lipstick and then blotted it with the tissue. I had no idea what it was doing on his desk.

Being up there where everyone could see me made me feel very self-conscious. The teachers were now certain something was going on. They stood back, trying hard to disguise their curiosity. Even the older children felt the tension and made quick glances at the stage. They must have all thought I had done something bad, as Mr. Carlos looked very angry indeed.

His eyes were even redder than usual. I sat nervously in front of him with my head bent, afraid to hear what he had to say. Mr. Carlos then proceeded to tell me that if I did not listen to what he had to say or do what he wanted me to do, he would report me to the education authorities and have me thrown out of the school under the shadow of a big scandal. He would report that I was sleeping around with all the teachers on school premises.

Then his tone softened. He told me he knew my hesitation to be 'friends' with him was because I was afraid of the consequences. He reassured me that he knew what to do and he took out the condom again. As he opened up the packet, he proceeded to tell me in graphic details how and when he would use it. As he was talking, he kept looking at me. Every now and then he would pick up the tissue and press it to his lips. He was sweating profusely and had a wild look in his eyes.

I was too afraid to say or do anything and tried to keep from bursting into tears. Somehow I managed to keep a straight face and say nothing at all. He then smiled his gentle smile, patted my arm, and told me we would talk more on the way home. He ended by telling me that I must realize he cared deeply for me and would never hurt me. He said I would love what he was going to do to me.

I was worried and pre-occupied for the rest of the day. Mr. Carlos, however, appeared to be in a friendly, relaxed mood, as he joked with the older students and teachers. Rupert, who was observing all this, made an excuse to come over to my desk. He quietly asked me if I needed a ride home after school. I told him I would very much like that but was not sure how I could manage it with Mr. Carlos right there in front of us. Rupert lived in the opposite direction from where I lived, but at that point I was too scared to go home with Mr. Carlos. Rupert told me not to worry, that he would fix it.

From time to time, teachers would go to talk to Mr. Carlos for a few minutes after the school bell rang. When that happened I would usually wait outside for him and then we would leave. Rupert must have said something to some of the other teachers because just as the bell rang, two teachers went up to Mr. Carlos and began an earnest conversation with him. With a nod of his head, Rupert gave me the signal to casually walk outside. I walked out and headed straight for his car. Just as I sat down, Mr. Carlos came out of the school building. I knew then that he had seen through the plot. I pretended I did not see him as we left the school.

Within minutes of arriving home, Mr. Carlos's car came screeching up to the house. He had to have driven very fast to reach the house so quickly. I had not said anything to Victor, as I was too scared. But when I saw the car, I rushed off to have a shower, wondering nervously what he would say to Victor. I stayed in the shower for a long time until I was sure Mr. Carlos had left. When I saw Victor later he was his usual self, so I knew Mr. Carlos had said nothing. Mr. Carlos had obviously chased after me to see if I had come home or gone off with Rupert. He probably had a jealous fit.

I always got home before Mom, and that day was no different. I anxiously waited for her to come home so I could tell her what had happened. I needed to talk to someone and she was the only one I had. I felt too ashamed to talk to anyone else about it.

When Mom came home that evening, I told her everything. She told Victor because we did not know how to handle the situation. Victor's first reaction was to pick up the gun he had not touched in years threaten to shoot Mr. Carlos when he turned up the next morning. Mom and I struggled to hold him back, trying to reason with him at the same time. After a while he calmed down.

Now that both Mom and Victor knew the truth and did not hold me responsible, I felt strong enough to cope. I told them I was not going to quit the school. We had a lot of our own contacts in the Education Ministry and there was nothing that Mr. Carlos could do to jeopardize my reputation. I thought of a plan. The next morning I would go earlier to school and see what he would do. Let him make the first move. I was ready.

The shameless Mr. Carlos stopped for me as usual the next morning. Mom greeted him in a polite manner and told him I had already left for school. He drove off in a screech of burning tires. When he arrived at the school he said nothing to me but stormed up to his desk and sat there glowering until the bell rang. The other teachers all looked at me but were too afraid to ask what was going on. I appeared cool, so they thought everything was under control.

When the bell rang for the morning assembly, Mr. Carlos stormed over to where I was and told me to take the assembly. I had never done so before and with nearly three hundred children present, I was very nervous. I somehow got through it and everyone dispersed. But that was just the beginning. Mr. Carlos sent me a note informing me that I would have to take the Standard Eight class in Biology that morning. The topic I would have to teach was human reproduction. I was taken aback, but I had decided I would overcome this. I would not let him get the better of me and I taught the subject as best as I could while he paced up and down at the back of the class.

Mr. Carlos summoned me to his 'office' and reprimanded me for embarrassing him in front of the teachers. He was sure the whole village would soon know how badly I had behaved by running off with another teacher. I listened without saying a word and glared at him with cold, hard eyes. I was not afraid of him anymore. As he predicted, the whole village became aware of the tension between us and speculated about what had happened. Mr. Carlos was the object of much ridicule and jest.

A few days later Mr. Carlos went to see Victor. He said he wanted to explain. Victor decided to hear him out. Mom was on hand in case she had to remind Victor to stay cool. Mr. Carlos told them he was a reformed alcoholic and that he still suffered from withdrawal symptoms. He added that he also suffered from high blood pressure, which sometimes caused him to say and do things that people could take the wrong way. He suspected that I, in my immaturity, had misunderstood his concern for my well being. To help me along in school, Victor and Mom let him think they had accepted his version of what had happened.

During school Mr. Carlos continued to watch me closely, ready to reprimand me for no apparent reason. I suspect he did this to prove to the children and teachers that he was not intimidated by me. I played along. The children were important to me and I knew I was making a significant contribution to their lives. They also cared for me, which was all that mattered. One of the older boys once quietly asked me if I wanted to have Mr. Carlos beaten up. I pretended not to understand him. Mr. Carlos still tried to pressure me in subtle ways.

One day the older boys were helping to burn down the wasp nests, as they were creating a health hazard. Kerosene was used to make the flambeau for the burning. One little boy thought the kerosene was water and drank some. My instinctive reaction was to rush the child to the hospital to have his stomach pumped out. Mr. Carlos refused permission for any teacher to leave the school. I stood my ground. I picked up the little boy and rushed off in a taxi to the nearest hospital, which happened to be ten miles away. It was just as well I did because it apparently saved the child's life.

When I went back to school the next day, I was summoned to Mr. Carlos. He tried to reprimand me but before he could get started on his tirade, I decided I would give him a piece of my mind. I told him what I thought of him and the things he had done. I told him that if he bothered me again, I would go to the Ministry and tell them everything about him and he would lose his job. I reminded him that he was a 'reformed alcoholic,' hardly someone to be taken seriously. I also reminded him that between Noman and Victor, I had some pretty big heavyweights behind me, so he had better watch out. He saw my wrath and knew enough about me and my family to know this was no idle threat. He never bothered me again.

Being the only female teacher in a staff of eleven had other challenges as well. Of the ten male teachers, only two were married. The bachelors all competed for my attention. Although it was rather sweet and amusing, I was not at all interested. I was only seventeen and these fellows were well into their twenties.

At the age of seventeen anything over twenty-one seemed old. I had nothing in common with anyone I had met at the school. Once again I felt different. I wondered if there was anything wrong with me. I was still hoping that when my Mr. Right came along, I would know it the instant I saw him.

On day Rupert came over to my desk and told me he was hoping to get married soon because he had found the girl of his dreams. I congratulated him, relieved that he would no longer be waiting on me hand and foot at school.

That evening Rupert came to the house with a huge bouquet of flowers and a jeweler's box in his hand. Mom went out to meet him. He told her he had come to ask for my hand in marriage. Mom came in to warn me. When she told me, I was shocked to say the least and refused to come out. In the jewelry box was a beautiful pair of amethyst earrings as an engaged-to-be-engaged present. I refused to accept the present, although Mom said I should at least accept the flowers so he would not feel too bad.

I reluctantly went out to meet him and told him in no uncertain terms that I was not interested. Mom thought I could have been gentler. I was afraid to be too kind; he might have mistaken it for hope. Rupert did not take my refusal seriously. He left the earrings on the centre table in the drawing room and departed.

I left the present on the table and told Mom it would stay there until he took it away. I knew he would be coming back. He came back every day for about two weeks. Every day he would see the box lying there. I would not come out to speak to him. He would sit for about an hour and then leave.

At school we were just as we always were—friendly colleagues. No one at school knew. Mom eventually managed to convince him he should take the box away since I was stubborn enough to leave it there, and he did. Rupert vowed to love me forever and wait his whole life for me in case I had a change of heart. He got married three years later. So much for his love-me-forever promise.

I had many experiences during that first year of teaching. I met the most wonderful, generous people in the village and managed to make a difference in their lives; I helped to save a life; I received my first proposal of marriage; and I learned to cope with another nasty side of the world, thanks to Mr. Carlos. My biggest gift, however, was finding my true vocation. Sometime, somewhere, I knew I would go back to being a teacher.

Chapter 23

Arnie decided he would have to study Medicine when he realized Uncle Larry would never agree to his being an Opera Singer or, rather, the Opera Star he believed he was born to be. He applied to the medical faculty of the University of the West Indies in Jamaica and was accepted. Arnie was a little apprehensive, about leaving, as this would be his first time away from home. He was not as ready as he should have been to face the challenges of new surroundings alone.

Arnie was the "good child" of the family. He did very well in school, listened to his parents and never argued with them, helped in the house, assisted old people to cross the road, and was exceedingly polite to grown-ups.

Arnie talents included a rich tenor voice and an above-average ability to play the violin and the piano. But we children knew that Arnie was not all he made himself out to be. He was a mischief-maker, a show off and a tattletale and he loved being the centre of attention. He would complain to the grown-ups if he did not like or approve of some of the things we did or if we had not included him in any of our activities. He reveled in being the favourite and he did all he could to show himself in the best possible light to the grown-ups. He did everything he could to get praise and accolades even at the expense of Ricky or me. He actually appeared to enjoy the commotion and quarrels that ensued.

Many times he would tell Mom about things I was supposed to have done and then hang around to see the results. One could almost see his shiny halo gleaming as he puffed himself up with smug, sanctimonious innocence while I received the brutal punishment that left me sore for days. He also carried the careless mutterings from grown-up to grown-up. If he overheard someone making a casual remark, you could be certain he would pass the information on, hoping to show his loyalty and gain points. I suppose he did this to get attention from the adults, since he liked to ingratiate himself with them at every opportunity. This invariably caused tensions between Mom and Auntie Dora over the years.

At this stage of his life, Arnie saw himself as the star of the family. Perhaps it was his way of adding a bit of melodrama to his confused life. Indeed, Arnie treated his everyday life like a dramatic, Oscar-winning performance. Marleen found Arnie's behavior ugly, vulgar and embarrassing. Arnie could not understand why Ricky, Marleen, and I found his theatrics quite stupid. He talked about he and I being 'milk siblings,' remembering that Mom had shared her milk with him. "That makes us special," he would say. Arnie did not really love anyone but himself, but if he did he would have loved Marleen the most. Viv was still too young to be a part of our group, so she was not a part of all these goings on.

Ricky, on the other hand, was a totally different character. At sixteen he studied because he had to. He did not do that well in his "O" level examinations because he was too busy skipping classes to visit his many girlfriends at their homes when their parents were at work.

Whenever he had a new girlfriend in his life, he would be moody and quiet and play tennis longer and harder. He would sit and think for long periods in the rocking chair. I was the only one he could confide in. If he talked to Arnie, Arnie would surely tell Auntie Dora and he would be grounded and that would have meant disaster for him. Marleen would not understand, she was a year younger than he was and besides, she could not see these things rationally. Marleen had very strong ideas on what she thought was morals and could be quite harsh and rigid. That was the last thing that Ricky needed or wanted.

On one occasion he came back from an early morning tennis match totally exhausted. He sat under the porch for what seemed like ages, still wearing his damp, soiled tennis clothes. He had his head down looking very thoughtful and uneasy as he rocked slowly back and forth on the rocking chair.

I knew something was wrong, so I went to sit with him. He told me that one of my friends had invited him over to her house that evening because her parents were going to be away. She had also told him that he should come prepared because she did not want to risk getting pregnant. Ricky was desperate to go that night, but he was also scared. How should he do "it?" What if he made a fool of himself? Where would he go to buy the 'French Letter?' And most importantly, what if his parents found out? Ricky said he had played tennis very early that morning hoping to get the tempting thoughts out of his mind, but he could not. He did not know what to do.

I was shocked. How could a friend of mine—this nice girl who looked so sweet and innocent—be so provocative and wild? Why would she invite him to her home when her parents were out? And worse still, how could she even suggest that he come prepared to do it? I was sure she must have done this before; she sounded so knowledgeable about what to do.

I immediately advised Ricky not to go. "You would surely get caught. What if her parents came home early?" I was very worried for him. That whole day I was restless. Auntie Dora noticed that both Ricky and I were moody, but she put it down to us having one of our fights. We didn't tell her otherwise.

I decided to discuss the situation with Marleen. It was the worse thing I could have done at that time because she took it as a personal attack. How could he even think of doing that sort of thing with someone who was our friend? She was very judgmental and called him rude names. I think that was the beginning of her resentment of him and his morals. She accused him of being loose and without character. The animosity stemming from this would intensify, as they grew older.

I don't think Ricky went to see my friend that day, but it set the pattern for his love life. At some point soon after that he must have lost his virginity. He made no secret of the fact that he wanted and needed girlfriends. He had a very cute smile and was considered ruggedly handsome. He was also very charming and gentle around his girlfriends, so I could see why they found him attractive. I think he must have had relationships with most of my friends as well as Marleen's. While these liaisons did not bother me, Marleen did not approve of them at all and she expressed her views very clearly. She and Ricky had many arguments about this. She did not like the fact that he was pursuing her friends and tempting them to doing things that were not right.

Many times Auntie Dora would have to intervene to make peace. Marlene, of course, would misunderstand Auntie Dora's motive on these occasions. She was convinced her mother preferred the boys to her. But Auntie Dora loved all her children. Marleen was just more difficult to reach and had some fixed ideas that she would not talk about or share with anyone except me from time to time. She was afraid to show love because she didn't want to get hurt. She also did not want to be tempted by passionate affairs, which appeared to be rampant. That is why she reacted so strongly to Ricky's affairs with her friends; it felt like she was the one being tempted.

During the next two years Ricky somehow got his act together. He performed so brilliantly in his "A" level examination that he was given a scholarship to study Aeronautical Engineering at the University of Manchester in the United Kingdom. Uncle Larry was delighted. Both his sons had done well and were about to embark on very lucrative careers.

Marleen was not a gifted student and had to work hard for her grades. She found studying very tedious but was tenacious enough to work hard every day and get reasonably good grades. Marleen had a flair for languages and decided she would major in Spanish.

She was convinced that everyone thought she was peculiar because she was so quiet. She had her own views, which she hardly ever shared because she thought no one would understand them. And she maintained the silly notion that Auntie Dora did not like her. She knew that Uncle Larry adored her, but no one could convince her that she was just as important as everyone else. She was prone to severe bouts of depression, especially when she saw Mom beat me.

As we were growing up, we became close and began to share our thoughts and feelings more. I think I was able to help her through the times when she felt alone and cast off from the family. Although I did not always agree with her views on morality or her severe judgement of people, we both shared a desperate need to search for a spiritual existence. This bonded us very tightly together.

My own personal search began when I was about ten years old. She began her search when she was around the same age. We spent hours talking about what we felt was the meaning of life. Sometimes Arnie and Ricky would join in on our discussions, but they usually thought we were silly and did not know what we talking about. In their minds, they knew everything and had all the answers. Typical youthful male arrogance!

Although I was unable to open up and joke around with Mom, I could easily do that with Auntie Dora. We laughed a lot together. She let me help her with the cooking and taught me the basics of cake making. The boys were always pulling her leg. Arnie, in particular, teased her a lot, calling her Tubby or Fats. Not that she was ever fat or even plump; she was just round and soft. Auntie Dora understood my problems with Mom and would tell me so. That made me feel much better, as I would sometimes wonder if I really was wrong and deserved to be treated the way Mom treated me. I wondered, though, why she never stood up to Mom when Mom acted wild and hysterical.

Underneath Auntie Dora's quiet support of her family and her tidy housekeeping skills, she was a sad, suppressed person who lacked the confidence to emerge from her shell. This insecurity had begun when she was a child. At that time Clara had taken her in hand and had guided her through her growing-up years. Whatever she did had to meet Clara's high standards. Since her efforts rarely ever did, Clara would end up having to do "everything" herself. Poor Dora just could not win. Then she married this slick, handsome town boy, who was worldly and knew how and what he wanted for the children he brought into this world. Auntie Dora's main contributions to their life together were a clean house, their four children and regular well balanced delicious meals.

Uncle Larry was always working late. He had to earn enough money so he could send all his children to the best universities. Ricky, of course, had eased the situation by winning a scholarship, but there was still Arnie, Marleen, and Viv to save for. No one thought anything of his late hours. We were all aware of his obsession and he was always home every night. Auntie Dora could call him anytime at the office and he would always be there, even on those late-night jobs. There was never any gossip or talk about Uncle Larry, but Auntie Dora hid a deep, uneasy feeling in her heart. For many years, she did not share it with anyone. Then one day when she felt it very strongly, she talked to Mom about it. Mom immediately dismissed it and said her unfounded suspicions were just the work of an idle mind with not enough problems to worry about. She reminded Dora that she should be thankful to have a husband who lived for the good of his children and reminded her about Winston and his lack of interest in me, my education, and in providing a home for us.

One day soon after that, Uncle Larry, very confident that his children loved him for all the support he had given them thus far, called a family conference around the kitchen table. He announced that he was in love with another woman who worked in his office and that they had been having a deep relationship that was full of emotional and intellectual compatibility. He refused to call it an affair but said that the relationship had been going on from five years before. He now wanted a divorce so he could marry this woman, as she needed him.

Auntie Dora appeared shocked and unbelieving that he would spring something like that on their seemingly perfect family. She thought he should have had the decency to warn her first. To tell her in front of the children was unforgivable, but she took this humiliating blow with little real surprise. She had had a nagging, gut feeling. A wife always knows.

The children, however, were outraged. They all got up and stood behind Auntie Dora. In a quiet and controlled voice, Arnie told Uncle Larry that he could do what he wanted but that they would have nothing more to do with him if he left the house and married that woman. That was the end of the conversation and the end of the relationship. Uncle Larry never talked about leaving again, and no more reference was made to the affair or the woman involved. Life went on as if nothing had happened.

Three years later Uncle Larry came home late one evening. He told Auntie Dora he was late because he had gone to the funeral of the woman he had loved. She had died of tuberculosis. He then opened up to Auntie Dora about the affair.

This woman had been his secretary and they worked closely for many years. She was a good, kind person who cared deeply for him. He knew she was ill and that she was going to die, so he wanted to give her something in return for the loyalty she had shown to him. He felt somewhat responsible for her because she was in love with him and had never married. Marriage was the one thing he felt would have made a difference to her, especially as she was not well. He agreed that marrying her had been an emotional, spur-of-the-moment decision. He admitted his surprise at the children's ultimatum when he had announced his intentions those years before. In retrospect, he realized they had done the right thing and was grateful for the strength and support they had shown their mother. It made him realize that he could never leave his children or the mother of his children.

Janice, the woman he loved, had understood. Although she continued to be his secretary, their affair had ended. He cried in Auntie Dora's arms for all the pain he had caused all his loved ones. Auntie Dora said nothing. She held him in her arms and comforted him as a mother would comfort a child.

Their relationship grew stronger after that. Uncle Larry, who had never been outwardly affectionate towards her, now made a great show of love and affection when ever possible. He went out of his way to demonstrate how much he appreciated her gentle, quiet ways and her understanding of his indiscretion.

Shortly after that although only seventeen, Arnie left home

to attend university. His departure was hard on all of us. We had grown up with each other—arguing, fighting, singing, discussing—and now one of us was leaving the nest. We would miss him terribly. We all cried openly at the airport, except for Marleen, who had her face firmly set until we got home, when she fled to her bed and sobbed. Everyone knew then that she had cared deeply and wondered why she was so afraid to show the love she felt.

She did tell me that though she cared for him, he often embarrassed her with his show-off ways. She was sort of glad he was gone, as she would not have to see him do the things he did. She was crying because it was a new beginning, not only for him but also for all of us. Things would change and she did not know how it would affect everyone, especially Arnie because he was the first to leave. It was a strange feeling to hear her echo the very thoughts I was having. We both held each other and cried for our uncertain futures. We voiced our hopes and prayed that Arnie would survive and that we would also survive when it came time for us to leave.

Auntie Dora took Arnie's departure in stride. She was weepy for a few days and then most likely wept in the privacy of her room. As her eyes often looked red. We were consoled by the fact that Fifi and Uncle Noman often traveled to Jamaica for his numerous conferences and that many close friends in Jamaica were available in case of an emergency.

Life carried on. I taught; Ricky completed last-minute preparations for his finals, Marleen prepared for her "O" levels, and Viv struggled with school.

Uncle Larry wanted to a build a new home for his family. The house on Eemrie Street was outdated and had been built on a tight budget. He bought a large plot of land in one of the new, upscale suburban areas of town. As it turned out, the plot was opposite the Ramsey's house on Coconut Drive. Uncle Larry was very pleased with the location, but Auntie Dora believed that such close proximity to family might eventually breed contempt. Of course Mom endorsed that view. She was not too keen on Ramsey and Lucille anyway. Their close and happy bond, coupled with the fact that they appeared to be totally self-sufficient, was enough to put Mom off.

Uncle Larry was not to be put off, though. He liked the location of the plot and did not believe there would be any friction. And so a wonderful, modern house was built and the family moved in. Auntie Dora was still apprehensive, but everyone else was thrilled and excited, especially Uncle Ramsey who lived across the street.

Mom was agonized by all this. She did not have a husband to build a house for her. "Look at Fifi . . . Noman bought her dream house for her birthday. Look at Dora . . . Larry built this wonderful, modern house for his family. Look at me . . . I have no home." Mom became more and more obsessed with the idea that she must have a house of her own. It was all she talked about. She would get all worked up and then slip into a deep depression.

Somehow it ended up being my fault. If it weren't for me, she could have gotten married again and had a wonderful husband who would have given her all these things. Mom's hate for me festered. She could no longer wildly beat me with the belt, as I was much taller and stronger than she, so her attacks on me were mostly verbal, punctuated with stinging slaps across my face.

Her hatred for Winston also intensified. She blamed him for the utter mess her life was in. She invited him over to talk about the piece of land they had bought downtown. I tried to reason with her. I told her that she should let it be, as we were content in Diamond. Rachel was behaving all right and we were comfortable there. Victor had told me that the house would be mine, so we actually did have our own home. But Mom did not listen. She continued to rant and rave.

When Winston came over he told her that the land downtown was now in his sister Ena's name because his mother had wanted it so. To add fuel to the fire, he told her that the only way out would be for her to give her half of the plot to Ena.

Mom wanted to ask Victor for some of the land he had on the north side of town. This upset me because she really had no right to do that. Papa had already said he had given us the Diamond house, so I thought her request was unethical. Mom did not listen and did what she thought was right. She asked him and to my horror, used me as the trump card. I did not have a father to care for me, she said, and I should not have to suffer for that. The very next day Victor went to Noman's office and transferred the deed to her name.

This did not matter at all to Fifi, but Dora did not approve. She had four children who needed all she could get for them. She was too afraid to tell Mom how she felt, but she discussed it with me. What could I say? For my own reasons I did not like it I was embarrassed and I was hurt that Auntie Dora should have burdened me with that extra guilt. To be honest, I felt ashamed for Mom and for me.

With this plot of land now in Mom's name, Mom began to feel paranoid. She and Winston had never divorced. If anything should happen to her, he could lay claim to all her possessions, her bank account, and the land. Winston was once again summoned to the house. This time she asked him to give her a divorce. The laws of the land were such that they both had to consent to a divorce before a divorce could be granted. If, however, only one wanted a divorce, he or she could only get it if they could prove the other party had committed adultery. Winston bluntly refused to give her the divorce. He swore that he would always love her and could never bring himself to sever their ties, however tenuous, through divorce.

Now Mom was frantic. How could she get a divorce? She knew that Winston had a young housekeeper and had heard rumours there was an affair going on. She devised a plan. In the dead of night she, along with several witnesses and her lawyer would go to Winston's flat and catch them both in a compromising position. We all tried to dissuade her from committing this foolish, desperate act, but she would not listen.

That night, at 11.30 p.m., Mom, her lawyer, and two witnesses, Noman had refused to be apart of it, knocked on the door of Winston's flat. Winston opened the door and was most amused when Mom charged in and demanded that the housekeeper come out of the bedroom. Of course the housekeeper was nowhere to be seen. Mom was humiliated but still desperate. She did not know how to get that divorce.

A month later Winston came over and very calmly told her he would grant her the divorce. He said she should apply for it and he would not contest it. With that, he turned and walked away.

The next day Mom started the proceedings. Several months later the final divorce came through. Winston came to the house in Diamond that day. Without saying a word, he sat at Mom's feet like he usually did, put his face in her lap, and sobbed loudly as if his heart had been broken. It was the first time I had ever seen a man cry like that. I did not know what to do. They were oblivious to me, locked in a world of their own, no doubt re-living their pathetically sad married life. I was certain that I, their only child, was not a part of those memories.

I felt very sorry for myself. I thought about my mother and

the man who was my father. I did not seem to have much to be proud of. I lamented over the fact that I had not been blessed with the jump start that most people had. Since I had not inherited any qualities I could be proud of, I would just have to develop my own personality. I prayed I would not be like my parents. I was ashamed of them and ashamed of myself for feeling that way. I could not wait to distance myself from them.

Chapter 24

Victor settled nicely into retirement. He seldom went into town and had arranged to hand over all his property to Clara, Fifi, and Dora. Rachel was very much in control of the home situation but it was not the kind of control she had first set out to achieve all those years before. Now she was kind, helpful, and supportive to all, even to Nan and Little Sparrow's side of the family. Apart from Clara, who still treated her with some reserve, everyone was comfortable with her and appreciated her help. Rachel had finally become an important part of the family and for the first time was accepted as Victor's wife. There was just one dark cloud on her horizon—was she was still not legally married to Victor.

Having lived with Rachel as his common law wife for nearly fifteen years, Victor decided it was time he put the past behind him and did the right thing by her. After all, she had had his child and was a good, dutiful wife. He would now put the record straight and legally marry her before he died.

And so Victor finally married Rachel in a quiet, discreet ceremony at the registry office with Mom, Fifi, and Dora present as witnesses. No one talked about it and no announcement was made. This was not only for the benefit of Dawn, who did not know that her parents were not legally married when she was born; it was also for the public at large. No one ever knew that Victor and Rachel had never married, and it was not the time to reawaken old gossip. A new birth certificate was also arranged for Dawn, with no mention of her illegitimate birth.

Victor decided to arrange some financial security for Dawn. He took out a large insurance policy for her in case something happened to him before she completed her studies. Dawn was a naturally bright student, and everybody had high hopes for her to do great things with her life.

By this time Dawn and I had developed a warm and close relationship, although we were never as close as Marleen and I. Dawn and I both liked to dance, so when no one was home we would turn up the radio and dance to the latest pop music. Dawn liked to sit next to me during meals. She said the way I ate my food with such relish made her think mine tasted better than hers did so she would always ask to eat from my plate.

I was Dawn's big sister, even though she was really my aunt. I found out later that she wanted to be closer to me, but we were both afraid of how Rachel would have reacted to our close bond. I was still afraid to trust Rachel; my earlier experiences with her had not been happy ones. She was always so cold, hard, and nasty with me and I was too afraid to let down my protective shield.

Also by this time Merle was well settled with her husband and new baby boy. Shortly after the birth of her son, she started to work at Noman's Farmers Association office. Because she was efficient and very reliable, she quickly became Noman's right arm and handled all his personal matters. She was the best as- sistant any boss could ever have and Noman rewarded her with a high salary. The Farmer's Association now a very large and important association had sister associations in all the agricul- tural based countries. Noman, sometimes accompanied by Fifi, was traveling more than ever; therefore, Merle had the added responsibility of running the office when he was away.

Noman was very popular with the masses because of all the work he had done to bring improvements into their lives and because he was a just and fair man. But his fame also brought him a few enemies. Some people were jealous of his achievements and his close relationship with the then Prime Minister of the island. Noman was a special advisor to the Prime Minister and, as such, the Prime Minister would listen to and invariably follow his advice. Noman reluctantly decided that he needed a bodyguard because of the occasional kidnapping and death threats he received. He never thought he would actually need protection. The bodyguard was primarily for show. Noman thought that some form of protection would act as a deterrent for anyone who might want to create a noisy disturbance.

That was as much trouble as he expected. He suspected the threats might have come from disgruntled politicians who envied his position or from people involved in a lawsuit he happened to be working on. Neither Noman nor Fifi believed his life would ever really be in danger.

But then one evening, while Noman was addressing an outdoor meeting of some five hundred farmers, a shot was fired at him. Dave, his bodyguard, who also happened to be his friend, jumped in front of him and took the bullet in the spine. Dave became paralyzed and never walked again.

Totally shocked Noman and Fifi felt responsible for Dave's injury and realized the death threats really had been real. Now it was unthinkable for Noman to have another bodyguard. They did not want that any more innocent people to suffer because of Noman and his activities. The only way Fifi could cope with the situation was for them to support Dave's family for the rest of their lives.

Fifi and Noman spent a small fortune getting the best medical help for Dave, but nothing could be done and he remained in a wheelchair. Dave told Noman and Fifi that they should not feel guilty, as this was meant to happen to him. It was his fate, what God had planned for him. His kind understanding and fatalistic acceptance of his fate made Fifi and Noman feel even worse and quite humbled.

Noman now decided to keep a low profile. He gave up practicing law and let his new, young partners handle his cases. He resigned as President of the Trinidad & Tobago Farmers Association but continued to be involved with them in an advisory capacity. He stayed on as President of the International Farmers Association based in Geneva so he could continue supporting the farmers and the farm workers. He took on less Government jobs and curtailed his travel with the Prime Minister. Noman began a semi-retired life while in Trinidad but was still quite active at the international level.

Now that I was more grown up, I was spending more of my free time with Fifi and Noman. Even as child, I had worried about Fifi's inability to have children. I could not bear to see her yearn for a child, so I promised myself that I would be her daughter as well as my mother's. I wanted to fill that gap in her life. I spent many long weekends with them at their home and became part of their social crowd.

I was always at Fifi's side, helping her prepare for the many parties and meeting all their friends. I discovered I could hold my own with their fancy jet- set, party-loving crowd. Mom was not keen on this "high falutin' social scene," as she put it, but she could not refuse without appearing heartless or stubborn, so she had no choice but to allow me to go. She would sometimes get angry but there was no way she was going to refuse, lest Fifi or Auntie Dora accuse her of being overly possessive of me or wanting to control my life.

Mom desperately hoped I would have the good sense to re-fuse to go, but I never refused. This caused much tension at times but I pretended not to notice. I was old enough to have a mind of my own. When Mom got worked up enough to be violent, I at least had some good times to compensate for the punishment she still dished out from time to time when her temper got the better of her. I had had so much of Mom's pun-ishment while growing up that I had now become immune and hardened to it. I could take whatever verbal abuse or licks she dished out.

Marleen never took to Fifi's lifestyle or social 'to-do's' as I did and always chose to remain in the background. Sometimes when I begged her, she would go with me to stay with Fifi but would remain close to my side.

Auntie Dora was a little jealous of the attention Fifi gave me. She was always worried that I would get more things like clothes or jewelry from Foie than her children would. In actual fact I never did get anything extra from Fifi, she was very fair that way and what so ever she gave me she made sure that Marleen and Viv got the same. Since Marleen was not the type to bond with Fifi easily, Auntie Dora began to encourage Viv to do so. I thought Viv was still too young to go with me to Fifi's parties. The environment was not suitable for a little girl but I did not say anything for fear that Auntie Dora would misunder-stand. Besides, I did not mind Viv's company. She was the cute baby sister I never had and I while I enjoyed having her tag along, I still believed that it was not always right for her to be a part of the around grown up parties.

Fifi loved taking us out to eat at fancy, expensive restaurants and hotels on the island. On one of these outings, we met one of the world's most famous ballet dancing couples. We went up and spoke to these exalted performers and had our pictures taken with them. Several years later when I was in London, I went to see them perform at Convent Garden.

Fifi always took it for granted that Noman would die before her. She was certain that God would not force poor Noman to cope if she was not around. She also assumed that all Noman's wealth would be left to her, as she was his wife and they had no children. On many occasions, Fifi would tell us that her money would be shared equally amongst the five of us—Arnie, Ricky, Marleen, Viv, and me—and that the house she lived in would go to Viv, since Marleen and I would both be given homes of our own. It did not matter to us; we never thought about money or property.

Auntie Dora however talked about this from time to time. She did not think it was fair that Fifi should share her money equally with me as well as her children. She would sometimes verbalize that Mom had only one child and plenty of money for that one child, but she and Larry had four children to provide for. In all fairness, she said, Fifi could leave me a small token but should leave the bulk of the money to her children. I would feel very embarrassed and guilty about this. Why did people—my family, in particular—think so much about money? Money was not everything. Besides, you received whatever God had in store for you. If it were your kismet to have it, it would come your way. I could never understand this desire to get money from other people. Auntie Dora's calculating and mercenary attitude surprised me, it disappointed and distressed me.

Meanwhile, life in Diamond continued. I was enjoying my teaching and coping with Mr. Carlos while Mom went to her job in town from Monday to Friday. She still enjoyed this job and continued to stay in touch with some of her old friends. Mom still went to the cinema most Sundays. It was her special time and she enjoyed getting dressed up and going into town to see the latest movie.

Either on Saturday or Sunday evenings Fifi would pick up Auntie Dora and Viv and take a slow drive to see us in Diamond. The other children—Arnie, Ricky, and Marleen—hardly came at that time, as they were all busy studying, playing tennis, or participating in other activities with their friends.

Victor was instrumental in the construction of a community centre in Diamond where people could gather and discuss village matters. It was no surprise that the centre was also used for debates or when well-known speakers gave discourses and speeches.

Victor himself was very often invited to the centre as a speaker. He always spoke about his favorite topic, "The Need for a Universal Religion or Way of Life." Victor would quote from his religious books to prove that all religions had the same message. This did not make him very popular with the followers of the latest craze to hit Trinidad, the American Evangelists, who, with their born-again fervor, tried to convert the natives. Many of these Evangelists would make a point of coming over to our house to argue with Victor or try to convert him. Victor always won his arguments.

I wanted to go to one of these crusades to see for myself what they were all about. I was on my own quest for answers to spiritual questions, so I was curious to hear what these people had to say. Too self-conscious to go alone, I arranged to go with my old friend Pamela. Her mother, Silvia, was a confirmed believer and a born-again Christian, whose Hallelujahs and Amens were always the loudest and most fervent at those gatherings.

I did not tell Victor I was going. I knew he would not approve, especially since he had had all those altercations with the missionaries. That first time I went, I thought the preacher sounded more like a politician than an evangelist did. I was shocked to see the propaganda movies that he and his entourage played.

These movies showed tribes in Africa, India, and the East Indies living in what was considered uncivilized and dirty conditions with strange customs and traditions. He called them 'devil worshipers' and 'pagans,' and told the congregation that the only way to be civilized was to accept the Lord Jesus Christ as their saviour to be free of sin and go to heaven.

I was overwhelmed and disgusted by the twisted, barbaric manner in which these tribes were portrayed. The Evangelists began to preach about salvation and rescuing people from these scenes of hell. Horrified, I looked at the faces of the people in the congregation and was amazed to see that they were lapping up all the rubbish that was being fed to them.

Many at the gathering had come from Africa and India. How could they accept these terrible insults about their century-old traditions and customs without a word of protest?

The meeting ended with the lusty, robust singing of one hymn after another, accompanied by loud, brassy music. At the end of the crusade, the crowd slowly dispersed. They felt cleansed, their sins forgiven. They had released all their tension by singing loudly until they were exhausted and relaxed, and had made enough of a financial contribution to appease their conscience.

I came out feeling drained and sad. The masses were being fooled and they could not see it. Some manipulative preacher man in America was getting rich on the hard-earned money of these poor, ignorant people. To coerce people in the name of religion was, to me, the biggest sin ever committed. In my heart, I cursed them for what they were doing.

I went again the following week. I wanted to see more, to confirm that the feelings I had had from the previous week were in fact correct and I had not misjudged these so-called do-gooders. This second time around I was even more horrified. I went home very upset and distraught. I wanted to do something for those people. I wanted to shout out aloud and tell them that the secret of God was in their own hearts and that all they had to do was listen and trust their inner instinct. I became depressed and angry with them. How could they not see they were being conned?

I had not told Victor I was going to the crusade or that I had gone the week before, so I was very surprised to find Victor was waiting for me on the veranda when I got home. He had been told I was seen there the week before and again that day. The fact that I went back again a second time was like throwing mud in his eye. At least that is what he told Mom. But all he asked me was where had I gone? I did not lie. I told him I went to see what the whole crazy thing was all about. Victor did not speak to me for about a week, but he soon got over it and things returned to normal.

Victor never knew that I went to parties or danced with boys. He would have been very cross indeed and may have even hit me. Victor had strong convictions that he saw no reason to hide.

I was helping to water the garden one morning when Harold, a boy from the village, walked by. He stopped to chat with me through the picket fence as I watered. Mom knew his mother, they met at the village festivals and at weddings and his sisters were friendly with me. Harold and I often met at the various parties we went to, so we had gotten to know each other quite well. As we were talking, Victor kept walking back and forth. I did not think anything of it because there was really nothing to think about.

Finally, Victor could take no more. Fuming, he charged up to the garden tap, turned it off, and then stormed over to me. In a loud voice that Harold could hear he told me I had watered the garden long enough and I must go inside immediately. I could have died at that moment. To be reprimanded like that in front of someone—especially a male—was just too embarrassing. I wanted the ground to open up and swallow me. I never wanted to see Harold after that. I was sure he would tell everyone about it and they would make fun of me. I stopped going to parties after that. I was too ashamed to see anyone.

Fashion was a big thing in our lives during the middle to late 1960's. The new fad was paper dresses. Everyone wanted to own one of the bright, gaudy psychedelic, A-line, paper dresses from trendy Carnaby Street in London. Then there were those short, short mini skirts worn with contrasting flowery tops and matching big, plastic dangly earrings. We all devoured the latest fashion and music magazines to see what was in and what was out. None of us wanted to be out-of-date.

Most of my friends wore very short skirts, which I was not allowed to wear. My skirts had to be just to my knees. So except for the length of my skirt, I was pretty much at the height of fashion. But I soon figured out that to fit in with my friends' skirt length, all I had to do was roll up my skirt from the top when I left the house and roll it back down before I got home.

One day when I got home, Mom was waiting for me. It seemed that Victor had seen me downtown but could not believe his eyes, as I was wearing such a short skirt. Mom had assured him that all my skirts were the proper length. Perhaps he had made a mistake. "Vee was never one to disobey," she pointed out. Just to be sure, Mom thought she should check the top of my skirt. Sure enough, she saw the rolled-up marks at the top. I felt so ashamed to have been caught like that. Fortunately for me, she did not tell Victor, so he was left to still think that his eyes really had deceived him after all.

Despite my fashionable hair and clothes, I was uncomfortably aware of my unattractive my looks. My big nose was still the object of much teasing and it was obvious boys did not find me as attractive as they did my friends. Still I remained patient. I could wait. My Mr. Right would come along in due course and see me for who I was deep inside and my looks, for what little they were worth then, would not matter.

Every year there was as Annual County Fair in a different part of the island. That year Niala decided I should attend. She thought I was just too good to be true and I should believe in myself. She was always encouraging me to do something wild. "There is life and passion in you," she would insist. Niala was always trying to get me to meet her boyfriends' friends and go out on dates.

Niala pestered my mom so much that she finally agreed I could go to the fair. To make sure I did go, Niala insisted on picking me up at home. The fair was fun and there was a lot to see. Niala's boyfriend and a whole string of his friends, no doubt especially picked for me, accompanied us. I felt flattered and important. I began to realize that this boy thing could be fun. So many cute boys to choose from!

I decided I would be bold and agree to have tea at the tea pavilion with the first one who asked me. Niala was pleased. I was breaking loose. I had been good for too long.

As I sat and had tea with 'the chosen one,' I gazed at my surroundings. This fair was the largest on the island and people had come from far and wide. There must have been over ten thousand people milling about. People in Trinidad always dressed formally for functions, so most of the young girls were nicely dressed and looked beautiful. I was having a good time and the tea was delicious. I found myself laughing and blushing at the compliments the young man was paying me. I noticed that many people were looking at me too. Perhaps I was not that bad looking after all, I quietly thought to myself.

By late evening when the Fair was ending, I heard my name announced. I was asked to report to the stage. I got very worried. Something terrible must have happened. It must be bad news. I rushed to the information desk and was told I had to climb onto the stage for the message. I rushed up to the stage and over to the Master of Ceremonies. As I crossed the stage I saw the whole crowd of people watching me but I was too worried to feel embarrassed. Just as I got near centre stage where the MC was standing, the band struck up some loud music and the MC announced that I was the Queen of the Fair.

I had been selected from all the young girls there that day. There was a loud burst of applause. I was shocked. Me? Before I could say anything, a sparkly rhinestone crown was placed on my head and I was loaded with presents. I was nervous. What would I tell my mother? She would think I had paraded on stage for this. I would die. Of course Niala thought it was great fun and did not give me a chance to object or say anything to ruin the occasion.

Fortunately that was the last item of the day, so I was able to go home soon afterwards. I went home laden with towels, bed linen, a Hoover vacuum cleaner, various cosmetics, and several other gifts. Niala explained to Mom how it happened. Mom took the news quietly and did not say anything. I was relieved. Maybe she would finally see that I was not the unattractive person she always told me I was. Hopefully she would see me differently now and be happy for me.

The next day there was a news item and photographs in the papers and an announcement on the radio with the weekly round up of social events. Before Victor could get wind of it and would have to face his warth, I escaped to Auntie Dora's for a few days.

Chapter 25

I was lucky to grow up in the company of many dogs. Victor had a passion for them. I remember having as many as twelve dogs in our yard. Like our family members, our dogs had their own personalities and idiosyncrasies. Some were amusing and entertaining, while others were rather grouchy and irritating.

The first dog I can recall was Brown. He was called Brown because he was a warm, chocolate brown colour all over. Brown was a gentle, loving dog with soft, kind eyes. He listened and obeyed and had a secret, quiet understanding with Victor. He would follow Victor around, always staying close by, and looking up into Victor's face when he spoke as if he understood each and every word. Brown would rub his head again Victor's leg and put his soft, velvety wet nose against the palm of his hand in silent communication.

Mom had a good friend called Mrs. Ali who lived in San Fernando. One day when Victor was passing Mrs. Ali's house, he thought he would drop in for a while, as it had been quite a while since he had seen her. No sooner had he opened the gate than an enormous German shepherd came bounding out of the yard. The dog galloped straight up to Victor and began to jump all over him, making quite a noisy racket with his playful yelping. Mr. Ali rushed out of his house to see what the ruckus was all about and tried to call the dog off, but the dog was not at all interested in listening to his master. He continued to jump all over Victor, barking excitedly.

Flustered and embarrassed, Mr. Ali apologized to Victor and told him that getting the German shepherd had been the worst mistake of his life. He admitted to not knowing anything about dogs or how to train and look after them, but that he had heard people say German shepherds were quite ferocious and made the best watchdogs. With robberies on the increase, he thought a big, fierce dog like a German shepherd would be just the thing to frighten off potential thieves or burglars. Mr. Ali had paid a lot of money for the dog, which his children had named Jacky, and they hoped he would have been a good watchdog.

However the whole family was very disappointed when Jacky had grown from a tiny, playful, puppy into this big monster of a dog that thought he was still a puppy. They were fed up with him chewing up slippers and pieces of wood, dragging things all over the yard, running out on to the road to make friends with any Tom Dick or Harry, and generally being an absolute nuisance. They had reached the stage where they would be quite happy to give him away. The trouble was that no one wanted a dog that ate too much and did not earn his keep. They had no choice but to hang on to him. They did not have the heart to throw him out on the street or put him down.

Victor had always wanted to own a shepherd so he jumped at the chance and offered to take the undisciplined beast off their hands. Mr. Ali was delighted to pass the dog on to Victor, knowing that he would not only be ridding himself of his big headache, but that the wretched beast would go to a home where he would be loved and well looked after. And so that day Victor came home with Jacky, the German shepherd.

When we saw Jacky we were surprised to see such a fine, handsome animal and shocked that he would have been given away. He must have been worth a lot of money. Jacky it seemed, was a show off too, as if reading our minds, he held himself taller, with his ears erect and his long, hairy tail at just the right angle. There was a mischievous twinkle in his eyes as he observed his new owners, fully expecting to be loved. We did not disappoint him. We fell in love with him immediately, but were a little concerned about how he would adjust to his new home as well as to Brown and the other dog we had at the time.

We need not have worried. Jacky was friendly and playful and took to his new home like it was meant to be his. He fit in from the moment he arrived, making friends with all of us and attaching himself to Brown as though he were his shadow. Good-natured Brown did not seem to mind sharing his bowl or his special restingplace with this new, boisterous addition to the family.

Brown was a common mongrel with no special looks except for his unusual coloring and gentle eyes. It was quite an amusing sight to watch this huge, handsome German shepherd follow the smaller, less attractive dog with obvious hero worship and then sit as close to him as he could possibly get. Jacky would not eat unless Brown was around. He scratched and groomed Brown as if Brown were his own puppy. Brown was kind, patient and indulgent with Jacky, even when Jacky performed his mischievous pranks. Occasionally, if Brown sensed that Jacky had overstepped his boundary and that Victor would be cross, he would nip Jacky's tail in warning. Surprisingly, Jacky would sit quietly and submissively in shameful remorse.

Directly behind the house in Diamond were rolling fields with lush savanna grass, good for grazing the animals that many of the village people kept for meat or milk. The people in the village would often tie up their animals there and leave them there to feed. Everyone knew which animals belonged to whom and there were very few misunderstandings. Everyone looked after everyone else's animals—a peaceful tropical pastoral scene if there ever was one.

Living opposite our house in Diamond was Mr. Gool, his wife, and nine unkempt, uncouth, loud children. Mr. Gool was a quiet, thin little man who seldom smiled but worked very hard to support his large family. After a long, hard day of working in the fields, he would go to the rum shop for a quick drink to ease his aching body. Invariably, as with most of the men who worked so hard, one drink was never enough, and by the end of the evening he would be well and truly drunk. After his drinking spree, Mr. Gool would return home late at night to noisily awaken his wife for sex. If she resisted, he would beat her up.

Their bedroom was at the front of their wooden house near the road. The windows were always left open to catch the cool breezes. Many nights we could hear them through the open windows. First they would argue because Mrs. Gool was tired from working all day and coping with the string of children, and did not want the sloppy, smelly attentions of her drunken husband. The blows would follow. Then, finally, the noisy sex would begin. Mr. Gool's loud grunts, groans and ahaas were familiar sounds all over the village. Curiously, by that point in time, Mrs. Gool herself would be caught up in the moment and her soft giggles and moans would often accompany her husband's ecstatic chorus.

By morning reality would strike, bringing Mrs. Gool to Victor to seek his advice. She would repeatedly beg Victor to talk to Mr. Gool, to explain to him that he could not drink away the little money they had, especially since their nights of heated passion had already resulted in nine children and she was worried the tenth would soon be on its way. Mrs. Gool was certain her husband would listen to Victor because he respected Victor.

Victor had never taken to Mr. Gool, finding him to be withdrawn and up tight, so he never had that talk with Mr. Gool. But one day after Mrs. Gool begged and pleaded, Victor reluctantly agreed to talk to him. Later that morning, he called him over and they chatted or, rather, Victor chatted and made suggestions while Mr. Gool listened.

Mr. Gool did not seem to be taking it too well. His thin, bony face was set and he kept his eyes down and did not say much. He looked like he wanted to tell Victor to shut up and mind his own business but did not dare say it to Victor's face, as Victor was always there to hand out small loans when his family was in need. Victor quickly realized he had failed to get through to him. He had no choice but to tell Mrs. Gool he would not speak to Mr. Gool about their personal life again.

The night Mr. Gool got totally plastered as usual. He came to the front of our house and shouted a long string of abusive words that he could not dare say when he was sober. He cussed and swore using the foulest language. "Ah go teach that Mr. know it all, fix it up, wife-stealing mother fucking son of a bitch a lesson. Who he tink he is, telling mey how to treat mey woman?" In his drunken state, Mr. Gool had lost all reason. We all woke up from his shouting; in fact, half the village must have woken up, fearful that Victor would get angry, lose his temper, and most probably grab his gun.

Fortunately this was one instance when Victor remained calm. He was, confident that by the next morning Mr. Gool would have no recollection of what he had said or done. Meanwhile, Mrs. Gool, knowing that she was the one who had insisted Victor to talk to her husband, called out to Mr. Gool and invited him to hurry home, as she was anxiously waiting for him in their warm, cozy bed. Mr. Gool lumbered off to his wife's bed, still grumbling and cussing under his breath. Relieved, we all went back to sleep.

Veena Masud

The next morning we could not find Brown or Jacky anywhere. It was time for their morning feed, a meal they normally enjoyed and were always anxiously awaited. We called out, yelled, looked up and down the road, but they were nowhere to be found. The other house dogs followed us around, looking lost, sad, and confused. We were anxious and unsettled.

Later that morning one of the young children from the village came to tell us that he had seen Jacky in the fields at the back when he went to tie out his goats for grazing that morning. He had called out to Jacky, who was always ready to play, but Jacky had just sat there whimpering and moaning with his head hung low. He thought Jacky must be hurt, so he rushed over to tell us.

We were surprised to know that Jacky had been seen in the field, as normally he never ventured out there. Our dogs loved to be around people, so we never thought of looking for them there. Victor and I hurried out to the fields calling, "Jacky! Jacky! Brown! Brown!" Mom followed closely behind. As we approached a small ditch, we heard a soft moan and saw Jacky sitting in the long, damp grass with his head down. We rushed up to him and saw Brown lying in the deep grass with his head smashed in. Jacky sat there looking lost and very sad, heaving long sighs between mournful whimpers.

Victor was enraged. "Who could have done this? Who could be so heartless and cruel as to hurt an innocent dog?" With heavy shoulders and tears streaming down his face, he tenderly picked up the broken body. We slowly trudged home. A weak, sad, and tired Jacky walked slowly behind us with his head down. I remember walking with my hand on Jacky's head so he would know I shared his grief.

Brown was buried under the mango tree at the side of the house near Victor's bedroom. Jacky was inconsolable. He did not move from Brown's grave. Two days went by and he still did not move. He gradually got weaker and weaker. Victor tried to feed him bread and milk. He tempted him with his favorite minced meat. But Jacky refused to eat or drink. He just moaned, sighed, and whimpered from time to time. Real tears ran down his face. I had never seen a dog cry; I did not know they had tears. I sat next to him for long periods, patting and stroking him, and he would put his sad head on my lap.

On the third or forth morning after the incident, we woke up to find Jacky lying over Brown's grave, dead. Victor dug up Brown's grave and buried the two dogs in the same hole. I have never seen or heard of a dog grieving like that. It was such human-like behaviour, so unusual for a dog. But then Jacky was an unusual dog. The whole house was in deep mourning. We all felt like we had lost our best friend.

Soon after we lost Brown and Jacky, a stray motley-looking mongrel moved into our yard and decided to adopt us. We called him Rex. Rex was white with little brown spots all over his body. He was quite an ugly-looking dog except for his intelligent eyes. Rex was bright; in fact, if he were a human being, he would have scored exceptionally well in any IQ test.

There was no doubt that Rex understood everything we said. Rex was the ideal watchdog. He guarded the property as if his life depended on it, making just the right amount of noise to arouse the household and frighten off the enemy. But Rex had another side to his character: he moonlighted as a ragamuffin. From time to time, Rex would somehow creep out of the yard, despite the wooden fence and the closed gates, and go for long walks. He would be spotted several miles from home, yet curiously he was always back home for his dinner and stayed home during the night. Perhaps he visited some lady friends. We never found out, but there were quite a few puppies that looked like Rex in and around the village.

As Rex got older his outings became more frequent. Strangely, while he was out on the road, he would never bark, attack or growl at anyone. He greeted everyone with a friendly wag of his tail. But if that very same person came to the yard or house, then he would growl and become decidedly furious and ferocious, snapping wildly at the heels of the 'intruder.' Even when he grew so old that all his teeth fell out, Rex pretended he could still bite or tear an intruder to pieces if he invaded his home.

Rex also understood English. When he sat at our feet as we chatted, he would look at whoever was speaking and nod and shake his head as if he understood everything that was being said. He escorted visiting friends and family in when they arrived and saw them out when they were leaving. He knew who was welcome and who was not. Rex was very entertaining and a favourite with everyone.

As Rex got older, unbeknownst to me, he began to suffer from rheumatism or arthritis. He would be very reluctant to move when he was asked to.

It was my job to sweep out the front porch. Rex's favourite place was right at the top of the steps....exactly where I had just cleaned. I would plead to Rex very politely to 'Please move." When he wouldn't budge, I would get more assertive. 'Rex, please go!' I'd say, but Rex still would not move. I knew he hated water, so I played my trump card. "Rex if you don't move, I will pour water all over you," I would say in a quietly menacing tone. Rex, whose eyes had been closed all this time, would now slowly open his eyes and stare at me. I would repeat the threat again, looking straight into his eyes. Rex would now slowly and, upon reflection, painfully begin to pull himself up. If, by chance, Mom had heard me threaten Rex, she would call out, "Vee, let the dog be. He is old. Don't harass him." Rex would then turn around and hurry back to his warm place, with no apparent discomfort and a smug grin of triumph on his face.

Rex ran away one day on one of his jaunts and got run over by a car about 200 yards from the house. He dragged himself until he was outside the gate and then died.

Just before Rex died Victor brought home a playful puppy he had found. We called him Sparky. Sparky, who was mostly Labrador with a bit of Beagle thrown in, was full of fun and not at all interested in being a watchdog. He loved going to the beach with us. On one of our beach trips we lost Sparky. We searched everywhere and when after several hours we still had not found him, the family decided they would not look any more and would go home.

I thought it was cruel and unfair, and cried as we drove off. We were forty-five miles from home. How would Sparky find his way home? I complained, but no one listened. They were all tired and bad tempered because they had wasted so much time looking for a silly, wayward dog that hadn't had enough sense to stay with his family in a foreign place. They would put an ad in the papers, they said, and someone would be sure to find him and bring him home.

I remember not saying much to anyone for the next few days, as I mourned the loss of Sparky. A week went by and I had resigned myself to the fact that we had lost Sparky forever. No one had responded to the ads in the papers. Someone had either found or adopted him, or he had died somewhere, alone and lost. I was inconsolable.

One afternoon I was sitting in the front gallery of the house, rocking in my favourite Bentwood rocking chair and reading a book, when I saw a frail, tired, dirty Sparky wearily walking up towards the house. When I excitedly called out to him, despite his tiredness, he broke into a doggy trot as he approached the gate. It was a miracle that Sparky had found his way home. It was 'doggy willpower.' With great authority, Mom announced that she had known all along that Sparky would somehow find his way home. Sparky never ran away again after that and lived to a ripe old age of fifteen.

Victor went to visit a friend in a nearby village, who had a purebred female pointer to give away. Victor brought home a half-starved and sickly-looking female. Victor changed her name to Lottie from the undignified name of Slutty that her previous master had given her. Lottie was so grateful to be loved and to be a part of a family of dog-lovers that she became totally devoted to all of us, Victor in particular. She soon put on weight and her coat took on a beautiful, shiny gloss. Victor paraded her around at dog shows and although she never came away with the top prize, she attracted a lot of attention. Over the years she was bred with prize-winning male pointers. Victor always gave her puppies away to loving homes.

For the first few days after the old extension of the house burned down, Lottie remained at Victor's side. When he suffered his heart attack, she refused to eat until one day I sat next to her and spoon-fed her tiny morsels at a time, as Victor had done when he first brought her home to live with us.

But Lottie had a major idiosyncrasy—she hated black people. If a black person came close to the fence, she would go berserk, almost wild with rage. For a dog that was so gentle all the time, this was unusual behaviour. We were almost taken to court once when she bit a black man whose face had been pressed up against the picket fence. Lottie sneaked quietly up to the fence, pushed her long snout and sharp teeth through the space, and bit the man on the cheek. It was a huge gash and blood was everywhere. The women in the house panicked. What to do? What would happen? Fortunately Victor arrived home soon after that and solved the problem by giving the man some money to have the wound looked at. We thought that was that.

The next day, however, the man arrived back at the house sporting a huge bandage and a letter from the doctor, saying he had to have twelve stitches on his face and informed us that he was now taking us to court. His lawyer had said that since the man was outside the yard when he was bitten, we should pay him compensation and have the dog put down. Victor was angry but had an ace up his sleeve or, rather, a son-in-law who was one of the best lawyers on the island. Victor won the case, which was thrown out. The fact that the dog had bitten the man's face from inside the fence meant that the man had been too close to the fence and was, in fact, acting in a very suspicious manner. Why did he have his face pressed so close to the fence? Noman asked. Neither the man nor his lawyer had an answer and they ended up having to pay Victor's legal costs.

The silliest dog we ever owned was Raja. Raja, a Doberman Pincer, whose parents were 'Overall Dog of Dogs' Champions. After being totally taken in by a very impressive advertisement in the Sunday paper, Victor decided he had to have a pup from that litter and immediately went to see the puppies. Being the first potential buyer, Victor was given the pick of the litter. He chose very carefully and selected the pup that he believed was the most intelligent. The fact he was also the biggest pup of the litter was secondary, Victor insisted. He was determined to have a bright-eyed, friendly puppy. He christened him Raja even before he had arrived home.

We were all excited. Here was the pup of the Champion right here in our home. Victor had a beautiful, cozy kennel made for him. Raja was fed, toilet- trained by Victor himself, he was so proud of Raja. We soon became familiar with the latest doggie vitamins, health food, and grooming methods. Raja's tail was docked perfectly and his ears clipped to perfection. Raja had the makings of a prize specimen. He was pampered and spoiled.

Victor hoped his Raja would be a future Dog of Dog Champion, or so he boasted to all who had the patience or incline to listen to his endless praise of Raja.

We also had many cats roaming around our compound. Some of them were quite friendly and would steal food from the dog's bowls when they were not around, or eat tidbits left out especially for them. There was one particular cat we called Fluffy. With a name like Fluffy, you might think it was soft and cuddly, but this cat was quite the opposite. Fluffy was huge with short, stubby orange-coloured, wiry hair. I cannot remember why she was called fluffy because she was not fluffy by any means. Dawn, who loved cats, must have named her. Quite the tyrant, Fluffy bullied all the other cats in the yard and made sure she got first pick of the leftover dog food.

When Raja was a puppy, Fluffy thought he was just another cat, so she took him under her wing. It was not unusual to see them sitting together. When Raja got bigger, Fluffy continued to bully him as though he were still a small puppy or kitten. When Raja was given his dinner, he would sit patiently, mouth drooling, while Fluffy slowly ate her fill. When he forgot his patience to wait and tried to eat out of the same bowl, Fluffy would slap him. He would then ashamedly pull back and patiently wait until she had finished eating before making his move.

Raja grew to be almost as tall and as big as a Great Dane, and would gallop around the house like a young pony. Mom, who liked gardening, was not amused to see huge paw prints all over her garden. He would dig up plants and bury anything he could find, sometimes right in the middle of the beautifully manicured lawn. He knew when Mom was angry with him and would hide under the stairs and wait for her to go to work. As soon as she left, he would come boldly out of hiding, looking very pleased that he had fooled her once again.

We had a couple of clotheslines near the washing area at the back of the house. If we made the mistake of forgetting to bring in the clothes that had been left on the line to dry that day, the next day we would often find the clothes muddy and dirty and stuffed in a bucket. We were very curious to know how the clothes got off the line and into the bucket and why they were so dirty. One night we decided to investigate the thud, thud sounds we had been hearing. We soon realized that during the night, Raja pulled the clothes off the line, put them in a bucket, and dragged the bucket with the clothes half-spilling out. We now understood why the clothes from the line were so muddy. It was not some naughty kids prank; it was only Raja amusing himself or perhaps helping us.

As big as he was, Raja was a coward. He would run and hide if he heard a loud noise or people shouting. Rain and thunder would cause him to seek shelter behind one of us, except Mom. He avoided her because she shouted at him when she caught him doing naughty things. I think he was also afraid of her because she seldom smiled and he had seen her uncontrollable rage and wrath when she beat me. Raja would come to me when I was alone after those episodes. He would look at me and rest his paw on me. We would sit like that until I felt better and could face the world again.

Despite all Raja's trying episodes, Victor loved him more than all his dogs. He insisted that Raja had personality. I think he loved him because he was just plain good-looking. Victor never did show Raja at the Dog of Dog Championships. I'm sure it was because he did not want to lose and have to admit that Raja was not the perfect specimen of good doggie behaviour he thought he was.

We were not the only dog lovers in the family. Fifi and Uncle Noman also had dogs, which they treated like the children they did not have. There was Sputnik, Lunic, Prince, and Pretty Boy.

Sputnik liked a nip of brandy now and then. Fifi's heart was broken when she accidentally ran over him as she was backing out her long car.

Although not as dog crazy as the rest of us, Auntie Dora and Uncle Larry also had quite a few dogs over the years. There was Becket and Brutus, Ceasar and Cleo. Their children clearly admired the heroes of ancient Rome.

But Uncle Ramsey and his daughter Camille Anne took the cake when it came to dogs in our family. Their whole life revolved around their many, many dogs. Uncle Ramsey could often be found with one of his dogs on his lap, picking ticks and other bugs out of its fur. He saw nothing wrong with sharing bites of his snacks with his dogs. Camille Anne's bed reeked of dog and was full of dog hair. Even though we loved dogs, we found it difficult to spend a night in their house because of all the dogs. It was not unusual to have as many as six dogs all boisterously vying for our undivided attention whenever we visited. Thirty years later, Camille Anne would have to choose between her husband and her fourteen dogs. The dogs would win.

Chapter 26

As my year of teaching drew to a close, I began to think more about furthering my studies. I did not know how to ask Mom if she was prepared to support me so I could study abroad and fulfill my secret dreams, so I kept quiet. I had no one else to ask and did not for a moment consider that Winston, my father, would want to support me. I remembered all too vividly his penny- pinching habits and his devotion to the needs and wants of his mother and his sister Ena, rather than his daughter. Having largely ignored me for most of my life I knew I did not have the kind of relationship that I could ask him if he would finance my further studies.

I was painfully aware that Victor was not my father; therefore, no matter how much he may have loved me, I could not expect him to support me. This would be sure to cause a rift in the family, in particularly with Dora and Rachel. Besides, he had already split his money between Mom, Fifi, and Dora, and had made provisions for his last responsibility, Dawn.

I felt lost and alone, and spent many sleepless nights wondering what to do about my career. There was always the option of going into law with Norman but there, too, I would need money for tuition and exams. Eventually I would also need to travel to London for the Bar. While Norman was keen for me to join him as an articled clerk, he never mentioned any financial assistance.

Banking was another option, but I was not at all interested in high finance and could not see myself having a mundane desk job, calculating money or talking about money matters. Since I was already teaching, I was eligible for a further Teacher's Training Degree having already completed the Teachers Training Courses, I was therefore more or less reconciled to becoming a professional teacher. It would be a good second choice for me, as I enjoyed children and had already proven that I could make a difference in their lives. But I also knew that the decision to become a teacher like Winston would not go down well with Mom.

Then one day Mom unexpectedly brought the subject up herself. She began to talk about the fact that Arnie had left to study medicine and "in a few years he would be a big shot doctor earning a lot of money." Ricky would be leaving in another year or so to study aeronautical engineering, with Uncle Larry's full support.

Also all her friends' children were going or had already gone abroad to study. Perhaps, she suggested, I should also be thinking of going abroad for further studies. "Unless, of course," she continued with contempt, "you want to follow in your father's footsteps and take up teaching as a profession. I know you enjoyed teaching in that school. There is no doubt that you are a chip off the old block. It must be in your blood." I knew she would react that way to my becoming a teacher, so I quickly informed her I was not interested in teaching. I did not want to have to live with that taunt for the rest of my life.

I could see Mom was very relieved to hear me say that. She then went on to say that she did not want people accusing her of keeping me back, that she was the one who did not want send me abroad, or that she was possessive and tight-fisted with her money.

In her own way, she wanted to show Winston that she could be both father and mother to me, and that I did not need him. He may have abandoned me as a child, she said, but she would ensure that I did not lose out because of it. I was her only child and I had to make something of myself. I would be no less than anyone, she promised. By that Mom meant I would not be any less than Dora's children. People would see what a good mother she was and what huge sacrifices she had made for me. She was also determined not to give Uncle Larry the upper hand, enabling him to shove his foreign educated kids in her face at every family gathering. Mom had this competition thing going with Uncle Larry.

In fairness to her, perhaps the competitiveness came from him. His children had to be better than everyone else's kids particularly me. The way those two taunted and made snide remarks about each other and each other's weakness, I sometimes wondered if they even liked each other.

I was glad and relieved that Mom had brought up the subject of my studying abroad. I wondered if this might be an indication that she was prepared to financially support me. With Mom one could never be sure. Sometimes her words and feelings would confuse me and I would often misunderstand her mixed signals. But she did seem happy at the prospect of my going abroad to study.

This was a surprisingly new side to Mom and I was filled with hope. Could this be the beginning of a new era for Mom and me? For the first time in my life, my mother was actually saying she accepted the responsibility of being my parent and was prepared to help me with my future. I knew she could afford to support me. All my family and friends had had that same kind of support from their parents. This was how parenting was supposed to be and more so in the East Indian community of

Trinidad.

I now felt encouraged to look forward to getting to know my mother all over again. I was prepared to wipe out the bad memories of the beatings and the physical and verbal abuse. I wanted to be her friend, share stories and jokes, to be comfortable with her, and confide in her the way other daughters confided in their mothers. I was the happiest I had ever been in my life. Maybe I could now learn to love my mother instead of just feeling sorry for and fearful of her. Perhaps she had finally outgrown her hysterical, crazy behaviour. Thank God Mom had finally grown up I kept thinking again and again.

Perhaps I would now tell her about my dreams. She would understand how I felt about living in a country with a civilization that was less than five hundred years old and that that was the reason I was so fascinated by ancient civilizations and their culture and religious beliefs. I could share with her that I lived and breathed the life of Ancient Babylon with its mysterious ziggurats and the Egypt of Cheops, Menes, Akhenaton and Nefertiti, and how the yet-to-be deciphered script of the Indus Valley civilization fascinated me. This simple, peace-loving, agricultural people completely disappeared when the fierce Aryans came charging down from the Steppes on their swift horses. I devoured every article I could find on the subject, longing to know every detail.

In my imagination I lived during these ancient times. I saw myself wearing flowing robes of vibrant colours and walking in the cool gardens. Inhaling the scent of fragrant flowers and animals. I strolled along foot worn paths that curled around exotic flowering shrubs and wild vegetation. I could clearly see the sprawling palaces and pristine white mansions of the rich. When I looked at the fields below I saw huts made of baked mud and bricks where the working classes lived. I could smell the damp earth and feel the mud between my toes as I toiled the earth with ancient tools alongside the sun beaten, muscular farm workers.

In the cities I would look up at the magnificent temples that in my mind's eye were built high above and separate from the biggest and highest houses, and be awestruck by the gigantic images of gods and goddess that decorated these edifices. What caused these people to have so much faith that they were inspired to create such beautiful works of art? I wanted to know more about the earthy colours and hues of vegetable dyes that were used to paint their exotic images and symbols. The terra cotta pots and urns all seemed so real and familiar to me. I could almost taste the food in those times—the rice, cracked wheat, vegetables cooked with strong and bitter herbs, the dark gray biscuits with sweet fruit.

I had an all-too-familiar understanding of these people's need to worship nature and their gods and goddesses. I was sure these people of ancient times possessed certain psychic abilities and a spiritual understanding of nature that we, in this day and age, have somehow lost. I was certain the answers to my questions regarding the meaning and understanding of life and how we got to be here on earth lay somewhere in those ancient, buried cities and texts. I had a desperate thirst and hunger to know and understand those times.

I also had a natural curiosity about my faraway ancient homeland on the sub-continent of India and Pakistan. I wanted to know more about the Aryans who swept down to colonize these parts and then spread to Europe where they were known as Huns. I was always amused at the irony of Hitler's silly racist dreams. There he was, propagating the idea of a true, blue-blooded and pure race, when he and his people were, in fact, descendents of these nomadic, barbaric conquerors who had moved west from central Asia. After intermarrying and copulating with the people they conquered, they left behind a whole race of people with a mixed up bloodline. His people, Hitler claimed, were the true Aryan Race. In reality, they were probably more like my own bloodline—people whose skin tones ranged from the palest brown to almost black-brown. I wondered if he knew that his swastika, the symbol of his pure Aryan race, was taken from those ancient people. This spiritual symbol is still revered by Buddhists and Hindus all over the subcontinent.

This fascination with ancient civilizations and old religions urged me to study Anthropology and Archeology and related subjects. I was obsessed by the subjects and believed that with this as a base, I would get the knowledge that would help me confirm my instinctive feelings and thoughts. I was anxious to lose myself in the archives of a university or museum, devouring old artifacts and ancient texts.

I was also looking forward to meeting people who shared my interest. Because there was no one around me who understood my passion, I was reluctant to talk about it or let anyone see the depth of feeling and emotion the subject stirred in my soul. When I tried to talk about how I felt, my friends and family would call it my stupid day-dreaming nonsense. I had always wanted to discuss it with Winston; I wondered if he would have understood.

I guess that was the first time I regretted not knowing him. I suspected he would have understood, but I never did get the opportunity to ask. Anyway, I was sure I would meet a nice old professor who would nurture and feed my interest and be that longed-for father figure.

I told Mom all these things, except the part about wanting to share my feelings with Winston; she would not have liked to hear that. I was so eager to share these inner thoughts and was happy that I was actually talking to her for the first time in my life. I was sure she would understand, now that she was going to be kind and supportive. I was also certain that Mom would agree at once to my chosen course of study when she saw how keen my interest was.

But I was wrong. Mom had strong reservations and decided to talk it over with Uncle Larry. He would know what to do. He had done a lot of research and had advised his children. I was not so sure that Uncle Larry would see my point of view or understand my ideas, and I told her so.

I remembered that Uncle Larry had never been there for me when I had needed help or advice with my studies. I was not happy that Mom insisted he advise us. I was very upset with her for sharing my deepest thoughts and secrets with him. I knew his family would not understand and would make fun of my fanciful thoughts. I was not as intellectually gifted as his children were and they would make sure that Mom and I understood that.

Uncle Larry not only endorsed Mom's reservations but also expressed such strong arguments against the idea that I lost all hope of ever changing Mom's mind. His stance reinforced my belief that he did not want me to be successful. I was certain he would prefer it if I just took up a simple teaching job or, better still, became an ordinary shop assistant, just so I would not be as successful as his children would be.

He told Mom I would likely end up digging ditches and trenches with a lot of free-spirited people, who indulged in loose morals. He told me I would end up with a low-paying job and no prospects and that it would sully my reputation and lower my standard of living. And to top it all it was definitely not the kind of career for a woman.

There were three professions that met my Mom's approval: medicine, law, and chartered accountancy. Medicine had the edge over the others because if you became a doctor, it meant you were a bright student who was capable of doing those difficult science subjects. Once you qualified, you were assured of earning a very good living and, most importantly, you had the added privilege of having a 'Dr.' before your name. It was prestigious being a doctor. So it was a fait accompli. Mom suggested that medicine would be a good field for me and that if I wanted to go abroad to study, it would have to be to study medicine. There was no way she was going to waste her hard-earned money on a silly, fanciful hobby that I could indulge in by simply reading books in my spare time.

In reality Mom wanted me to study medicine only because she wanted me to achieve the same status that Arnie would achieve so that Uncle Larry could not look down on her. She also told me that I must keep my new ambition secret and not tell anyone. "Let us surprise them." She looked forward to seeing their faces when I came back a full-fledged doctor. She would surely have the last laugh then. Everyone would know that Clara was an achiever. She had not only overcome the problems that plagued her life—no husband and no man for companionship—but she had made her one and only daughter a woman of respect. Her Vee, who did not have a father to love or care for her, had a mother who had made the ultimate sacrifice for her.

I gave up arguing with Mom, as nothing I could say would change her mind. I sadly agreed because at that time I felt I had no other choice. According to her, she had had a hard life and had made too many sacrifices for her only child. She had lived only for me, she reminded me. I should not hurt her anymore. I had done enough of that, being the child of my father. God alone knew the patience she had to have to deal with me with the kind of no good father I had, and me being a chip of the old block.

I hated when Mom talked like that, but I could not say anything. I quietly listened to her, sadly realizing that Mom would never change and that she saw the world only through her twisted narrow vision.

I knew only too well that my chronic aversion to blood and the thought of injections, surgery, childbirth, and the other bloody gory things that doctors had to do in order to help save a life, would be major challenges for me. I tried to tell Mom this, but she reassured me that most people felt that way at the beginning. Even Arnie had felt that way, she whispered in a smug, conspiratorial tone. She was sure I would get used to it. I was not sure at all.

Arrangements began surreptitiously lest the family found out, and I was enrolled for a pre-medicine course in a college in London. I still had reservations, but I kept them to myself. Perhaps I would get used to it. Medicine was a noble profession and I would be able to help people. Perhaps I may just have found my forte. I consoled myslef.

Chapter 27

My applications were sent off. I was required to do a one-year, pre-medical course to make me eligible for medical school. Mom could not contain her excitement. She no longer wanted to hide the fact that I would be studying medicine. She wanted every-one to know that she was going to spend her money to support me through medical school. She told everyone she met that I was soon to be leaving for the UK to begin studying Medicine. "My daughter, the doctor-to-be," she boasted.

I was depressed and had a niggling feeling that her dream would come true at my expense. Knowing I was not strong enough to confront her with my fears, I made up my mind that I would try to be the doctor she wanted. I would study medicine. Hopefully, I would become accustomed to the blood and the needles. I kept telling myself it could be done. Before too long, I had convinced myself that I could and would be the doctor she wanted.

Uncle Larry demonstrated his disapproval of my studying medicine by making sarcastic comments. Even Auntie Dora was more than a little surprised, and kept asking Mom if she was sure that medicine was the right thing for me. "After all, Vee is a girl. Would you want her studying for so many years and then working in such conditions?" she asked. "It is a tough life," she continued. "medicine is not the life or profession for a woman. Too much studying, too many long hours. How would she find a husband? Who would want to marry someone who was on call all the time and did not have time for a home or a family?" Mom just smiled, comforted by the thought that I would soon be leaving and there was nothing anyone could do to stop me.

Fifi did not join in the pros and cons of the discussions; she was busy with her own life. She was quite happy for Mom and me, if that was what we wanted. She helped me to get my new passport and took me to the British Council to take care of the last-minute requirements. Fifi, the most traveled member of the immediate family, also took it upon herself to offer me insight and advice on living in London, which she called her 'home away from home.'

Mom listened with great discomfort as Fifi shared her intimate knowledge of London. She told me where the fancy shops were and where I needed to go to get the best bargains. She reminded me about the interesting historical places we had read about in our history books- the Tower of London, Kew Gardens, then there were charming places like Trafalgar Square, Regents Street, and the lights of Oxford Street at Christmas time. And if it was books I was looking for, I must be sure to go to Foyles on Tottenham Court Road.

She also thought it prudent to advise me about the places I should avoid at all cost. "Stay away from the seedy Soho area. It's bad, with nothing but strip shows and peep shows with dirty men in raincoats," Fifi had also heard that the owners of these clubs and their henchmen were known to lure young, innocent young girls from abroad into their dirty clubs, drug them, and make them work as prostitutes. "You have to be very careful," Fifi warned.

Fifi also provided details on what to do when I got to London and how to get through immigration. She had valuable advice on how to hail taxis, how much to tip, and so on. She also thought it wise to provide me with the names of some of her dear, dear friends, who would always be on hand if I needed help. I wasn't the only one who found Fifi's advice so interesting and informative; the cousins also sat and listened attentively to Fifi's stories and experiences. She sounded like a tourist guide. As always, we were very impressed with Fifi and everything she had to say. Every one of us wanted to go to London. It seemed familiar, despite being so remote. I felt fully prepared and certain that I would have no problems at all.

Mom's euphoria was soon to hit a slump. When it came time for her to send off the fees for the first session, she slipped into a deep depression. I quietly observed her struggle. She could be seen sitting with her bankbook, confused and wondering whether or not she should withdraw the money for the draft. I could see the turmoil going on in her mind. What would happen if she just dropped the idea? What would people say if Vee did not go abroad? How could she live down the boasts she had made about her daughter being a doctor? She would never be able to show her face if she did not go through with it now. People would talk and, worst of all, Winston would laugh. She had made her bed; now she must lie in it. She, sadly, had no choice.

I tried to talk to her about it and give her the option of withdrawing her offer to support me at university. I even offered to say that I was the one who did not want to go. But she said nothing. In the end she made the payment just before the due date. She did so quietly, but I could tell she was now regretting the decision she had made in a moment of weakness when her pride and ego had gotten the better of her.

After the draft was sent, she could no longer contain herself. Her innermost thoughts began to come out, slowly at first. Then, as she got used to verbalizing them, they became more frequent and vehement. Mom began to tell me very sadly about how much money it was going to cost her, the poor discarded wife who had no one at her side. This was a major sacrifice she was making for me, she said, and she hoped I appreciated it. "I have had many, many people interested in me. If not for you, I could have been married by now, with a loving husband, financially secure, and with a happy life of my own.

How many single mothers have made the sacrifices I have made and will continue to make? How many mothers have given up their lives like I have? Who in their right mind would send their only child abroad to study medicine? It had better be worth it," she threatened. "I have little money left. Your selfish, uncaring father deserted you and now I am left with you on my hands. I have no choice but to give up my life for you. If I don't, people will talk. They do not understand how much I have given up for you. Of course you are my child and I love you, but this is so unfair. My life has been one long sacrifice. No one has helped me, yet I have to help everyone. I hope you realize that I don't have to do this for you, but out of the goodness of my heart I am doing it. That father of yours will pay. This was his responsibility and he left it on my doorstep."

I kept quiet and listened to her go on and on. Yet in front of everyone else, she alleged she was making all these sacrifices with the generosity of a loving mother. I began to dread being alone with her because all she would talk about was this big sacrifice she was making, and she would remind me that I must always be grateful. I promised I would be grateful to her always. It was the easiest way to shut her up for awhile.

I had to buy an overcoat and some warm clothes suitable for the cooler, wetter British climate. Once again Fifi took control, this time advising me about the mercurial British weather. "Warm one minute and wet and cold the next," she said. "The cold, foggy mornings can be depressing and the smog and fog so thick you can't even see the front gate. A real 'pea souper,' as the British would say."

That Dickens-like description of the weather actually excited me. How wonderful it will be to experience different kinds of weather! Four seasons seemed so much more civilized and fun than our boring old tropical warm and wet seasons. No more monotonous, balmy evenings. No more humid, sticky summer days or wet 'winter' days that are almost as warm as summer days.

Oh, how I looked forward to experiencing those climatic changes. In my mind I saw cool, lemon-smelling springtime with fresh, green leaves on thin, green stems with lots of pale yellow flowers. I imagined warm, emerald green summers with lush shrubs and a profusion of scented flowers, including the wide varieties of English roses I had heard so much of, and big, fat, red strawberries with thick, clotted cream that was synonymous with tennis at Wimbledon. Autumn would be breezy with dark yellow, golden-brown leaves gently falling, crunchy under my feet, quietly followed by the quiet crisp, white winters. I imagined tasting the soft, powdery flakes of snow falling on my tongue and my face, building a snowman, and rolling around in the snow with sleigh bells ringing in my ears. I could not wait get lost in all that. I day dreamed a lot during those days.

The cousins teased me, calling me the English lady. They said I had always assumed the airs of a grand English lady. I preferred to eat bland English fare with a knife and fork, dress up for dinner, strut around with a superior air looking tall and speaking in what they called my soft affected voice while I devoured Charles Dickens, Jane Austin, or the works of the Bronte sisters. "No slang Trinidad talk for Vee, she an she queen's english, good she go go dere and fit right in!"

They told me I was going home to England and reminded me to take my overcoat whenever I left the house. "Just in case the weather should change." But all this was done in good fun and I did not mind one bit. I put Mom's taunting, depressing remarks out of my mind and played out the role they had created for me. I would soon be far, far away from all of this. My world had become a stage and I played my parts very well.

Mom woke up one morning with a determined, cold look in her eyes. I knew she had a plan in mind. Sure enough, she ordered me to go and visit Winston before I left. "After all, Vee, he is your father and he should know you will be leaving to study in England. He needs to know you are not suffering and that you are not less than anyone, despite the fact that he does not care about you or your future. Tell him that I am being both father and mother to you. Tell him about the sacrifices I am making for you. Let us see if he is man enough to feel any guilt or if he will remember that you are his own flesh and blood and he has neglected you all your life."

I was taken aback. I did not want to go to see Winston. I knew what I was letting myself in for. I dreaded it but could not argue with Mom. She was by now quite hysterical. And so, with Mom's words heavy in my heart, I reluctantly went to see Winston. I did not call him before I left because I felt it would be better if I dropped in unexpectedly. I was hoping against all hope that he would not be home.

It was about 4.30 in the afternoon when I got there. Winston was gardening in the front yard of the new house he had quietly built a few months before. He was taken by surprise when he saw me, as it had been years since I had ventured to visit him. If I had not seen him first, I was sure he would have pretended he was not home.

Moon, his live-in housekeeper and rumoured mistress, came forward to open the front gate as she asked me why I had come and if there was something I wanted. I remember feeling very awkward and resentful while silently cursing Mom for making me do this terrible, embarrassing thing. I decided I would never let this housekeeper know how unnerved I was. I confidently pushed past her and said I had come to see Winston. With that, I walked over to him. He was wearing faded, loose cotton shorts and a string vest, which was a little damp with sweat and smelled of mud and cigarettes. That was the first time I realized that Winston smoked.

Winston had stopped what he was doing. As I approached him he said, "So, Vee, why have you come? Why don't you come in and sit down. How's your mother?" He did not seem genuinely interested. I could hear Mom's taunts that my own flesh and blood,- the person from whose loins I had sprung, as she liked to put it,- did not want me. In a voice that was hoarse from suppressed anger and resentment, I told him that I only came to say good-bye, as I was leaving in a few days to study in the UK.

Winston took a long look at me before asking me why I had thought to come over to say good bye. "Are you expecting me to support you and pay for your education? Is it money you have come for?" he asked pointedly. I bent my head with shame and cursed Mom again for making me go through this indignity. "Why oh why must I have to listen to this kind of thing all my life?" I silently questioned God.

After taking a minute or so to compose myself, I told him in a soft, clear voice that I had come over to say good-bye because he was my biological father and it seemed to be the correct and expected thing for me to do. I assured him I had never wanted anything from him and that I still did not want anything from him. I told him that I did not ever want him to think that that was why I had come to see him.

Moon hovered in the background, listening to the conversation. I could see her sly grin of satisfaction. I said a hasty and strained good-bye. Just as I was about to leave I heard Rookie, my grandmother, calling out to ask who had come over.

Winston told her that I had come over to say good-bye, as I was leaving for the UK to study. She called for me to go up to her. I hesitated, unsure if it would be the thing to do. Winston told me it was okay. By this time Rookie was very old and frail and had shrunk even smaller from arthritis. I did not know what to say to her. Before I could say anything, she called me over and for the first time in my life, asked me to kiss her. She held on to me and cried, her thin, bony shoulders shaking with deep, long, dry sobs. "Tell yur modder to come back. Tell she to forgive meh and come back to mey son. I have done she wrong. Promise mey you go talk to she and make she come back."

To say that I was shocked by this plea would be an understatement. The strong-willed, controlling, hardened, tyrannical witch of a woman that I had always known had now become this withered, feeble, sad, repentant, desperate old lady wanting forgiveness before she died. I could not believe my ears.

How could I tell Mom what this senile old lady was asking? She and Winston were already divorced. Besides, I was fed up with the whole thing and believed it was none of my business. I was never treated as though I were a part of their married life. It was their problem and they had chosen to solve it their own way. No one had ever asked me how I felt, so why should I intervene now? Their marriage was a matter they had made their own private affair. I was always an outsider and wanted to remain so.

But it was a strange feeling for me to hear this pathetic old woman, my estranged grandmother and the main cause of my parents' and, thus, my problems, ask me this. Pity and sadness overwhelmed me. Pity for what might have been and for what we had all lost. It had come to this after eighteen long years. But it was futile now. I told her gently but firmly that there was nothing I could do, but that I would tell Mom what she had said. I quickly removed her bony arms from me and I left. Winston did not attempt to stop me.

As I walked away I felt cold and alone and quite disgusted. I remember taking a deep breath of relief. I told myself that that part of my life was now over. I would never see my grandmother or my father again. I felt a sudden sense of lightness. It was finally the end of that chapter in my life.

Mom was waiting for me when I got home, anxious to know Winston's reaction. I remember thinking she looked like a magpie with her beady, shiny eyes full of expectation and curiosity, anxiously waiting to see if Winston had committed to helping me and if he had given me any money. In a low, emotionless voice, I told her everything that was said. I did not allow her to interrupt me. When I was finished I told her that she had made me do something I had never wanted to do and that she had made me lower myself to go to people who had preconceived ideas of what I wanted or expected. I had embarrassed myself and had lost my pride, all because of her. I felt humiliated and belittled. I told her that never again should she insist that I go to see Winston because I had no intentions of ever going there again.

Mom immediately became very contrite, stating that she only wanted to do what was right, to give Winston the opportunity to do right by me in case later on he accused her of depriving him of the chance of being a father. "I want nothing on my conscience," she said sanctimoniously. She then told me that she knew all along he would behave as he did, and that she wanted me to see him for what he really was. She had done me a favour. Now I would know who was on my side. She said perhaps now I would appreciate the sacrifice she was making for me. "Look what your own flesh and blood has done to you, Vee? Look how your father has humiliated you, his one and only child? I could have done the same to you, but instead I have made, and will continue to make sacrifices for you, you are my child."

I looked long and hard at Mom. She missed the sarcasm in my voice as I told her I would never ever forget all she had done for me as long as I lived. I then quickly turned and walked away, anxious to be alone with my tears. I felt cold and hard, devoid of any feelings for either of my parents.

Chapter 28

The last few days before I was due to leave were pretty hectic. Worried about my leaving the warm, humid climate of tropical Trinidad, Fifi and Mom were frantically trying to get me some suitable clothes so I would have something warm to wear in England. They dragged me from one shop to another to choose from the limited selection of warm clothes available. As always, Victor, my grandfather, gave me all the money I needed to buy a basic wardrobe. I was still embarrassed to accept money from him, as he was not my father, but I had no choice since Mom readily and eagerly accepted it on my behalf.

The most trying time of all, however, was when Mom insisted I had to visit the whole family—including extended relatives—to say good-bye. Of course Mom would accompany me and no doubt boast that she was the one who was making the ultimate sacrifice to support me, not my "useless, good for nothing father." I dreaded the visits. I could hear her voice with her perfect diction ringing inside my head.

The sooner we started the ordeal, the sooner it would be over. The first family I chose to visit was Nan and Nas Tante, who happened to be in Trinidad in between her many foreign trips.

Nas Tante could not contain her excitement about my going abroad, especially to England, her favorite country. "Yu goin to

live and study in Queen Lizabet home country. How nice for yu."
It was obvious to all of us that Nas Tante had more than a mild
obsession with Royalty and that going to England was for her a
step closer to actually being Royal. "Remember, yu must promise dat yu go to see de Palace. It so big and beautiful. It have
more dan one hundred rooms wid so many guards all dressed
up in red and black with big furry hats on top of dey head. Dey
job is to help guard and watch out for de place, you know. Den
dey is a big balcony in de front of de palace. If yu lucky, yu go
get to see de Queen. She does stand dey, right in the middle of
de balcony and she does wave to she people whenever she in
London. She does have so much wok to do, bein' her majesty
of all dem countries. And yet she does still fine time to come
out to greet she people. But dey say she husband is a wile man,
yu know. We does hear all kinda talk about how he does carry
on wid odder women. People even say he might have a bastard
child somewhey in South America. All dem sailorman does have
de same kinda bad habit, always chasing skirt. It muss have
someting to do wid bein in de sea for so long, shut up on a
ship wid only men for company. What a terrible ting for she to
have to face. Imagine how she muss feel. She so beautiful wid
she pink rosy cheeks and queen of nearly de whole world and
she husband is a randy womanizer who karnt keep he ting in
he pants. Poor woman. God go bless she, for sure. And so yu
see, Vee, let dis be a lesson to yu. Life so unfair. Yu could have
de whole world at yu feet an still doe have happiness inside yu
heart or a honest man at yu side," a solemn Nas Tante advised,
nodding her head sadly.

Older now, and no longer interested in housework, Nas Tante
still insisted on cooking that last meal for me. The chicken she
cooked this time, though, was not caught in the backyard, but
was bought already dressed from the supermarket. Despite the
elaborate spread with my favourite dishes, somehow the meal
was not the same. The wonderful memories of those bygone
days when we youngsters roaming all over the farm in Moruga

gave me a warm, nostalgic feeling. I remember feeling a deep sense of loss for those long-gone, carefree times when life was still filled with hope.

Now that Nas Tante had returned from her foreign trips, Nan was back with her, but Nan was very quiet as she sat there in the rocking chair. Although she did not fully understand what was going on or that I was leaving for London, she sensed that something different was happening that day. Lost somewhere in the past, big, fat tears silently streamed down her face. Nan looked so much older now, very much like a dried-up walnut, all brown, leathery, and lined. She looked at us, lost and helpless, perhaps wanting to ask something but not remembering what. Her look of utter confusion and dejection touched me deeply.

I looked at Nan and wondered if and when I would ever see her again. She had to have been almost ninety at that time. For the first time in my life, I was aware of a great, indescribable emotion welling up inside me. I wanted to hug her close and protect her. She had had such a great influence on my life, more than she could have known. Through her I had learned about the many lives, peoples, and stories I have related in this book. And while she now was lost in her own world, I knew for sure that she was reliving every moment of her life, particularly those times she had had with her husband. It was a comforting and reassuring feeling to still have her with us. She was the last connection we had with our roots. Nan was an example to us all. She had had a hard life, but had been blessed with a sense of humour, enabling her to cope with all the trials and tribulations in her life. She had accepted that it was what God had destined for her and, as such, had never complained or felt bitter.

One of my favourite people in the family was Auntie Savi, Ismat's youngest daughter. Auntie Savi had had cancer when she was young. In a way she was lucky because even though she was not in remission, at least her condition was not worsening.

The radiation treatment she had undergone had killed not only the cancer but irreparably damaged many of her other internal organ. She was now a shell of the woman she once was. The wonderful thing about Auntie Savi was that despite all that she had been through with her illness, she had not lost her terrific will to live and sense of humour and was still full of naughty jokes. No one was safe from her cutting humour. Auntie Savi had a way of telling you hard truths but in such a funny way that you did not mind her straightforwardness.

Auntie Savi invited Mom and me for a farewell lunch. Not one to stand on formality, Auntie Dora also decided to join us. Both she and Auntie Savi were always close, Auntie Savi having spent many months with Auntie Dora and Uncle Larry while she was going to college. Once Fifi came to know that we three were going for lunch, she decided she would also come with us. Auntie Savi ended up with a few extra lunch guests that day!

Auntie Savi was an amazingly good cook. She insisted this was because of the generous amounts of good, sweet, Spanish olive oil and imported New Zealand butter she used. "There is no substitute for delicious food, and to get delicious food you have to use good, rich ingredients," she would announce. Auntie Savi was skinny. For the rest of the family, eating at Auntie Savi's meant gaining a few extra pounds.

For lunch that day Auntie Savi prepared her very own specialty—curried cascadura. Cascadura is a freshwater fish encased in its own soft-shell. As far as we Trinidadians know, it is found only in the muddy waters of Trinidad rivers. As a child I thought it was a kind of undiscovered living fossil, as it certainly looked like one. Auntie Savi had deliberately cooked the cascadura for me that day because, as the story goes, whoever eats the cascadura will surely return to Trinidad to die. Auntie Savi was taking no chances with me. She made sure I had eaten the cascadura and was firmly convinced that no matter how far I traveled, I would eventually return to Trinidad one day. Auntie Savi outdid herself that day.

The meal was exceptionally delicious. After nearly thirty-seven years, the taste of that curried cascadura is still fresh in my mouth. I can still smell the wonderful, slightly warm and nutty, herbal curry aroma of the cascadura that filled the room that day. After lunch we sat back and relaxed and Auntie Savi lectured me on the dos and don'ts of big city life. She hugged me tightly and gave me one last warning. "Don't fall in love too quickly, you hear? Man means trouble!"

I have no idea who told Rupert I was leaving but he somehow found out and arrived with an armful of flowers, the amethyst earrings he had tried to give me some months earlier, and a well-prepared speech. "You are leaving me," he said, "but if you feel you need to do this then I understand, as long as you always remember that I love you and always will. I shall be waiting here for you when you come back. I have loved you before in another life and if I can't have you in this life, I will surely have you the next time around. But for now, I want to hold you just once, please. Just one kiss before you go, something that I can hold on to until you come back."

I was disgusted. How dare he come here and tell me that he loved me! And who did he think he was to demand a hug and a kiss? Had I not made it clear to him that I was not interested? How dare he tell me he would be waiting for me in this life and in the next! Was he saying that just to make me feel bad and put me on a guilt trip? The cheek of him, I thought, telling me these things in front of my mother. Did he not have any respect? He did not know me. He had no idea of how I felt and the things I believed in. How could he love me if he did not know the real me?

I could not waste my time with someone like that, someone who uses the 'love' word so easily. I was going to tell him these things, but Mom gave me a signal to be quiet and give him a brotherly hug. I gingerly leaned forward and offered him my cheek, but I was angry and it showed. How dare my own mother compromise me like this! She knew how I felt about Rupert, but she always had a soft spot for him. After that brief, cold hug, I tried to pull back but Rupert held on to my arm so tightly it hurt. He took a long look at me and said, "Remember what I said," and ran down the stairs, leaving behind the flowers and the earrings. I remember telling Mom they now belonged to her. I did not want them.

I was angry and upset. It felt like Rupert had threatened me. Mom's response was that I was leaving anyway and most probably would never see him again, so what was the harm in just being polite? After all, he had laid his heart at my feet in a most romantic way. Mom had been reading too many "Mills & Boon" love stories. I was not moved at all by Mom's pleas and did not feel the least bit guilty because I knew I had never encouraged him or led him on.

Victor, my Papa, the only father figure I had ever known, had become quiet over the past year and seemed even quieter during my days at home. Late in the evening on the day before I left, he called me aside to talk to me alone. We sat quietly on the dimly lit veranda, silently looking up at the stars through the ornate wooden arches of the eaves I loved so much. After some time he leaned back in the old, comfortable rocking chair and reminded me of how much he loved me and that he always thought of me as one of his own daughters. He went on to explain that in order to keep the peace with Rachel, he had not shown his feelings for me. He admitted that he always knew about Rachel's negative attitude and insecurities regarding me. He also realized that Mom was unwilling to even try to understand things that did not go her way, and that she had taken out all her frustration on me. I felt then what I had always suspected – that I had been the cause of most of the tension in the house. Dear God, I thought. Why, through no fault of my own, did I have this heavy burden to bear?"

Papa talked to me about the house we lived in. He told me that by rights the house should go to me because it was the house that he and my grandmother, Little Sparrow, had built together. Papa was adamant that Rachel would not have the house for the simple reason that, in his heart, it had belonged to Little Sparrow. By all that was fair, Rachel, the second wife, did not have a right to that house. He once again reminded me that he would leave the house to Mom first and that he had already told her she should then pass it on to me without delay. He apologized again for not being able to leave the house to me straightaway. He was afraid that if he did, Auntie Dora's children would feel he did not leave them anything, and that would seem unfair. He also knew that Auntie Dora felt her children needed more than I did.

Papa told me that he knew I loved his books, so he was going to leave me all the old religious books in his little library. I hugged him. I knew we shared something no one else had. I think I was more pleased with the gift of the books than the gift of the house. I could see myself all curled up, engrossed in the musty, fragile pages of those books, lost in deep philosophical, spiritual, and mystical thoughts.

Papa also spoke to me about Mom and Winston and how guilty he was that their marriage had not worked out. He admitted that he did not agree with Mom's violent, reckless, and irrational behaviour. He put it down to the fact that she must have been very distressed that her life had ended up in shambles. "She was always overindulged when she was small. She was spoiled. Her mother gave her everything, always gave in to her every demand. It was difficult for your mother to cope with her mother-in-law and the situation she was in," he said in defense of her.

I realized then that Papa was telling me I should forgive Mom for all she had put me through in my eighteen years. In his own way he was also apologizing for his weakness and inability to stop her when she beat me so badly. He was also sorry that he had not stood up for me when Rachel had been against me. I held him tightly and told him that I understood.

My Papa cried for me that day. I knew then that he really had loved me but that circumstances had not allowed him to show it as often as he would have liked. What a pity, though, for it would have made such a big difference to me and how I felt growing up. I looked at him and saw him for what he really was—a weak man who was too afraid of the women in his life to do the right thing to protect a defenseless, young child.

I slept very little that last night as I relived my life. I could feel Mom tossing in bed next to me, so she too may have been thinking about the events in her live and all that we had been through together. I suppose she knew this was the beginning of a different time for us. I thought of all the people in my family. People, who, according to all the natural rules of nature, should have had an instinctive, unconditional love for me but who either did not love me or were all too afraid to show it. I realized I did not understand what love was. I was curious to know how it felt to know someone loved you and what emotions you felt when you loved someone. I was confused. Love seemed to be elusive for me, yet other people seemed to find it easily, without even trying. I doubted I would ever love anyone.

Eventually morning arrived. I went outside at the break of dawn. It was cool and the grass was slightly misty with dew. Raja came bounding up to me, leaving a trail on the damp grass. He walked with me around the house, looking up at me questioningly as I paused to listen to the familiar but faint sounds of the approaching day. The sun was just peeping over the horizon. As I gazed at the fields and distant houses, I was once again taken with how beautiful and peaceful it was. How could a day end so sadly when it had begun so beautifully?

A faraway cock crowed his wake-up call, which set off a whole chorus of cocks with their answering cries. I guess this was the signal for the rest of the animal world to wake up because soon the dogs were barking and the sky was filled with a cacophony of whistling, chirping birds. It was a beautiful day. The sky was a soft, pale gold, dotted with little fluffs of soft, white, powdery clouds. This had to be a sign. A good omen, to be sure. I was suddenly overcome with euphoria. Everything felt right. Deep inside I knew I was doing the right thing.

Chapter 29

Janet, my friend from next door, insisted that, one of her elder brothers who had migrated to England a few years before and who lived just outside of London in the city of Leicester with his wife and two children, meet me at London airport. Mom had done a lot for them and this would be a good way to repay her kindness. Mom was very relieved to hear that someone she knew and who was almost like family would be on hand to greet me at the airport. This was one problem she would not lose sleep over.

Auntie Dora, Uncle Larry, Ricky, Marleen, and Viv had come over earlier that day, and Fifi brought Nas Tante. The house was full of noisy chatter. It was like a party. I was dressed in my smart new peach-colored, tailored suit that had been especially made for the occasion. I thought I looked like a stiff, awkward airhostess, but everyone else thought I looked the height of London fashion.

Mom was satisfied that she was sending me off with dignity. Just before we left for the airport, she called me aside and ceremoniously presented me with an envelope. Inside was the allowance for my living expenses for the first year in London, a grand total of three hundred and sixty pounds sterling. That was thirty pounds a month to live on. Even then Mom felt it necessary to remind me that it was the sum total of her whole savings and that she was making this big sacrifice so I must be economical and not waste. I was grateful. This was the first time Mom had given me anything. I tucked the envelope safely away at the bottom of my purse.

Many of the village people came by to see me off—Janet and Mollie, the older and still unmarried sister, their mother Tante Ella, my sad, lonely friend Pamela with her Mom, and surprisingly, many of the young boys—young men now—who used to tease me by sending me love notes with sprigs of flowers. I smiled shyly at them, remembering that I would refuse to speak to them for months because I was afraid they might have thought me forward. I could not believe that they all liked me enough to want to say good-bye. I felt a lump in my throat. I wanted to tell them that I did care for them and remembered each and every one of their puppy love letters, but then thought better of it. They might not understand what I really meant and I would look foolish. With so many people hovering outside the house waiting to see me off, I felt somewhat like the Queen of England as I graciously waved and stepped into the car.

It was more like a procession as the long line of cars slowly moved away from the only place I ever called home. First there was our car, with Papa, Mom, Rachel, and me; then came Fifi's car with Merle, Dawn, and Janet; following Fifi was Uncle Larry with Auntie Dora, Marleen, Ricky, and Viv; and then there was Uncle Ramsey with Auntie Lucille, Camille Anne, and Nas Tante.

This was Trinidad and the grand farewell that Trinidadians thought was a must. The whole family trooped off to the airport all dressed in their Sunday best to say good bye.

It was a quiet drive to the airport. The tension in the car was unbearable. I wanted to break the silence but did not know what to say. What do you say at a time like this? Should you be funny, reminiscent, matter-of-fact, emotional . . . or what? How does one say good bye? It was the longest one-hour drive ever.

When we arrived at the airport, Fifi, once again in her role as the experienced world traveler, took over the proceeding. She found porters, sorted out the luggage, grabbed my passport and ticket, and went to check in the luggage and get my boarding pass. The hustle and bustle of the airport was a comforting distraction. I was relieved that everyone else was caught up in the confused melee, as I did not know what to do or who to talk to. I felt nervous and a little disorientated. I stayed close to Mom because I knew she need that, then I saw Papa was standing at the back looking forlorn, so I thought I would go and stand with him for awhile. As I moved towards him, I felt someone reach out and touch my arm. When I turned around, I saw to my utter amazement that it was Mr. Carlos. Oh, dear God!

He was the last person I wanted to see. I did not need that kind of confrontation at this time. My mouth went dry and my face turned red. My heart started pounding with embarrassment and a touch of fear. Mom and Papa saw what was happening. They immediately moved to my side.

I look up at Mr. Carlos, unsure if I should say hello or just ignore him. Realizing I was confused, Mr. Carlos immediately began to talk. He first asked me how I was and what I was doing at the airport, and then without waiting for my answer, quickly went on to apologize for the difficult time he had put me through at the school. Again and again, he told me how very sorry he was. He explained that he had been a very sick man then. He had since been to see a doctor and found out that he had suffered some sort of mental breakdown caused by his years of heavy drinking and the fact that his family had deserted him. He was lost and lonely. It was by a happy coincidence that he was here at the airport and had this opportunity to see me and apologize. Now, he said, he would be able to rest in peace.

I did not know what to say. Seeing my bewilderment, he again saved me from having to speak to him by apologizing to Victor and Mom and telling them how sorry he was for all that had happened. He said he had wanted to contact our family for a while to clear the air but didn't have the courage to do so. He wanted our forgiveness. We were all surprised by this but also relieved that there had been no uncomfortable scene.

I looked at the sad, pathetic man and felt nothing, not even pity. I turned and walked away, I had no time for people who could not cope with the challenges of their lives and who sort release in drink or other mind numbing substance or indulgence.

I took a long, deep breath and thought for a moment, "Dear God, what is all this about? Why is it that people are telling me they are sorry? Is it a kind of end for me?" I began to feel scared. It could not be ominous, could it? Oh well, I will just place my trust in my great Divine, my protector, and my future will be guided by the trust I had in my beliefs. I prayed that I would be guided by my inner voice, that part of me that I truly believed was a minute part of my Divine and, therefore, the whole universe.

My old school friend Naila's arrival at that moment was a welcome relief. She rushed up with a loud cry of delight and enveloped me in a big good-bye hug. She chatted and laughed with everyone, her bubbly personality helping to immediately ease the situation and change the mood. Mr. Carlos immediately faded into the background and no one gave him a second glance.

Soon after that it was time to say good-bye and go through immigration and customs. I vaguely recall everything happening in a hazy rush. I think I must have hugged and kissed everyone before Fifi finally steered me towards immigration. I turned to wave. All I could see was Mom standing alone at the back with her face grimly set and her arms folded tightly. I realized then that I was crying.

Half an hour later as the plane taxied off, I felt all my fears, nervousness, and apprehension suddenly evaporate. It was as if I had removed a tightly fitting dress and exhaled long and hard. I felt relaxed, comfortable and full of hope. It was my new beginning. I would discover and know me for the person I really was, not the person everyone thought they saw. I would no longer have to play a part to survive or be under the shadow of my confused and frustrated mother, heartless, uncaring father, or my bright, shining cousins. I would be me. The new people I would meet would see only me, the beautiful rosebud who was ready and waiting to blossom and bask in the knowledge that people would recognize the wonderful person she really was. I knew I would be homesick for the familiar, but I also knew I was strong enough to survive.

The twelve-hour flight was long and I could not sleep. Mom lingered in my thoughts as I relived my eighteen years with her. I thought of each member of the family and of all the nice times I had, despite the emotional and physically trying times I endured. I felt close to Fifi, who had always been there, happy and jolly, doing all she could to help us have a good time. Then there was Auntie Dora and Uncle Larry. I was grateful that they let me stay with them, but I knew they were a tight little family and totally devoted to their children. Papa cared for me, but was too afraid to show it. I prayed that Nan would not know pain and that she would slip from this world peacefully, without suffering. I thought about my last visit with Winston, my biological father, and decided I would never think about him again.

The airhostess's announcement that we must all fasten our seatbelts and prepare for landing brought me out of my deep thoughts. I could feel the plane descending slowly through the mist and fog. I would soon be landing in 'Queen Lisabet's' own country to begin the next chapter of my life.

Veena Masud

Born in Trinidad, West Indies, Veena is an educationalist by profession and has been living in Pakistan for the past 28 years. Veena has worked relentlessly in her adopted homeland for the uplift of young people. She was the first woman to be elected onto the Pakistan Olympic Association and has been instrumental in the promotion of Pakistani women in domestic and international competitive swimming. Veena has represented Pakistan in numerous international sports seminars, and as Team Official at various elite international sporting events. Veena's contributions and achievements to the cause of women in sport in Pakistan in has been recognized and acknowledged by the International Olympic Committee.

ISBN 141206114-8

9 781412 061148